Praise for *Common System and S[...]*

"Firesmith's collection of actionable practices for real-world, non-trivial testing and the processes in which they're applied is comprehensive and uniquely valuable. Nothing published about software testing in recent years provides anything like it."

—**Robert V. Binder**, robertvbinder.com

"Don's compilation of real-world testing problems, symptoms, and solutions is the most comprehensive available. You can use it early in your project to prevent these problems. Or you can use it at the end, as a ready list of costly lessons you could have avoided, had you used it early on. I'm afraid this book's publication will undermine a lot of excuses for repeating these mistakes."

—**Vince Alcalde**, National Australia Bank

"Excellent, Excellent, Excellent! This book should be mandatory reading for anyone involved in product development. Donald's book addresses the pitfalls that need to be understood and allowed for in all product development verification and validation planning. While the focus of the book is on software projects, most of the pitfalls are equally applicable to any size project that involves both hardware and software."

—**Louis S. Wheatcraft**, Requirements Experts Inc.

"The potential impact of this book cannot be overstressed. Software systems that are not adequately tested do not adequately evolve. I highly recommend this book as a must-read for people directly involved in the development and management of software-intensive systems."

—**Dr. Kenneth E. Nidiffer**, Director of Strategic Plans for Government Programs, Software Engineering Institute, Carnegie Mellon University

"*Common System and Software Testing Pitfalls* identifies realistic testing pitfalls. More importantly, it also identifies solutions for avoiding them on your next project. Every manager should read this book and follow the recommendations."

—**Barry Stanly**, Enterprise Technology Alliance

"Whether you are a novice tester or a seasoned professional, you will find this book to be a valuable resource. The information on how to identify and prevent problem areas is clear, concise and, most importantly, actionable."

—**Allison Yeager**, Blackbaud

"First of all, this is great material! It contains probably all of the testing problems I have faced in my career and some that I wasn't aware of.... Thank you for the opportunity to read this superb material!"

—**Alexandru Cosma**, Frequentis

"As a tester, I consider *Common System and Software Testing Pitfalls* by Donald Firesmith to be a must-read book for all testers and QA engineers."

—**Thanh Huynh**, LogiGear

"Your book provides very good insight and knowledge. After working in IT for over thirty years, and focusing on software testing the past thirteen years, I still learned more tips and best practices in software testing."

—**Tom Zalewski**, Texas State Government

"This book is essential for the people in the cyber security business . . . I can see it becoming a classic. Don has done a great job."

—**Michael Hom**, Compass360 Consulting

"Awesome work. Very mature."

—**Alejandro Salado**, **Kaiser**, Threde Gmbh

"All in all, a great document."

—**Peter Bolin**, Revolution IT Pty Ltd.

Common System and Software Testing Pitfalls

Common System and Software Testing Pitfalls

How to Prevent and Mitigate Them

Descriptions, Symptoms, Consequences, Causes, and Recommendations

Donald G. Firesmith

✦✦Addison-Wesley

Upper Saddle River, NJ • Boston • Indianapolis • San Francisco
New York • Toronto • Montreal • London • Munich • Paris • Madrid
Capetown • Sydney • Tokyo • Singapore • Mexico City

The SEI Series in Software Engineering

For information about buying this title in bulk quantities, or for special sales opportunities (which may include electronic versions; custom cover designs; and content particular to your business, training goals, marketing focus, or branding interests), please contact our corporate sales department at corpsales@pearsoned.com or (800) 382-3419.

For government sales inquiries, please contact governmentsales@pearsoned.com.

For questions about sales outside the U.S., please contact international@pearsoned.com.

Visit us on the Web: informit.com/aw

Library of Congress Cataloging-in-Publication Data

Firesmith, Donald G., 1952–
  Common system and software testing pitfalls : how to prevent and mitigate them : descriptions, symptoms, consequences, causes, and recommendations / Donald G. Firesmith.
      pages   cm.
  Includes bibliographical references and index.
  ISBN 978-0-13-374855-0 (pbk. : alk. paper)
  1. Computer software—Testing—Automation. 2. Software failures—Prevention. I. Title.
  QA76.76.T48F58 2013
  005.3028'7—dc23   2013039235

ISBN-13: 978-0-13-374855-0
ISBN-10: 0-13-374855-3

Text printed in the United States on recycled paper at R.R. Donnelley in Crawfordsville, Indiana.
First printing, December 2013

CONTENTS

FOREWORD

As a general rule, about 50 cents out of every dollar spent on software projects goes toward finding and fixing bugs. About 40 cents out of that 50 is spent on various kinds of testing, of which there are more than twenty types in total.

Software testing is a curious part of software engineering. Given that it is the key cost driver for software projects, and that testing costs go up with application size, it is alarming that testing is seldom done well. And yet, the topic is covered by some of the best software engineering books by some of the best authors. A quick search of the web or online bookstores will turn up dozens of books about software testing, and many of these are quite good.

There seem to be some social reasons for why testing is not as sophisticated as it should be. One of these is that not every test team member actually reads any of the books on testing. Another is that tests by certified test personnel who do know how to test well are still outnumbered by amateur testers or developers who may lack training and who may not have read the testing books either. A third reason, addressed by this book, is that many of the older testing books cover only part of the problem of achieving good testing results.

Many testing books are, as might be expected, "how-to-do-it" books that step through a sequence of test planning, test-case design, test-case construction, test execution, defect identification, defect repair, and repair integration. These are all teachable skills, and they should be better known than they are.

Don Firesmith's new book on testing approaches testing from a different perspective. Rather than being another "how-to-do-it" book, this book examines testing from the opposite direction. It explains the errors and failures of testing that he has observed over his long career in software and his work with the Software Engineering Institute (SEI).

This reverse view makes Don's book a natural complement to "how-to-do-it" books. I think that this is the first book on testing that emphasizes what goes wrong and how these problems might be avoided.

In other fields, combining how to do something with avoiding common problems is a standard part of the instruction sequence. For example, when learning to play golf, modern golf schools have video cameras that film golf students during lessons. The golf instructors go through the videos with each student and show them exactly what they did well and what they did poorly. This is an effective training technique. It is actually much harder to stop doing the wrong things than it is to learn to do the right things.

Other fields, such as professional football, also divide training into what has to be done right and what happens when the basics are not done right. This is why coaches and players review films after every game.

Until this new book on software testing, the literature only emphasized doing things well; it was a bit short on what happens if things are not done well.

In this book, a "pitfall" is any action or decision that might lower the effectiveness of testing. Don identifies ninety-two of these pitfalls, which is certainly the largest number I've encountered to date.

This book somewhat resembles a classic medical textbook that defines various illnesses and then discusses the available therapies for them. Each of the ninety-two pitfalls is defined and discussed using a standard format and identical points, which makes the book very easy to follow.

The pitfall descriptions use common headings, such as:

- Descriptions
- Potential Applicability
- Characteristic Symptoms
- Potential Negative Consequences
- Potential Causes
- Recommendations
- Related Pitfalls

This format is similar to a book I wrote some years ago, entitled *Assessment and Control of Software Risks,* published by Prentice Hall. My book used an actual medical text, *Control of Communicable Diseases in Man,* published by the U.S. Public Health Service, as the pattern.

Having worked as a programmer and systems analyst for the U.S. Public Health Service, I was in close contact with medical diagnostic methods, and they seemed to be appropriate for diagnosing software problems.

Some of my topics are very similar to Don's, such as:

- Definition
- Severity
- Susceptibility and Resistance
- Methods of Prevention
- Methods of Control

Applying some of the diagnostic patterns from medical practice to software engineering problems is a useful way to understand serious and common conditions, and Don has taken this idea to a new level for software engineering, and especially so for testing.

Testing is the main form of defect removal for software applications, but it is not the only form. A synergistic combination of defect prevention; pretest removal, such as inspections and static analysis; and formal testing by trained and certified test personnel can approach or exceed 99% in cumulative defect-removal efficiency levels. Even better, these good results come with shorter schedules and lower costs since the main source of software project delay is excessive defects during testing, which stretches out test schedules to several times their planned durations.

I recommend *Common System and Software Testing Pitfalls* for project managers, test personnel, quality-assurance personnel, and software engineers at all levels. All of us in software should know the common problems that we face during testing and how these problems might be avoided or minimized.

Don's book is a very good addition both to the testing literature and to the literature on quality assurance and software engineering. It is likely to become a standard for test training as well as a good reference for professional testers and developers. It would be a good teaching aid for young software engineers and a good handbook for all of us

I would also recommend this book as background material for negotiating outsourced software contracts. I often work as an expert witness in litigation for software with very poor quality, and this book might well reduce or eliminate these lawsuits if it were consulted before contract negotiations.

—Capers Jones, VP and CTO
Namcook Analytics LLC

PREFACE

There are numerous good books on systems and software testing, and most testers probably already have several on their shelves. There seems to be no scarcity of how-to books on testing, and they are full of excellent advice on how to test software-reliant systems. They cover test planning, the many different types of tests, how testing fits in to the development cycle, test-case design—including test-case-selection and test-completion criteria—test tools and environments, and many other interesting and useful topics.

Yet we spend a huge amount of time and effort testing, and in spite of this, we deliver systems with dozens if not hundreds of residual defects. In addition to being a tester, I have also taken part in numerous internal as well as independent technical assessments (ITAs) of system and software development projects, including their testing organizations and programs. And in every single case, regardless of whether I was a member of the test team or the assessment team, I have always observed several significant testing problems. More specifically, I have observed testers and other developers falling into the same pitfalls over and over again. Clearly, how-to books—while highly useful—are not sufficient to make testing either efficient or effective.

The frustration I experienced by enduring and observing these commonly occurring testing pitfalls led to this book. If the many how-to books are insufficient by themselves, then clearly it is time to try something different: a *how-not-to* book.

You can think of this book as a catalog and repository of testing anti-patterns: the pitfalls to avoid, how to mitigate their negative consequences if you can't avoid them, and how to escape from them once you've fallen in. Like a naturalist's field guide to wild animals, let this be your guidebook to the dangerous world of testing mistakes and its denizens—the many creative ways people have discovered to botch testing.

Scope

The scope of this book is *testing*, which is only one of several methods commonly used to validate that a system meets its stakeholders' needs and to verify that the system conforms to its specified requirements. Although other such methods (for example, inspections, demonstrations, reviews, analysis, simulation, reuse, and certification) exist and could be documented in a similar manner, they are beyond the scope of this book.

The scope of this book is also the testing of *software-reliant systems*, which often are heterogeneous aggregations of subsystems, hardware, software, data, facilities, material, and personnel. This includes the testing of pure software applications and their components. For simplicity's sake, I will use the term *system* to mean heterogeneous systems, software applications, and their architectural, design, and implementation components.

The pitfalls in this book primarily apply to large and medium-sized projects producing important systems and software applications that require at least a quasi-rigorous testing program and process. The pitfalls do not necessarily apply to very small and simple projects producing relatively trivial systems or software programs that (1) are neither business-, mission-, safety-, nor security-critical; (2) will be used only in-house with close collaboration between stakeholders and developers; (3) will be used once and not maintained; or (4) are prototypes that will not be placed into operation. Such systems often can be adequately tested in a highly informal and ad hoc manner. Some of the pitfalls apply only or primarily to testing systems having significant hardware, and these pitfalls therefore do not (primarily) apply to testing software-only applications.

Intended Audience

This book is written primarily for testers and their technical managers. It is intended to help you recognize and avoid potential testing-related pitfalls.

This book is also written for all stakeholders in system development and sustainment who need a better understanding of what can go wrong with testing, both when preparing for testing and during the actual testing. This includes customer and user representatives, project managers and technical leaders, requirements engineers, architects and designers, implementers, maintainers, and specialty engineers (such as configuration managers, quality engineers, reliability engineers, and human factors engineers).

Finally, this book is written for testing subject-matter experts, whether academics or consultants, who need a more organized and comprehensive understanding of what can go wrong with testing.

How to Use This Book and Its Contents

The primary goal of this book is to provide the information you need to

- Avoid falling into any of the commonly occurring testing pitfalls
- Recognize when you have already fallen into one or more testing pitfalls
- Escape from these pitfalls while minimizing the resulting negative consequences

This book provides detailed information on the commonly occurring testing pitfalls, and it can be used

- To improve understanding of and communication about commonly occurring testing pitfalls
- As training material for testers and the stakeholders of testing
- As checklists[1][1] when
  - Developing and reviewing an organizational or project testing process or strategy
  - Developing and reviewing test planning documentation, such as:
    - Test and Evaluation Master Plans (TEMPs), System Test Plans (STPs), or Test Strategy Documents (TSDs)
    - The testing sections of planning documents such as the System Engineering Management Plan (SEMP) and the System Development Plan (SDP)
    - Test planning presentations (for example, for training and status reporting)
    - Testing wikis, SharePoint sites, and Application Lifecycle Management (ALM) tool repositories
  - Evaluating the testing-related parts of contractor proposals
  - Evaluating test planning documentation, test descriptions, and test results (quality control)
  - Evaluating the actual as-performed testing process (quality assurance)[2]
  - Identifying testing risks and appropriate risk-mitigation approaches
- To categorize testing pitfalls for metrics collection, analysis, and reporting

---

1. Notes are identified by a bracketed number ([#]), and are located in Appendix C, Notes.

- To help identify testing areas potentially needing improvement, both during a project and at its conclusion, such as during project postmortems

Organization of This Book

This book is organized as follows:

- **Preface**

  This preface begins with a brief introduction to the book, followed by a description of the book's scope and its intended audience. Next, it offers brief advice on how best to use the information provided here. Finally, I acknowledge the book's many technical reviewers, without whom it would not be half as good.

- **Chapter 1: Foundational Concepts**

  The first chapter defines the most important concepts in this book: testing, defects, and testing pitfalls. It presents the system-engineering V Models that explain how different types of testing are associated with the project's work products. It addresses why testing is so important as well as explains why it has some significant limitations. Finally, it explains how the testing pitfalls are categorized and documented to make them easier to locate and to understand.

- **Chapter 2: Brief Overviews of the Testing Pitfalls**

  The second chapter identifies and summarizes ninety-two commonly occurring testing pitfalls. The purpose of Chapter 2 is to provide a *very* brief, high-level overview of each pitfall, making it easy for readers to search for and identify pitfalls relevant or specific to their situations.

- **Chapter 3: Detailed Descriptions of the Testing Pitfalls**

  The third chapter provides detailed descriptions of each of the commonly occurring testing pitfalls. Specifically, it documents each pitfall as follows: its name, description, applicability, characteristic symptoms, potential negative consequences, potential causes, and associated recommendations for avoiding the pitfall or limiting its consequences. Chapter 3 is intended to be used primarily as a handy reference once relevant pitfalls are identified via either the Contents section or Chapter 2. Thus, I suggest that you read this chapter as you would read the patterns in a patterns book: once through rapidly to get a basic understand of the pitfalls, then examine the detailed specifications of individual pitfalls on an as-needed basis.

- **Chapter 4: Conclusion**

  The fourth and final chapter provides a holistic summary of the pitfalls before concluding with a brief look at potential future research that might make this categorization of testing pitfalls even more useful.

- **Appendixes**

  The appendixes start with a glossary of terms and a list of acronyms. In order to keep the descriptions of the individual pitfalls reasonably short—especially for the experienced tester, who will recognize the majority of these pitfalls— Appendix C provides extensive notes for those who might desire a little extra information. The notes are identified by bracketed numbers [#] throughout the text. The book's relatively short list of references comes next. The final appendix is a checklist that can be used when planning testing and assessing testing programs and organizations.

Acknowledgments

I am grateful for the interest of the more than 350 testers, testing subject-matter experts (SMEs), and academics from forty-six countries who volunteered to review various draft versions of this book. I am extremely grateful to the following individuals who provided excellent review comments and recommendations, often several times, while reviewing different drafts of the manuscript:

Dimpy Adhikary, Amagi Media Labs, India
Vince Alcalde, Independent Consultant, Australia
Stephanie Benedetti, AIPSO, US
Laxmi Bhat, Minerva Networks, US
Robert V. Binder, System Verification Associates, US
Peter Bolin, Revolution IT Pty Ltd, Australia
Michael Bolton, DevelopSense, Canada
Paul Carvalho, Software Testing and Quality Services, Canada
Alexandru Cosma, Frequentis, Romania
John Dannenberg, Compuware Corporation, US
Jorge Alberto De Flon, Servicio de Administración Tributara (SAT), Mexico
George Despotou, University of York, UK
Lee Eldridge, Independent Consultant, Australia
Eliazar Elisha, University of Liverpool, UK
Robin Goldsmith, Go Pro Management Inc., US
Jon L. Gross, Software Engineering Institute, US
Paolo Guolo, Private Consultant, Italy
Kobi Halperin, Ceragon Networks, Israel
Sam Harbaugh, Integrated Software Inc., US
John Hawrylak, Software Engineering Institute, US
M. E. Hom, Compass360 Consulting, US
Thanh Cong Huynh, LogiGear, Vietnam
Capers Jones, Namcook Analytics, US

Ronald Kohl, Independent Consultant, US

Wido Kunde, Baker Hughes, Germany

Seth Landsman, The MITRE Corporation, US

Philippe Lebacq, Toyota Motors Europe, Belgium

Stephen Masters, Software Engineering Institute, US

Ken Nidiffer, Software Engineering Institute, US

Anne Nieberding, Independent Consultant, US

William Novak, Software Engineering Institute, US

Mahesh Palan, Calypso Technology, US

Dan Pautler, Elekta, US

David C. Peterson, Protengent, US

Mark Powel, Attwater Consulting, US

James Redpath, Sogeti, US

Sudip Saha, Navigators Software, India

Alejandro Salado, Kayser—Threde GmbH, Germany

David Schultz, NASA, US

Matt Sheranko, Knowledge Code, US

Oleg Spozito, Independent Consultant, Canada

Barry Stanly, Independent Consultant, US

Amit Wertheimer, EMC Corporation, RSA, Israel

Lou Wheatcraft, Requirements Experts, US

Kerry Wilkerson, Private Consultant, US

Allison Yeager, Blackbaud, US

Thomas Zalewski, Texas State Government, US

Although the vast majority of the comments and recommendations from each of the reviewers made it into this book in one form or another, that does not mean that every reviewer would necessarily agree with everything in it. Further, I naturally take responsibility for any errors that slipped past my diligent reviewers and made it into the final book.

I would like to thank John Foreman, an SEI fellow and member of the management team, who provided the funding and time I needed to finalize the manuscript for publication.

Finally, I would like to thank the acquisition and production teams at Addison-Wesley for their strong support in publishing this book. Deserving special mention are Bernard Goodwin, my acquisitions editor, and Vicki Rowland, who copyedited the manuscript and created a very high level of consistency of both content and format. Both worked closely with me through several iterations of the book's cover and contents, thereby making this the most enjoyable of my books to bring to completion.

ABOUT THE AUTHOR

Donald G. Firesmith, a senior member of the technical staff in the Software Solutions Division at the Software Engineering Institute (SEI), helps the US Department of Defense and other governmental agencies acquire large, complex, software-reliant systems. He is an internationally recognized subject matter expert who has published seven software and systems engineering books in the areas of requirements engineering, architecture engineering, situational method engineering, testing, and object-oriented development. With thirty-five years of industry experience, he has also published dozens of technical articles, spoken at numerous international conferences, and has been the program chair or on the program committee of several software conferences. He has taught several hundred courses in commercial and governmental settings (both civilian and military, as well as numerous tutorials at international conferences. Copies of his numerous papers and presentations are downloadable from his personal website: http://donald.firesmith.net.

CHAPTER 1

OVERVIEW

1.1 What Is Testing?

Testing is the activity of executing a system, subsystem, or component under specific preconditions (for example, pretest mode, states, stored data, and external conditions) with specific inputs so that its actual behavior (outputs and postconditions) can be compared with its required or expected behavior.

Testing differs from other verification and validation methods (for example, analysis, demonstration, and inspection) in that it is a dynamic, as opposed to a static, analysis method that involves the actual execution of the thing being tested.

Testing has the following goals:

- Primary goal:
  - Enable the system under test (SUT) to be improved by:
    - "Breaking" it (that is, by causing faults and failures)
    - Exposing its defects so that they can be fixed
- Secondary goals:
  - Provide adequate confidence based on sufficient objective evidence regarding the SUT's:
    - Quality
      A system's quality is not just its lack of defects or its correctness (in terms of meeting its requirements). A system must also have the necessary levels of relevant quality characteristics and attributes; for example, availability, capacity, extensibility, maintainability, performance, portability, reliability, robustness, safety, security, and usability.
    - Fitness for purpose
    - Readiness for shipping, deployment, or being placed into operation

1

1.2 Testing and the V Models

Figure 1.1 illustrates a common way of modeling system engineering: the traditional V Model of system engineering activities.[1] On the left side of the V are the analysis activities that decompose the users' problem into small, manageable pieces. Similarly, the right side of the V shows the synthesis activities that aggregate (and test) these pieces into the system that solves the users' problem.

While useful, the traditional V model does not really represent system engineering from the tester's viewpoint. The next three figures show three increasingly detailed V models that better capture the testing-specific aspects of system engineering.

Figure 1.2 illustrates a V model oriented around work products rather than activities. Specifically, these are the major executable work products because testing involves the execution of work products. In this case, the left side of the V illustrates the analysis of ever more detailed executable models, whereas the right side of the V illustrates the corresponding incremental and iterative synthesis of the actual system. This V model shows the executable things that are tested rather than the general system engineering activities that generate them.

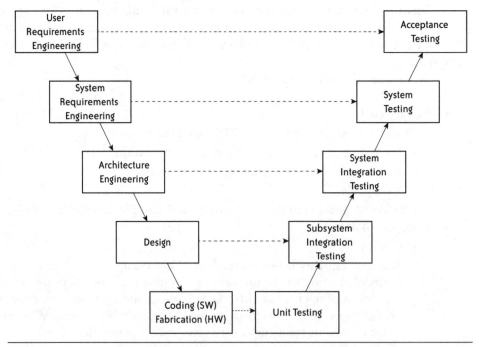

FIGURE 1.1 Traditional Single V model of system engineering activities

1. V stands for both validation and verification.

Figure 1.3 illustrates the Double-V model, which adds the corresponding tests to the Single V Model [Feiler 2012]. The key ideas to take away from this model are:

- Every executable work product should be tested. Testing need not, and in fact should not, be restricted to the implemented system and its parts. It is also important to test any executable requirements, architecture, and design. In this way, associated defects are found and fixed before they can migrate to the actual system and its parts. This typically involves testing executable requirements, architecture, or design models of the system under test (SUT) that are implemented in modeling languages (typically state-based and sufficiently formal) such as SpecTRM-RL, Architecture Analysis and Design Language (AADL), and Program Design Language (PDL); simulations of the SUT; or executable prototypes of the SUT.
- Tests should be created and performed as the corresponding work products are created. The short arrows with two arrowheads are used to show that (1) the executable work products can be developed first and used to drive the

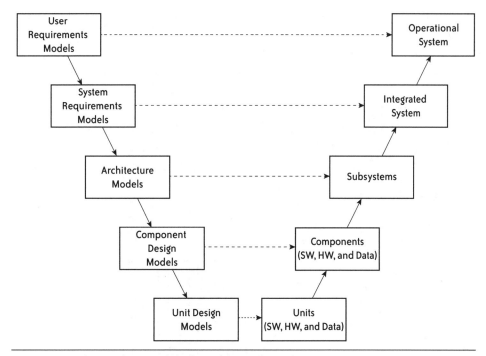

FIGURE 1.2   The Single V model of testable work products

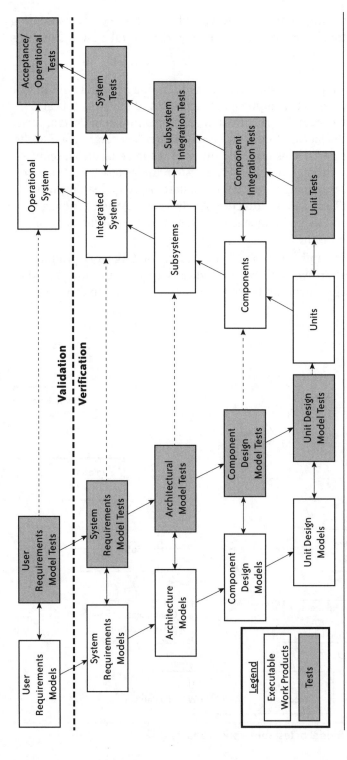

FIGURE 1.3 The Double V model of testable work products and corresponding tests

creation of the tests or (2) Test Driven Development (TDD) can be used, in which case the tests are developed before the work product they test.

- The top row of the model uses testing to *validate* that the system meets the needs of its stakeholders (that is, that the correct system is built). Conversely, the bottom four rows of the model use testing to *verify* that the system is built correctly (that is, architecture conforms to requirements, design conforms to architecture, implementation conforms to design, and so on).

- Finally, in practice, the two sides of the bottom row typically are combined so that the unit design models are incorporated into the units and so that the programming language is used as a program design language (PDL). Similarly, the unit design model tests are incorporated into the unit tests so that the same unit tests verify both the unit design and its implementation.

Figure 1.4 documents the Triple-V model, in which additional verification activities have been added to verify that the testing activities were performed properly. This provides evidence that testing is sufficiently complete and that it will not produce numerous false-positive and false-negative results.

Although the V models appear to show a sequential waterfall development cycle, they also can be used to illustrate an evolutionary (that is, incremental, iterative, and concurrent) development cycle that incorporates many small, potentially overlapping V models. However, when applying a V model to the agile development of a large, complex system, there are some potential complications that require more than a simple collection of small V models, such as:

- The architecturally significant requirements and the associated architecture need to be firmed up as rapidly as is practical because all subsequent increments depend on the architecture, which is difficult and expensive to modify once the initial increment(s) have been based on it.

- Multiple, cross-functional agile teams will be working on different components and subsystems simultaneously, so their increments must be coordinated across teams to produce consistent, testable components and subsystems that can be integrated and released.

Finally, it is interesting to note that these V models are applicable not just to the system under development but also to the development of the system's test environments or test beds and its test laboratories or facilities.

1.3 What Is a Defect?

A system *defect* (informally known as a bug) is a flaw or weakness in the system or one of its components that could cause it to behave in an unintended, unwanted manner or to exhibit an unintended, unwanted property. Defects are related to, but are different from:

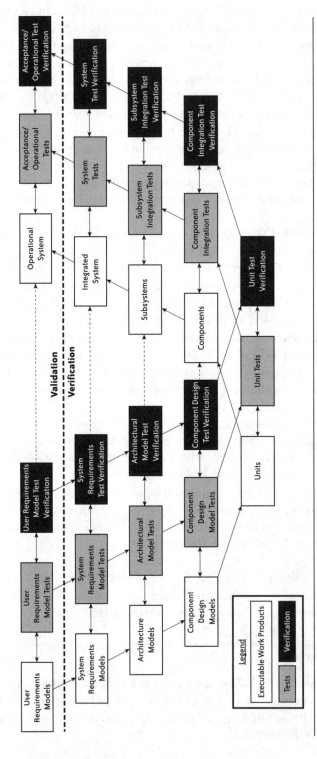

FIGURE 1.4 The Triple V model of work products, tests, and test verification

- **Errors**   Human mistakes that cause the defect (for example, making a programming mistake or inputting incorrect data)
- **Faults**   Incorrect conditions that are system-internal and not directly visible from outside the system's boundary (for example, the system stores incorrect data or is in an incorrect mode or state)
- **Failures**   Events or conditions in which the system visibly behaves incorrectly or has incorrect properties (that is, one or more of its behaviors or properties are different from what its stakeholders can reasonably expect)

Common examples of defects include the following flaws or weaknesses:

- Defects can cause the SUT to violate specified (or unspecified) requirements, including:
  - Functional requirements
  - Data requirements
  - Interface requirements
  - Quality requirements
  - Architecture, design, implementation, and configuration constraints
- Defects can also result when the SUT conforms to incorrect or unnecessary requirements.
- Defects can cause the SUT to:
  - Fail to behave as it should
  - Be missing characteristics that it should have
  - Behave as it should not behave
  - Have characteristics that it should not have
- Defects can cause the SUT to be inconsistent with its architecture or design.
- Defects can result from incorrect or inappropriate architecture, design, implementation, or configuration decisions.
- Defects can violate design guidelines or coding standards.
- Defects can be safety or security vulnerabilities (for example, using inherently unsafe language features or failure to verify input data).

1.4   Why Is Testing Critical?

A National Institute of Standards & Technology (NIST) report [NIST 2002] states that inadequate testing methods and tools cost the US economy between $22.2 billion and $59.5 billion annually, with roughly half of these costs borne by software developers, in the form of extra testing, and half by software users, in the form of failure avoidance and mitigation efforts. The same study notes that between 25% and 90% of software development budgets are often spent on testing.

Testing is currently the most important of the standard verification and validation methods used during system development and maintenance. This is not because testing is necessarily the most effective and efficient way to verify that the system behaves as it should; it is not. (See Table 1.1, below.) Rather, it is because far more effort, funding, and time are expended on testing than on all other types of verification put together.

According to Capers Jones, most forms of testing find only about 35% of the code defects [Jones 2013b]. Similarly, on average, individual programmers find less than half the defects in their own software.

For example, Capers Jones analyzed data regarding defect identification effectiveness from projects that were completed in early 2013 and produced the results summarized in Table 1.1 [Jones 2013a]. Thus, the use of requirements inspections identified 87% of requirements defects and 25.6% of all defects in the software and its documentation. Similarly, static analysis of the code identified 87% of the code defects and 33.2% of all defects. Finally, a project that used all of these static verification methods identified 95% of all defects.

As Table 1.2 shows, static verification methods are cumulatively more effective at identifying defects except, surprisingly, documentation defects.

TABLE 1.1 Average Percentage of Defects Found as a Function of Static Verification Method and Defect Type

Verification Method	Defect Type (Location)					Total Effectiveness
	Requirements	Architecture	Design	Code	Documentation	
Requirements Inspection	87%	5%	10%	5%	8.5%	25.6%
Architecture Inspection	10%	85%	10%	2.5%	12%	14.9%
Design Inspection	14%	10%	87%	7%	16%	37.3%
Code Inspection	15%	12.5%	20%	85%	10%	70.1%
Static Analysis	2%	2%	7%	87%	3%	33.2%
IV&V	12%	10%	23%	7%	18%	16.5%
SQA Review	17%	10%	17%	12%	12.4%	28.1%
Total	95.2%	92.7%	96.1%	99.1%	58.8%	95.0%

Source: Jones 2013a

TABLE 1.2 Cumulative Effectiveness at Finding Defects by Static Verification Methods, Testing, and Both

Verification Method	Defect Type (Location)					Total Effectiveness
	Requirements	Architecture	Design	Code	Documentation	
Static	95.2%	92.7%	96.1%	99.1%	58.8%	95.0%
Testing	72.3%	74.0%	87.6%	93.4%	95.5%	85.7%
Total	98.11%	98.68%	99.52%	99.94%	98.13%	99.27%

Source: Jones 2013a

1.5   The Limitations of Testing

In spite of its critical nature, testing has a number of pitfalls that make it far less effective and efficient than it should be. Testing is relatively ineffective in the sense that a significant number of residual defects remain in a completed system when it is placed into operation. Testing is also relatively inefficient when you consider the large amount of effort, funding, and time that is currently spent to find defects.

According to Capers Jones, most types of testing find only about 35% of the software defects [Jones 2013]. This is consistent with the following, more detailed analysis of defect detection rates as a function of test type and test capabilities, as shown in Table 1.3 [McConnell 2004].

As Table 1.4 shows, no single type of testing is very effective at uncovering defects, regardless of defect type. Even when all of these testing methods are used on an average project, they still only identify four out of five of the code defects.

TABLE 1.3 Defect Detection Rate

Test Type	Defect Detection Rates		
	Lowest	Mode	Highest
Unit Test	15%	30%	50%
Component Test	20%	30%	35%
Integration Test	25%	35%	40%
System Test	25%	40%	55%
Regression Test	15%	25%	30%
Low-volume Beta Test	25%	35%	40%
High-volume Beta Test	60%	75%	85%

Source: McConnell 2004

TABLE 1.4 Defect Detection Rate

Static Verification	Project Defect Detection Rate		
	Worst	Average	Best
Desk Checking	23%	25%	27%
Static Analysis	0%	55%	55%
Inspection	0%	0%	93%
Static Subtotal	19%	64%	98%

Testing	Project Defect Detection Rate		
	Worst	Average	Best
Unit Test	28%	30%	32%
Function Test	31%	33%	35%
Regression Test	10%	12%	14%
Component Test	28%	30%	32%
Performance Test	6%	10%	14%
System Test	32%	34%	36%
Acceptance Test	13%	15%	17%
Testing Subtotal	72%	81%	87%
Cumulative Total	81.1%	95.6%	99.96%

Source: Jones 2013b

1.6 What Is a Testing Pitfall?

A testing pitfall is any decision, mindset, action, or failure to act that unnecessarily and, potentially unexpectedly, causes testing to be less effective, less efficient, or more frustrating to perform. Basically, a testing pitfall is a commonly occurring way to screw up testing, and projects fall into pitfalls when testers, managers, requirements engineers, and other testing stakeholders make testing-related mistakes that can have unintended negative consequences.

In a sense, the description of a testing pitfall constitutes a testing antipattern. However, the term pitfall was specifically chosen to evoke the image of a hidden or not easily identified trap for the unwary or uninitiated. As with any trap, it is better to avoid a testing pitfall than it is to have to dig one's self and one's project out of it after having fallen in.

1.7 Categorizing Pitfalls

Many testing pitfalls can occur during the development or maintenance of software-reliant systems and software applications. While no project is likely to be so poorly managed and executed as to experience the majority of these pitfalls, most projects will suffer several of them. Similarly, although these testing pitfalls do not guarantee failure, they definitely pose serious risks that need to be managed.

This book documents 92 pitfalls that have been observed to commonly occur during testing. These pitfalls are categorized as follows:

- **General Testing Pitfalls**
  - Test Planning and Scheduling Pitfalls
  - Stakeholder Involvement and Commitment Pitfalls
  - Management-Related Testing Pitfalls
  - Staffing Pitfalls
  - Test Process Pitfalls
  - Test Tools and Environments Pitfalls
  - Test Communication Pitfalls
  - Requirements-Related Testing Pitfalls

- **Test-Type-Specific Pitfalls**
  - Unit Testing Pitfalls
  - Integration Testing Pitfalls
  - Specialty Engineering Testing Pitfalls
  - System Testing Pitfalls
  - System of Systems (SoS) Testing Pitfalls
  - Regression Testing Pitfalls

Although each of these testing pitfalls has been observed on multiple projects, it is entirely possible that you might have testing pitfalls that are not addressed by this document. Please notify me of any new testing pitfalls you stumble across or any additional recommended changes to the current pitfalls so that I can incorporate them into future editions of this book.

1.8 Pitfall Specifications

Chapter 2 gives high-level descriptions of the different pitfalls, while Chapter 3 documents each testing pitfall with the following detailed information:

- **Title**   A short, descriptive name of the pitfall
- **Description**   A brief definition of the pitfall
- **Potential Applicability**   The context in which the pitfall may be applicable
- **Characteristic Symptoms (or, How You Will Know)**   Symptoms that indicate the possible existence of the pitfall
- **Potential Negative Consequences (Why You Should Care)**   Potential negative consequences to expect if the pitfall is not avoided or mitigated[3]
- **Potential Causes**   Potential root and proximate causes of the pitfall[4]
- **Recommendations (What You Should Do)**   Recommended actions (prepare, enable, perform, and verify) to take to avoid or mitigate the pitfall[5]
- **Related Pitfalls**   A list of other related testing pitfalls

A few words on word choice and grammar are probably appropriate before you start reading about the individual pitfalls:

- **Potential Applicability**   You may fall into these pitfalls on your project, but then again you may not. Some pitfalls will be more probable and therefore more relevant than others. Of course, if you have already fallen into a given pitfall, it ceases to be potentially applicable and is now absolutely applicable. Because potential applicability currently exists, it is described in the present tense.
- **Characteristic Symptoms**   You may have observed these symptoms in the past, and you may well be observing them now. They may even be waiting for you in the future. To save me from having to write all three tenses and, more importantly, to save you from having to read them all, I have listed all symptoms in present tense.
- **Potential Negative Consequences**   Once again, you may have suffered these consequences in the past, or they may be happening now. These consequences might still be in the future and avoidable (or subject to mitigation) if you follow the appropriate recommendations now. These consequences are also listed in the present tense.

Note that sometimes the first symptom(s) of a pitfall are the negative consequence(s) you are suffering from because you fell into it. Therefore, it is not always obvious whether something should be listed under symptoms, consequences, or both. To avoid listing the same negative event or situation twice for the same pitfall, I have endeavored to include it only once under the most obvious heading.

- **Potential Causes**   Finally, the causes may also lie in your past, your present, or your future. However, they seem to sound best when written in the past tense, for they must by their very nature precede the pitfall's symptoms and consequences.

CHAPTER 2

BRIEF OVERVIEWS OF THE TESTING PITFALLS

This chapter provides a high-level descriptive overview of the testing pitfalls, including the symptoms by which you can recognize them.

2.1 General Testing Pitfalls

These general testing pitfalls are not primarily specific to any single type of testing.

2.1.1 Test Planning and Scheduling Pitfalls

The following pitfalls are related to test planning and scheduling:

1. *No Separate Test Planning Documentation (GEN-TPS-1)*
There is no separate testing-specific planning documentation, only incomplete, high-level overviews of testing in the general planning documents.

2. *Incomplete Test Planning (GEN-TPS-2)*
Test planning and its associated documentation are not sufficiently complete for the current point in the system development cycle.

3. *Test Plans Ignored (GEN-TPS-3)*
The test planning documentation is ignored (that is, it becomes "shelfware") once it is developed and delivered. It is neither used nor maintained.

4. *Test-Case Documents as Test Plans (GEN-TPS-4)*
Test-case documents that document specific test cases are mislabeled as test plans.

5. *Inadequate Test Schedule (GEN-TPS-5)*
The testing schedule is inadequate to complete proper testing.

6. *Testing at the End (GEN-TPS-6)*

All testing is performed late in the development cycle; there is little or no testing of executable models or unit or integration testing planned or performed during the early and middle stages of the development cycle.

2.1.2 Stakeholder Involvement and Commitment Pitfalls

The following pitfalls are related to stakeholder involvement in and commitment to testing:

7. *Wrong Testing Mindset (GEN-SIC-1)*

Some testers and testing stakeholders have an incorrect testing mindset, such as (1) the purpose of testing is to demonstrate that the system works properly rather than to determine where and how it fails, (2) it is the responsibility of testers to verify or "prove" that the system works, (3) the system is assumed to work, and so there is no reason to show that it doesn't work, and (4) testing is viewed as a cost center (that is, an expense) rather than as an investment (or something that can minimize future expenses).

8. *Unrealistic Testing Expectations (GEN-SIC-2)*

Testing stakeholders (especially customer representatives and managers) have unrealistic testing expectations, such as (1) testing detects all (or even the majority of) defects, (2) testing *proves* that there are no remaining defects and that the system therefore works as intended, (3) testing can be, for all practical purposes, exhaustive, (4) testing can be relied on for *all* verification, even though some requirements are better verified via analysis, demonstration, or inspection, and (5) testing (if it is automated) will guarantee the quality of the tests and reduce the testing effort.

9. *Lack of Stakeholder Commitment to Testing (GEN-SIC-3)*

Stakeholder commitment to the testing effort is inadequate; sufficient resources (for example, people, time in the schedule, tools, or funding) are not allocated the testing effort.

2.1.3 Management-Related Testing Pitfalls

The following testing pitfalls are related to management failures:

10. *Inadequate Test Resources (GEN-MGMT-1)*

Management allocates an inadequate amount of resources to testing, including (1) test time in the schedule with inadequate schedule reserves, (2) adequately trained and experienced testers and reviewers, (3) funding, and (4) test tools, test environments (for example, integration test beds and repositories of test data), and test facilities.

11. *Inappropriate External Pressures (GEN-MGMT-2)*
Managers and others in positions of authority subject testers to inappropriate external pressures.

12. *Inadequate Test-Related Risk Management (GEN-MGMT-3)*
There are too few test-related risks identified in the project's official risk repository, and those that are identified have inappropriately low probabilities, low harm severities, and low priorities.

13. *Inadequate Test Metrics (GEN-MGMT-4)*
Too few test-related metrics are being produced, analyzed, reported, and used in decision making.

14. *Inconvenient Test Results Ignored (GEN-MGMT-5)*
Management ignores or treats lightly inconvenient negative test results (especially those with negative ramifications for the schedule, budget, or system quality).

15. *Test Lessons Learned Ignored (GEN-MGMT-6)*
Lessons learned from testing on previous projects are ignored and not placed into practice on the current project.

2.1.4 Staffing Pitfalls

These pitfalls stem from personnel issues in one way or another:

16. *Lack of Independence (GEN-STF-1)*
The test organization or project test team lack adequate technical, managerial, and financial independence to enable them to withstand inappropriate pressure from the development (administrative and technical) management to cut corners.

17. *Unclear Testing Responsibilities (GEN-STF-2)*
The testing responsibilities are unclear and do not adequately address which organizations, teams, and people are going to be responsible for and perform the different types of testing.

18. *Inadequate Testing Expertise (GEN-STF-3)*
Some testers and testing stakeholders have inadequate testing-related understanding, expertise, experience, or training.

19. *Developers Responsible for All Testing (GEN-STF-4)*
There is no separate full-time tester role. Instead, every member of each development team is responsible for testing what he or she designed and implemented.

20. *Testers Responsible for All Testing (GEN-STF-5)*
Testers are responsible for all of the testing during system development. Developers are not even performing unit testing (of either their own software or that of their peers).

2.1.5 Test-Process Pitfalls

These pitfalls are related to the testing process rather than the people performing the testing:

21. *Testing and Engineering Processes Not Integrated (GEN-PRO-1)*
The testing process is not adequately integrated into the overall system engineering process, but is rather treated as a separate specialty engineering activity with only limited interfaces with the primary engineering activities.

22. *One-Size-Fits-All Testing (GEN-PRO-2)*
All testing is performed the same way, to the same level of rigor, regardless of its criticality.

23. *Inadequate Test Prioritization (GEN-PRO-3)*
Testing is not adequately prioritized (for example, all types of testing have the same priority).

24. *Functionality Testing Overemphasized (GEN-PRO-4)*
There is an overemphasis on testing functionality as opposed to testing quality, data, and interface requirements and testing architectural, design, and implementation constraints.

25. *Black-Box System Testing Overemphasized (GEN-PRO-5)*
There is an overemphasis on black-box system testing for requirements conformance, and there is very little white-box unit and integration testing for the architecture, design, and implementation verification.

26. *Black-Box System Testing Underemphasized (GEN-PRO-6)*
There is an overemphasis on white-box unit and integration testing, and very little time is spent on black-box system testing to verify conformance to the requirements.

27. *Too Immature for Testing (GEN-PRO-7)*
Products are delivered for testing when they are immature and not ready to be tested.

28. *Inadequate Evaluations of Test Assets (GEN-PRO-8)*
The quality of the test assets is not adequately evaluated prior to using them.

29. *Inadequate Maintenance of Test Assets (GEN-PRO-9)*
Test assets are not properly maintained (that is, adequately updated and iterated) as defects are found and the system or software under test (SUT) is changed.

30. *Testing as a Phase (GEN-PRO-10)*

Testing is treated as a phase that takes place late in a sequential (also known as waterfall) development cycle instead of as an ongoing activity that takes place continuously in an iterative, incremental, and concurrent (an evolutionary, or agile) development cycle.[6]

31. *Testers Not Involved Early (GEN-PRO-11)*

Testers are not involved at the beginning of the project, but rather only once an implementation exists to test.

32. *Incomplete Testing (GEN-PRO-12)*

The testers inappropriately fail to test certain testable behaviors, characteristics, or components of the system.

33. *No Operational Testing (GEN-PRO-13)*

Representative users are not performing any operational testing of the "completed" system under actual operational conditions.

34. *Inadequate Test Data (GEN-PRO-14)*

The test data (including individual test data and sets of test data) is incomplete or invalid.

35. *Test-Type Confusion (GEN-PRO-15)*

Test cases from one type of testing are redundantly repeated as part of another type of testing, even though the testing types have quite different purposes and scopes.

2.1.6   Test Tools and Environments Pitfalls

These pitfalls are related to the tools and environments used to perform testing:

36. *Over-Reliance on Manual Testing (GEN-TTE-1)*

Testers place too much reliance on manual testing such that the majority of testing is performed manually, without adequate support of test tools or test scripts.

37. *Over-Reliance on Testing Tools (GEN-TTE-2)*

Testers and other testing stakeholders place too much reliance on commercial off-the-shelf (COTS) and homegrown testing tools.

38. *Too Many Target Platforms (GEN-TTE-3)*

The test team and testers are not adequately prepared for testing applications that will execute on numerous target platforms (for example, hardware, operating system, and middleware).

39. *Target Platform Difficult to Access (GEN-TTE-4)*

The testers are not prepared to perform adequate testing when the target platform is not designed to enable access for testing.

40. *Inadequate Test Environments (GEN-TTE-5)*

There are insufficient test tools, test environments or test beds, and test laboratories or facilities, so adequate testing cannot be performed within the schedule and personnel limitations.

41. *Poor Fidelity of Test Environments (GEN-TTE-6)*

The testers build and use test environments or test beds that have poor fidelity to the operational environment of the system or software under test (SUT), and this causes inconclusive or incorrect test results (false-positive and false-negative test results).

42. *Inadequate Test Environment Quality (GEN-TTE-7)*

The quality of one or more test environments is inadequate due to an excessive number of defects.

43. *Test Assets Not Delivered (GEN-TTE-8)*

Developers deliver the system or software to the sustainers without the associated test assets. For example, delivering test assets (such as test plans, test reports, test cases, test oracles, test drivers or scripts, test stubs, and test environments) is neither required nor planned.

44. *Inadequate Test Configuration Management (GEN-TTE-9)*

Testing work products (for example, test cases, test scripts, test data, test tools, and test environments) are not under configuration management (CM).

45. *Developers Ignore Testability (GEN-TTE-10)*

It is unnecessarily difficult to develop automated tests because the developers do not consider testing when designing and implementing their system or software.

2.1.7 Test Communication Pitfalls

These pitfalls are related to poor communication with regard to testing:

46. *Inadequate Architecture or Design Documentation (GEN-COM-1)*[2]

Architects and designers produce insufficient architecture or design documentation (for example, models and documents) to support white-box (structural) unit and integration testing.

47. *Inadequate Defect Reports (GEN-COM-2)*

Testers and others create defect reports (also known as bug and trouble reports) that are incomplete, contain incorrect information, or are difficult to read.

---

2. Inadequate Requirements Documentation is covered in the next section, which concentrates on requirements.

48. *Inadequate Test Documentation (GEN-COM-3)*[3]

Testers create test documentation that is incomplete or contains incorrect information.

49. *Source Documents Not Maintained (GEN-COM-4)*

Developers do not properly maintain the requirements specifications, architecture documents, design documents, and associated models that are needed as inputs to the development of tests.

50. *Inadequate Communication Concerning Testing (GEN-COM-5)*

There is inadequate verbal and written communication concerning the testing among testers and other testing stakeholders.

2.1.8 Requirements-Related Testing Pitfalls

These pitfalls are related to the negative impact of poor requirements on testing:

51. *Ambiguous Requirements (GEN-REQ-1)*

Testers misinterpret a great many ambiguous requirements and therefore base their testing on incorrect interpretations of these requirements.

52. *Obsolete Requirements (GEN-REQ-2)*

Testers waste effort and time testing whether the system or software under test (SUT) correctly implements a great many obsolete requirements.

53. *Missing Requirements (GEN-REQ-3)*

Testers overlook many undocumented requirements and therefore do not plan for, develop, or run the associated overlooked test cases.

54. *Incomplete Requirements (GEN-REQ-4)*

Testers fail to detect that many requirements are incomplete; therefore, they develop and run correspondingly incomplete or incorrect test cases.

55. *Incorrect Requirements (GEN-REQ-5)*

Testers fail to detect that many requirements are incorrect, and therefore develop and run correspondingly incorrect test cases that produce false-positive and false-negative test results.

56. *Requirements Churn (GEN-REQ-6)*

Testers waste an excessive amount of time and effort developing and running test cases based on many requirements that are not sufficiently stable and that therefore change one or more times prior to delivery.

57. *Improperly Derived Requirements (GEN-REQ-7)*

Testers base their testing on improperly derived requirements, resulting in missing test cases, test cases at the wrong level of abstraction, or incorrect test

---

3. Incomplete test plans are addressed in Incomplete Test Planning (GEN-TPS-2). This pitfall is more general in that it addresses all testing documents, not just test plans.

cases based on cross cutting requirements that are allocated without modification to multiple architectural components.

58. *Verification Methods Not Properly Specified (GEN-REQ-8)*
Testers (or other developers) fail to properly specify the verification method(s) for each requirement, thereby causing requirements to be verified using unnecessarily inefficient or ineffective verification method(s).

59. *Lack of Requirements Trace (GEN-REQ-9)*
The testers do not trace the requirements to individual tests or test cases, thereby making it unnecessarily difficult to determine whether the tests are inadequate or excessive.

2.2 Test-Type-Specific Pitfalls

The following pitfalls are primarily restricted to a single type of testing:

2.2.1 Unit Testing Pitfalls

These pitfalls are related primarily to testing individual units:

60. *Testing Does* Not *Drive Design and Implementation (TTS-UNT-1)*
Software developers and testers do not develop their tests first and then use these tests to drive development of the associated architecture, design, and implementation.

61. *Conflict of Interest (TTS-UNT-2)*
Nothing is done to address the following conflict of interest that exists when developers test their own work products: Essentially, they are being asked to demonstrate that their software is defective.

2.2.2 Integration Testing Pitfalls

The following pitfalls are related primarily to integration testing:

62. *Integration Decreases Testability Ignored (TTS-INT-1)*
Testers fail to take into account that integration encapsulates the individual parts of the whole and the interactions between them, thereby making the internal parts of the integrated whole less observable and less controllable and, therefore, less testable.

63. *Inadequate Self-Monitoring (TTS-INT-2)*
Testers are unprepared to address the difficulty of testing encapsulated components due to a lack of system- or software-internal self-tests.

64. *Unavailable Components (TTS-INT-3)*
Integration testing must be postponed due to the unavailability of (1) system hardware or software components or (2) test environment components.

65. *System Testing as Integration Testing (TTS-INT-4)*

Testers are actually performing system-level tests of system functionality when they are supposed to be performing integration testing of component interfaces and interactions.

2.2.3 Specialty Engineering Testing Pitfalls

The following pitfalls are highly similar in nature, although they vary significantly in detail. This section could have been much larger because there are many different quality characteristics and associated attributes, each with its own associated potential symptoms, consequences, and causes.

66. *Inadequate Capacity Testing (TTS-SPC-1)*

Testers perform little or no capacity testing (or the capacity testing they do perform is superficial) to determine the degree to which the system or software degrades gracefully as capacity limits are approached, reached, and exceeded.

67. *Inadequate Concurrency Testing (TTS-SPC-2)*

Testers perform little or no concurrency testing (or the concurrency testing they do perform is superficial) to explicitly uncover the defects that cause the common types of concurrency faults and failures: deadlock, livelock, starvation, priority inversion, race conditions, inconsistent views of shared memory, and unintentional infinite loops.

68. *Inadequate Internationalization Testing (TTS-SPC-3)*

Testers perform little or no internationalization testing—or the internationalization testing they do perform is superficial—to determine the degree to which the system is configurable to perform appropriately in multiple countries.

69. *Inadequate Interoperability Testing (TTS-SPC-4)*

Testers perform little or no interoperability testing (or the interoperability testing they do perform is superficial) to determine the degree to which the system successfully interfaces and collaborates with other systems.

70. *Inadequate Performance Testing (TTS-SPC-5)*

Testers perform little or no performance testing (or the testing they do perform is only superficial) to determine the degree to which the system has adequate levels of the performance quality attributes: event schedulability, jitter, latency, response time, and throughput.

71. *Inadequate Reliability Testing (TTS-SPC-6)*

Testers perform little or no long-duration reliability testing (also known as stability testing)—or the reliability testing they do perform is superficial (for example, it is not done under operational profiles and is not based on the results of any reliability models)—to determine the degree to which the system continues to function over time without failure.

72. *Inadequate Robustness Testing (TTS-SPC-7)*

Testers perform little or no robustness testing, or the robustness testing they do perform is superficial (for example, it is not based on the results of any robustness models), to determine the degree to which the system exhibits adequate error, fault, failure, and environmental tolerance.

73. *Inadequate Safety Testing (TTS-SPC-8)*

Testers perform little or no safety testing, or the safety testing they do perform is superficial (for example, it is not based on the results of a safety or hazard analysis), to determine the degree to which the system is safe from causing or suffering accidental harm.

74. *Inadequate Security Testing (TTS-SPC-9)*

Testers perform little or no security testing—or the security testing they do perform is superficial (for example, it is not based on the results of a security or threat analysis)—to determine the degree to which the system is secure from causing or suffering malicious harm.

75. *Inadequate Usability Testing (TTS-SPC-10)*

Testers or usability engineers perform little or no usability testing—or the usability testing they do perform is superficial—to determine the degree to which the system's human-machine interfaces meet the system's requirements for usability, manpower, personnel, training, human factors engineering (HFE), and habitability.

2.2.4 System Testing Pitfalls

The following pitfalls are related primarily to the testing of completely integrated systems:

76. *Test Hooks Remain (TTS-SYS-1)*

Testers fail to remove temporary test hooks after completing testing, so they remain in the delivered or fielded system.

77. *Lack of Test Hooks (TTS-SYS-2)*

Testers fail to take into account how a lack of test hooks makes it more difficult to test parts of the system hidden via information hiding.

78. *Inadequate End-to-End Testing (TTS-SYS-3)*

Testers perform inadequate system-level functional testing of a system's end-to-end support for its missions.

2.2.5 System of Systems (SoS) Testing Pitfalls

The following pitfalls are related to testing systems of systems:

79. *Inadequate SoS Planning (TTS-SoS-1)*

Testers and SoS architects perform an inadequate amount of SoS test planning and fail to appropriately document their plans in SoS-level test planning documentation.

80. *Unclear SoS Testing Responsibilities (TTS-SoS-2)*

Managers or testers fail to clearly define and document the responsibilities for performing end-to-end SoS testing.

81. *Inadequate Resources for SoS Testing (TTS-SoS-3)*

Management fails to provide adequate resources for system of systems (SoS) testing.

82. *SoS Testing Not Properly Scheduled (TTS-SoS-4)*

System of systems testing is not properly scheduled and coordinated with the individual systems' testing and delivery schedules.

83. *Inadequate SoS Requirements (TTS-SoS-5)*

Many SoS-level requirements are missing, are of poor quality, or are never officially approved or funded.

84. *Inadequate Support from Individual System Projects (TTS-SoS-6)*

Test support from individual system development or maintenance projects is inadequate to perform system of systems testing.

85. *Inadequate Defect Tracking Across Projects (TTS-SoS-7)*

Defect tracking across individual system development or maintenance projects is inadequate to support system of systems testing.

86. *Finger-Pointing (TTS-SoS-8)*

Different system development or maintenance projects assign the responsibility for finding and fixing SoS-level defects to other projects.

2.2.6 Regression Testing Pitfalls

The following pitfalls are related primarily to regression testing:

87. *Inadequate Regression Test Automation (TTS-REG-1)*

Testers and developers have automated an insufficient number of tests to enable adequate regression testing.

88. *Regression Testing Not Performed (TTS-REG-2)*

Testers and maintainers perform insufficient regression testing to determine if new defects have been accidentally introduced when changes are made to the system.

89. *Inadequate Scope of Regression Testing (TTS-REG-3)*

The scope of regression testing is insufficiently broad.

90. *Only Low-Level Regression Tests (TTS-REG-4)*

Only low-level (for example, unit-level and possibly integration) regression tests are rerun, so there is no system, acceptance, or operational regression testing and no SoS regression testing.

91. *Test Resources Not Delivered for Maintenance (TTS-REG-5)*

The test resources produced by the development organization are not made available to the maintenance organization to support testing new capabilities and regression testing changes.

92. *Only Functional Regression Testing (TTS-REG-6)*

Testers and maintainers only perform regression testing to determine if changes introduce functionality-related defects.

CHAPTER 3

DETAILED DESCRIPTIONS OF THE TESTING PITFALLS

The commonly occurring testing pitfalls documented in this section are categorized as either general testing pitfalls or testing-type-specific pitfalls.

3.1 Common Negative Consequences

While different testing pitfalls have different proximate negative consequences, they all tend to contribute to the following overall ultimate problems:

- Testing is *less effective*.
  - More residual defects slip past testing into the deliverable system.
  - In spite of the extra cost and schedule time, the software-reliant system is still delivered and placed into operation with more residual defects than are either expected or necessary.
- Testing is *less efficient*.
  - More time and effort is needed to reach the same quality as would have been reached without the pitfalls.
  - The system is delivered late and over budget because of extra, unplanned time and effort spent finding and fixing defects during late stages of development.
  - The testers must work unsustainably long hours, causing them to become exhausted and, therefore, to make excessive numbers of mistakes.
  - Some defects are discovered later than they should be, when they are more difficult to localize and fix.
- Tester *morale* suffers.
  - The poor testing efficiency and effectiveness makes the tester's job longer and more difficult than it need be.
  - The poor testing effectiveness and the resulting increase in residual defects diminishes the testers' pride in their work.

In the following, detailed specifications of each testing pitfall, the typical severity of each of the three previously mentioned common negative consequences will be represented by a compact graphic. Note that the actual negative consequences for any specific program and system may vary based on many project-specific characteristics. As illustrated in Figure 3.1, the first column (thumbs down) represents the potential for decreased quality in terms of residual defects delivered; the second column (calendar) represents potential schedule (and thus, budget) overruns; and column three (sad emoticon) represents potential impact on tester morale. The higher the black bar, the greater the severity of the consequence. Note that poor quality may not immediately delay the development schedule and delivery if the corresponding defects are not discovered during development and become silent residual defects waiting to cause havoc when the system is in operation.

In the pitfall-specific versions of Figure 3.1, the specific and relative heights of the individual black bars that represent loss of quality, schedule slippages, and decreases in morale are merely rough approximations of the typical negative consequences of that pitfall, based on observing or technically assessing the testing efforts of numerous projects. I hope that someone will undertake a formal industry survey to determine more accurately the distributions of these characteristics for the individual testing pitfalls.

FIGURE 3.1 Example of the symbols used to summarize common negative consequences

3.2 General Recommendations

In addition to the individual pitfall-specific recommendations provided in the following pitfall specifications, the following recommendations are generally applicable to most of the common testing pitfalls.

- **Prevention Recommendations** These general recommendations can prevent falling into pitfalls in the first place.
  - **Update the testing process.** Testers, chief engineers, and process engineers update the testing process to help the project avoid falling into testing pitfalls and, failing that, detect when it has fallen into such pitfalls.

- **Treat pitfalls as risks.** When relevant, the pitfalls should be officially identified as risks in the project risk repository and managed accordingly.

- **Formally require the solutions.** Customer representatives formally require the solutions to the testing pitfalls in the appropriate documentation such as the request for proposal (RFP), contract, and statement of work (SOW).

- **Internally mandate the solutions.** Managers, chief engineers (development team leaders), or chief testers (test team leaders) explicitly mandate the solutions to the testing pitfalls in the appropriate documentation such as the System Engineering Management Plan (SEMP), System Development Plan (SDP), test planning documentation, or test strategy.

- **Provide training.** Chief testers or trainers provide appropriate amounts and levels of test training to relevant personnel (such as the acquisition staff, management, testers, and quality-assurance personnel) that covers the *potential* testing pitfalls and how to prevent, detect, and react to them.

- **Ensure management support.** Managers explicitly state (and provide) their support for testing and the need to avoid the commonly occurring test pitfalls.

- **Detection Recommendations** The following general recommendations enable existing pitfalls to be identified and diagnosed.

  - **Evaluate documentation.** Review, inspect, or walk through the test-related documentation (for example, the Test Plan and the test sections of development plans).

  - **Ensure oversight.** Provide acquirer, management, quality assurance, and peer oversight of the testing process as it is performed.

  - **Consider metrics.** Collect, analyze, and report relevant test metrics to stakeholders (for example, acquirers, managers, technical leads or chief engineers, and chief testers).

- **Reaction Recommendations** The following general recommendations help to mitigate existing pitfalls once they are detected.

  - **Reject inadequate test documentation.** Customer representatives, managers, and chief engineers refuse to accept test-related documentation until identified pitfalls are addressed.

  - **Reject delivery.** Customer representatives, managers, and chief engineers refuse to accept the system or software under test (SUT) until identified pitfalls (for example, in test environments, test procedures, or test cases) are addressed. Then rerun the tests after prioritizing and fixing the associated defects.

  - **Provide training.** Chief testers or trainers provide appropriate amounts and levels of remedial test training to relevant personnel (such as acquisition staff, management, testers, and quality-assurance staff) that covers the *observed* testing pitfalls and how to prevent, detect, and react to them.

+ **Update process.**   Chief engineers, chief testers, or process engineers update the test process documentation (for example, procedures, guidelines, templates, and tool manuals) to minimize the likelihood that the observed testing pitfalls will reoccur.

+ **Report pitfall occurrence.**   Testers should report the occurrence of the pitfall to project management, including the test manager, the project manager, and the technical leader.

+ **Treat pitfalls as risks.**   When relevant, the pitfalls should be officially identified as risks in the project risk repository and managed accordingly.

3.3   General Testing Pitfalls

The following types of testing pitfalls can occur regardless of the type of testing being performed:

- Test Planning and Scheduling Pitfalls
- Stakeholder Involvement and Commitment Pitfalls
- Management-Related Testing Pitfalls
- Test Organization and Professionalism Pitfalls
- Test Process Pitfalls
- Test Tools and Environments Pitfalls
- Test Communication Pitfalls
- Requirements-Related Testing Pitfalls

3.3.1   Test Planning and Scheduling Pitfalls

The following testing pitfalls are related to test planning and scheduling:

- No Separate Test Planning Documentation (GEN-TPS-1)
- Incomplete Test Planning (GEN-TPS-2)
- Test Plans Ignored (GEN-TPS-3)
- Test-Case Documents as Test Plans (GEN-TPS-4)
- Inadequate Test Schedule (GEN-TPS-5)
- Testing at the End (GEN-TPS-6)

No Separate Test Planning Documentation (GEN-TPS-1)

Description   Separate test planning documentation does not exist, regardless of whether test planning is addressed in:
- Documents such as a Test and Evaluation Master Plan (TEMP), System Test Plan (STP), or Test Strategy Document (TSD)

- Testing sections of the System Engineering Management Plan (SEMP) or Software Development Plan (SDP)
- Test planning presentations (for example, PowerPoint slides documenting the test program)
- Test planning section of a testing wiki or collaboration website (for example, SharePoint site)
- Test planning information stored in an Application Lifecycle Management (ALM) tool repository

---

Potential Applicability   This pitfall is potentially applicable anytime that a well-planned and well-documented, nontrivial testing program is justified because of the:
- Size of the project's budget, schedule, and staff
- Business-, mission-, safety-, or security-critical nature of the system or software under test (SUT)
- Geographic distribution of test and development teams
- Nature of the contractual relationship between test organizations, development organizations, acquisition organizations, subcontractors and vendors, subject-matter experts, and user representatives

---

Characteristic Symptoms
- There is *no* separate place to go to learn the project's plans for performing testing.
- There are only incomplete, high-level overviews of testing in the SEMP and the SDP.
  - The test planning parts of these other documents are not written by testers.
- Testing is not adequately planned.
- Many aspects of the testing program are not addressed in any test planning documentation.

Potential Negative Consequences

- The test plans are not adequately documented.
- It is difficult or impossible to evaluate the planned testing program.
- Testing is inefficiently and ineffectively performed:
  - Important types of testing are overlooked or cut short due to insufficient budget or schedule.

- Testing is not properly prioritized.
- Adequate testing resources are not allocated.

Potential Causes

- The customer has not required the developer to develop, use, or deliver separate test planning documentation.
- The customer was not willing to pay for the development of separate test planning documentation.
- Management, the customer representative, or the testers did not understand the:
  - Scope, complexity, and importance of testing
  - Value of separate test planning documentation
- The system engineering, software engineering, or testing process did not include the development of separate test planning documentation.
- There was no template for the content and format of a separate test plan.

Recommendations

- Prepare:
  - Determine what needs to be documented in written form and what can best be stored in ALM tools.
  - Reuse or create a standard template and content or format standard for test planning documentation.
  - Include the test planning documentation as deliverable work products in the contract.
  - Include the development and delivery of test planning documentation in the project's master schedule (for example, as part of major milestones).
- Enable:
  - Acquire an ALM tool set that supports testing (for example, by storing test-related information or automatically generating test planning documents from that information).
  - Provide sufficient resources (staffing and schedule) for the development of one or more separate test plans.
- Perform:
  - Develop and deliver separate test planning documentation.
  - Do not accept incomplete high-level overviews of testing in the SEMP or SDP as the only test planning documentation.
- Verify:
  - Determine whether separate test planning documentation exists.
  - Determine whether the separate test planning documentation has been approved.

- Determine whether the separate test planning document is being maintained.

Related Pitfalls Incomplete Test Planning (GEN-TPS-2), Testing and Engineering Processes Not Integrated (GEN-PRO-1), Inadequate Test Documentation (GEN-COM-3)

INCOMPLETE TEST PLANNING (GEN-TPS-2)

Description Test planning and its associated documentation are not sufficiently complete for the current point in the development cycle.

Potential Applicability This pitfall is potentially applicable anytime that a well-planned and well-documented nontrivial testing program is justified.

Note that the amount, rigor, size, and form of test planning documentation needed will vary greatly depending on the:

- Size of the project's budget, schedule, and staff
- Business-, mission-, safety-, or security-critical nature of the system or software under test (SUT)

Characteristic Symptoms

- The test planning documentation is *missing* some or all of the:[7]
  - **Test goals and objectives** Listing the high-level goals and subordinate objectives of the testing program
  - **Scope of testing** Listing the component(s), functionality, or capabilities to be tested (and any that are not to be tested)
  - **Test levels** Listing and describing the relevant levels of testing (for example, unit, subsystem integration, system integration, system, and system of systems testing)
  - **Test types** Listing and describing the types of testing such as:
    - Black-box, gray-box, and white-box testing
    - Developmental testing versus acceptance testing versus operational testing
    - Initial versus regression testing
    - Manual versus automated testing
    - Mode-based testing (system start-up[8], operational mode, degraded mode, training mode, and system shutdown)
    - Normal versus abnormal behavior (that is, nominal versus off-nominal, sunny-day versus rainy-day use case paths)
    - Quality-based testing such as the testing of availability, capacity (for example, load and stress testing), interoperability, performance, reliability,

robustness[9], safety, security (for example, penetration testing and red teaming), and usability

- Static versus dynamic testing
- Time- or date-based testing

◆ **Organizations** Test organizations, testing teams, and testers including responsibilities, authorities, reporting chains, associated qualifications (for example, expertise, training, and experience), and staffing levels

◆ **Test process** A description of the process or method for performing testing, including:

- **Testing work products** Listing and describing the testing work products to be produced or obtained, such as test documents (for example, plans and reports), test software (for example, test drivers and stubs), test data (for example, inputs and expected outputs), test hardware, and test environments
- **Testing tasks** Listing and describing the major testing tasks (for example, name, objective, preconditions, inputs, steps, postconditions, and outputs)
- **Test completeness and rigor** Describing how the completeness and rigor of the testing varies as a function of mission-, safety-, and security criticality
- **Subsystem source** Source of the subsystem, such as commercial-off-the-shelf (COTS), governmental-off-the-shelf (GOTS) or government furnished equipment (GFE), military-off-the-shelf (MOTS), open source, and developed in-house
- **Testing techniques** Listing and describing the planned testing techniques (for example, boundary-value testing, penetration testing, fuzz testing, alpha and beta testing) to be used, including the associated:
  - ➤ **Test-case-selection criteria** Listing and describing the criteria to be used to select test cases (for example, interface-based, use case path, boundary-value testing, and error guessing)
  - ➤ **Test entrance criteria** Listing the criteria that must hold before testing should begin
  - ➤ **Test-suspension and -resumption criteria** Listing criteria for stopping and restarting testing
  - ➤ **Test-exit or -completion criteria** Listing the test-completion criteria (for example, based on different levels of code coverage such as statement, branch, or condition coverage)
- **Test data** Listing and describing the types and amounts of test data to be produced

◆ **Environments** Listing and describing required computers (for example, laptops and servers), test tools (for example, debuggers, software simulators, hardware emulators, and test-management tools), test environments (software and hardware test beds), and testing facilities

- ◆ **Testing schedule**   Listing and describing the major testing milestones and activities in the context of the project development cycle, schedule, and major project milestones
- ◆ **Reviews, metrics, and status reporting**   Listing and describing the test-related reviews (for example, Test Readiness Review), test metrics (for example, number of tests developed and run), and status reports (for example, percentage and number of tests run and passed)
- ◆ **Dependencies of testing on other project activities**   Listing dependencies such as the need to incorporate certain hardware and software components into test beds before testing using those environments can begin
- ◆ **References**   Listing of all relevant documents influencing testing
- ◆ **Acronym list and glossary**
- On an agile project, the written test plan is replaced with an informal verbal discussion of what testing to do and how to do it at the beginning of each short iterative and incremental sprint.

Potential Negative Consequences

- Some levels and types of tests are not performed, allowing certain types of residual defects to remain in the system.
- Some testing is ad hoc and therefore inefficient and ineffectual.
- Mission-, safety-, and security-critical software is not sufficiently tested to the appropriate level of rigor.
- Certain types of test cases are ignored, resulting in related residual defects in the tested system.
- Test-completion criteria are based more on schedule deadlines rather than on the required degree of freedom from defects.
- Adequate amounts of test resources (for example, testers, test tools, environments, and test facilities) are not made available because they are not in the budget.
- Some testers do not have adequate expertise, experience, or skills to perform all of the types of testing that needs to be performed.
- Stakeholders will not be able to correctly make informed decisions regarding release and putting the system into operation if adequate testing is neither planned nor performed.

Potential Causes

- There were no templates or content and format standards for separate test plans.
- The associated templates or content and format standards were incomplete.
- The test planning documents were written by people (for example, managers or developers) who did not understand the:
  - Scope, complexity, and importance of testing
  - Scope, complexity, and application domain of the system being tested
- An agile development method is being used that recommends having a "zero-page test plan" and therefore confuses strategic project-wide test planning with tactical sprint-specific test planning.
- There was no review of, quality control process for, or acceptance criteria for test plans.

Recommendations

- **Prepare:**
  - Reuse or create a standard template or content or format standard for test planning documentation, including samples.
- **Enable:**
  - Provide sufficient resources (staffing and schedule) to perform test planning and develop adequate test planning documentation.
- **Perform:**
  - Base the completeness and rigor of the test planning documentation on the:
    - Size and complexity of the system being tested
    - Business, mission, safety, and security criticality of the system being tested
    - Number of testers and test teams
    - Geographic and corporate distribution of the testers and test team(s)
    - Nature of the contractual relationship (if any) between test organizations, development organizations, acquisition organizations, subcontractors and vendors, subject-matter experts, and user representatives
  - Use the form of documentation (for example, document, PowerPoint presentation, wiki) that:
    - Best communicates the test plans to the testers and testing stakeholders
    - Provides the appropriate level of maintainability
- **Verify:**
  - Determine whether sufficient resources are being used to develop and document the test plans.

- Determine whether the test planning documentation has the appropriate level of completeness and rigor.
- Determine whether the test planning documentation is in the appropriate form.
- Determine whether the test planning documentation is being updated as the plans are modified.

Related Pitfalls   Unclear Testing Responsibilities (GEN-STF-2), Inadequate Evaluations of Test Assets (GEN-PRO-8), Test Assets Not Delivered (GEN-TTE-8), Inadequate Capacity Testing (TTS-SPC-1), Inadequate Concurrency Testing (TTS-SPC-2), Inadequate Internationalization Testing (TTS-SPC-3), Inadequate Performance Testing (TTS-SPC-4), Inadequate Reliability Testing (TTS-SPC-5), Inadequate Robustness Testing (TTS-SPC-6), Inadequate Safety Testing (TTS-SPC-7), Inadequate Security Testing (TTS-SPC-8), Inadequate Usability Testing (TTS-SPC-9), Inadequate SoS Planning (TTS-SoS-1), Test Resources Not Delivered for Maintenance (TTS-REG-5)

TEST PLANS IGNORED (GEN-TPS-3)

Description   The test planning documentation is ignored (that is, it has become "shelfware") once developed and delivered.

Potential Applicability   This pitfall is potentially applicable anytime that test planning documentation exists.

Characteristic Symptoms
- The test planning documentation is neither being read nor used.
- The way the testers perform testing is not consistent with the relevant test planning documentation.
- The test planning documentation is never updated after initial delivery (that is, the test documents are not "living documents").

Potential Negative Consequences

- The test planning documentation is not used:
  - By the testers as a project-specific handbook for testing
  - To inform the testing stakeholders about the testing program
- The testing stakeholders (possibly including some testers) do not:

- ◆ Remember the contents of the test planning documentation
  - ◆ Understand the approved testing program
- The budget does not contain sufficient funds for adequate test resources (for example, testers, test tools, environments, and test facilities).
- Testers cannot effectively use the test planning documentation to justify their:
  - ◆ Requests for funds to acquire testing tools and environments
  - ◆ Requests for sufficient testers to achieve planned staffing levels
  - ◆ Insistence that certain types of planned testing are necessary and should not be dropped as soon as the schedule becomes tight
- New testers added to the project do not have adequate expertise, experience, or skills to perform all necessary types of testing.
- The test planning documentation becomes obsolete.
- Some levels and types of tests are not performed, thereby allowing certain types of residual defects to remain in the system.
- Some important test cases are not developed and executed.
- Mission-, safety-, and security-critical software is not sufficiently tested to the appropriate level of rigor.
- Test-completion criteria are based more on schedule deadlines than on the required degree of freedom from defects.

Potential Causes

- The test planning documentation was not very useful or easy to read or use.
- The testers thought that the only reason a test plan was developed was because it was a contract deliverable that was merely a box that needed to be checked off.
- Testing stakeholders (including testers) were unaware that they had forgotten certain parts of the test planning documentation.
- The test planning documentation was so incomplete and at such a generic high level of abstraction that it is relatively useless.
- Conversely, the test planning documentation was so complete and detailed that it was overwhelming.
- The testers were not involved in the development of the test planning documentation and therefore have no buy-in into it.
- Management did not know:
  - ◆ How much to budget for the planned test resources
  - ◆ What expertise, experience, and skills testers need to perform all of the types of testing and therefore were at a loss when determining staffing levels

Recommendations

- Prepare:
  - Project management (both administrative and technical), testers, and quality-assurance personnel read and review the test planning documentation.
  - Management (acquisition and project) signs off on the completed test plan documentation.
  - Use the test plan as input to the project's master schedule and Work Breakdown Structure (WBS).
- Enable:
  - Develop a short checklist from the test planning documentation to use when performing quality engineering assessments of the testing's performance.
- Perform:
  - The test manager periodically reviews the test work products and as-performed test process against the test planning documentation.
  - The test team updates the test planning documentation as needed.
  - Testers present their work and status at project and test-team status meetings.
- Verify:
  - Determine whether the test planning documentation has been reviewed.
  - Determine whether the test planning documentation has been approved.
  - Determine whether the project's master schedule and WBS are consistent with the test planning documentation.
  - Determine whether any quality engineering checklists are consistent with the test planning documentation.
  - Periodically determine whether the test work products (quality control) and as-performed test process (quality assurance) are consistent with the test planning documentation.

Related Pitfalls   Incomplete Test Planning (GEN-TPS-2)

TEST-CASE DOCUMENTS AS TEST PLANS (GEN-TPS-4)

Description   Test-case documents that document specific test cases are mislabeled as test plans.

Potential Applicability   This pitfall is potentially applicable anytime that:
- A well-planned and well-documented nontrivial testing program is justified.
- Test-case documents are being developed.

Characteristic Symptoms

- The "test plan(s)" contain specific test cases, including preconditions; and test inputs, including test data, test steps, expected outputs, and sources, such as specific requirements (black-box testing) or design decisions (white-box testing).
- The test plans do not contain the type of general planning information listed in Incomplete Test Planning (GEN-TPS-2).

Potential Negative Consequences

- Some levels and types of tests are not performed, allowing certain types of residual defects to remain in the system.
- Some testing is ad hoc and therefore inefficient and ineffectual.
- Mission-, safety-, and security-critical software is not sufficiently tested to the appropriate level of rigor.
- Test-completion criteria are based more on schedule deadlines than on the required degree of freedom from defects.
- Adequate amounts of test resources (for example, testers, test tools, environments, and test facilities) are not made available because they are not in the budget.
- Some testers do not have adequate expertise, experience, or skills to perform all of the types of testing that needs to be performed.

Potential Causes

- Some of the testers mistakenly believed that test planning was the same as designing and creating specific test cases.
- The test plan authors did not have adequate expertise, experience, or skills to develop test plans or know their proper content.
- There were neither templates nor content format standards for test plans and test-case documents.
- The test plan authors were under heavy pressure to minimize test documentation such that the actual test plans were not developed, which forced the test cases to document both test plans and test cases.
- Using an agile development method—with associated minimization of "unnecessary" documentation—led to dropping any separate test planning documentation the project had.

Recommendations

- Prepare:
  - ◆ Provide the test manager and testers with at least minimal training in test planning.
- Enable:
  - ◆ Provide a proper test plan template.
  - ◆ Provide a proper content and format standard for test plans.
  - ◆ Add the terms *test plan* and *test case* to the project's technical glossary.
- Perform:
  - ◆ Develop the test plan in accordance with the test plan template or content and format standard.
  - ◆ Develop the test-case documents in accordance with the test-case document template or content and format standard.
  - ◆ Where practical, automate the test cases so that the resulting tests (extended with comments) largely replace the test-case documents so that the distinction is clear (that is, the test plan is a document meant to be read, whereas the test case is meant to be executable).
- Verify:
  - ◆ Determine whether the test plan(s) conform to the associated template or content and format standard prior to accepting them.

Related Pitfalls   Incomplete Test Planning (GEN-TPS-2)

INADEQUATE TEST SCHEDULE (GEN-TPS-5)

Description   The testing schedule is inadequate to complete proper testing.

Potential Applicability   This pitfall is always potentially applicable.

Characteristic Symptoms

- The project's master schedule does not include sufficient time to perform all:
  - ◆ Testing activities (for example, automating testing, configuring test environments; developing test data, test scripts or drivers, and test stubs; and running tests and reporting their results)
  - ◆ Appropriate tests (for example, abnormal behavior, quality requirements, regression testing)[10]
- Change-request impact estimates do not include sufficient time for regression testing.
- Testing is behind schedule.

- The testing-related entrance criteria (for example, test-completion criteria) for milestone reviews are not being met.
- Testers complain that they do not have sufficient time to perform testing.
- Testers are working excessively and unsustainably long hours and days per week in an attempt to meet schedule deadlines.

Potential Negative Consequences

- There is a significant probability that the system will be delivered with an unacceptably large number of significant residual defects.
- Tester productivity (for example, importance of defects found and number of defects found per person-time normalized by the number of defects to be uncovered) is lower than it should be.
- Testing stakeholders (for example, customer representatives, managers, developers or testers) have a false sense of security that the system or software will function properly when delivered and deployed.
- The testers are overworked and exhausted and, therefore, are making an unacceptably large number of mistakes (for example, poor selection of test cases, incorrect test input data, incorrect oracle test outputs, false-positive test results, and false-negative test results).

Potential Causes

- More testing needed to be done than was originally recognized and planned for.
- The overall project schedule was insufficient for proper development, which thereby made the testing schedule insufficient.
- The size and complexity of the system were underestimated, thereby causing the effort to test the system to be underestimated.
- The project's master plan was written by people (for example, managers, chief engineers, or technical leads) who did not understand the scope, complexity, and importance of testing.
- The project's master plan was developed without input from the test team(s).
- Insufficient thought was given to testability during requirements engineering, architecture engineering, and design.
- The testing effort was reduced in order to meet one or more delivery or release deadlines.

Recommendations

- Prepare:
  - ◆ Provide evidence-based estimates of the amount of testing and associated test effort that will be needed (for example, based on cost models, historical records, statistical confidence levels, and research that identifies the most effective effort distribution for minimizing defects within project resource constraints).
  - ◆ Ensure that adequate time for testing is included in the program master schedule, test team schedules, and change-request impact estimates.
  - ◆ Include time for testing abnormal behavior and for the specialty engineering testing of quality requirements (for example, load testing for capacity requirements and penetration testing for security requirements).
  - ◆ Provide adequate time for testing in change-request estimates.
- Enable:
  - ◆ Deliver inputs to the testing process (for example, requirements, architecture, design, and implementation) earlier and more often (for example, as part of an evolutionary—incremental, iterative, parallel—development cycle).
  - ◆ Provide sufficient test resources (for example, number and types of testers, test teams, test tools, and test environments).
  - ◆ If at all practical, do not reduce the testing effort in order to meet a delivery deadline.
- Perform:
  - ◆ Automate as much of the regression testing as is practical, and allocate sufficient resources to create and maintain the automated tests.[11]
  - ◆ Negotiate a decrease in scope for the current release so that adequate resources can be applied to the testing of the reduced scope. However, be aware of the bow-wave effect that can occur when functionality is continually postponed to future releases without any schedule relief for the "last" release.
- Verify:
  - ◆ Determine whether the amount of time scheduled for testing is consistent with evidence-based estimates of need time.

Related Pitfalls   Lack of Stakeholder Commitment to Testing (GEN-SIC-3), SoS Testing Not Properly Scheduled (TTS-SoS-4)

TESTING AT THE END (GEN-TPS-6)

Description   All testing is performed late in the development cycle.

Potential Applicability   This pitfall is potentially applicable anytime that:

- A well-planned and well-documented nontrivial testing program is justified.
- The project has a nontrivial schedule that is sufficiently long to enable testing to be postponed.

Characteristic Symptoms

- Testing is scheduled to be performed late in the development cycle on the Project Master Schedule.
  - There is no testing of executable requirements, architecture, and design models, possibly because no such models were developed.
  - This is essentially testing only on the right side of the Single V Model (pages 2–3) when a sequential waterfall V model is used.
  - This is the opposite of Test Driven Development (TDD).
- Testers are only involved after requirements engineering, architecture engineering, design, and implementation, when all of the defects have already been created. Thus, testing is not used to help prevent any defects or to uncover the defects as they are produced.
- Little or no unit or integration testing is planned or is performed during the early and middle stages of the development cycle.
- There is insufficient time to perform testing during the current incremental, iterative build such that some or all of the testing of the current build is postponed until the following build.

Potential Negative Consequences

- There is insufficient time left in the schedule to correct any major defects found.[12]
- It is difficult to achieve and demonstrate the required degree of test coverage.
- Because so much of the system has been integrated before the beginning of testing, it is very difficult to find and localize defects that remain hidden within the internals of the system.

- Postponing testing from one build to another creates an ever-growing bow wave of testing that can never be performed unless the schedule is radically changed to postpone all work except for testing until testing gets caught up (often a necessary but not politically acceptable action).

Potential Causes

- The project used a strictly interpreted, traditional, sequential waterfall development cycle, whereby testing the requirements, architecture, and design does *not* occur (that is, a strict Single V model was used instead of a Double V model or Triple V model [see pages 5–6]).
- Management was not able to staff the testing team early during the development cycle.
- Management was primarily interested in system testing and did not recognize the need for lower-level (for example, unit and integration) testing.
- There was insufficient time allocated in an incremental, iterative build, both to develop an iterative increment and to adequately test it.

Recommendations

- **Prepare:**
  - Plan and schedule testing to be performed iteratively, incrementally, and in a parallel manner (that is, use an evolutionary development cycle), starting early during development.
  - Provide training in incremental, iterative testing.
  - Incorporate iterative and incremental testing into the project's system engineering process.
- **Enable:**
  - Provide adequate testing resources (staffing, tools, budget, and schedule) early during development.
- **Perform:**
  - Perform testing in an iterative, incremental, and parallel manner starting early during the development cycle.
  - Testers and developers collaborate and work closely together so that new or updated components can be unit and integration tested as soon as is practical.
- **Verify:**
  - In an ongoing manner (or at the very least, during major project milestones), determine whether testing is being performed iteratively, incrementally, and in parallel with design, implementation, and integration.
  - Use testing metrics to determine the status and ongoing progress of testing.

Related Pitfalls   Testing and Engineering Processes Not Integrated (GEN-PRO-1), Testing as a Phase (GEN-PRO-10), Testers Not Involved Early (GEN-PRO-11)

3.3.2 Stakeholder Involvement and Commitment Pitfalls

The following testing pitfalls are related to stakeholder involvement in and commitment to the testing effort:

- Wrong Testing Mindset (GEN-SIC-1)
- Unrealistic Testing Expectations (GEN-SIC-2)
- Lack of Stakeholder Commitment to Testing (GEN-SIC-3)

WRONG TESTING MINDSET *(GEN-SIC-1)*

Description   Some testers and testing stakeholders have an incorrect testing mindset.

Potential Applicability   This pitfall is always potentially applicable.

Characteristic Symptoms
- Some testers and other testing stakeholders believe that the purpose of testing is to demonstrate that the system works properly rather than to determine where and how it fails.[13]
- Testers believe that it is their job (responsibility) to verify or "prove" that the system works, rather than identify where and when it doesn't work.[14]
- Some testers and other testing stakeholders begin testing assuming that the system or software works, so testing is only performed to show this.
- Managers and acquirers believe that testing is a cost center (that is, an expense rather than an investment) because they do not see the value of the products produced (for example, test documentation, test cases, and test environments) or the costs avoided due to testing.
- Testers believe that the purpose of testing is to find out how the system actually behaves, without considering how it should or must behave. In this mindset, testing is unrelated to requirements, and defects are subjective and all in the "eye of the beholder."
- Only normal (primary and alternative) behavior is tested.
- There is little or no testing of:
  - Exceptional (error-, fault-, or failure-tolerant) behavior
  - Input data:
    - There is no testing to identify incorrect handling of invalid input values.
    - Test inputs include only middle-of-the-road values rather than boundary values and corner cases.

Potential Negative Consequences

- There is a high probability that:
  - The delivered system contains a significant number of residual defects, especially related to abnormal behavior (for example, exceptional use case paths)
  - These defects will unacceptably reduce the system's reliability and robustness (for example, error-, fault-, and failure tolerance)
- Customer representatives, managers, and developers have a false sense of security that the system will function properly once delivered and deployed.

Potential Causes

- Customer representatives, managers, and developers believe that testing can be exhaustive.
- Those performing testing were told (either implicitly or explicitly) that their job is to verify or "prove" that the system works.[15]
- Testers were simply unaware of the proper mindset.
- Developers tested their own software,[16] so that there was a "conflict of interest" (that is, they were to build software that works and then use testing to show that it does not work). This is especially a problem with small, cross-functional development organizations or teams that "cannot afford" to have separate testers (that is, professional testers who specialize in and have specialized expertise in testing).
- There was insufficient schedule allocated for testing, so there was only sufficient time to test the normal behavior (for example, normal, "sunny-day" use case paths).
- The organizational culture is very success oriented, and management gave the testers the strong impression that:
  - Management does not want to hear any "bad" news (that is, that any significant defects were found in the system).
  - They discourage testers from working "too hard" to uncover defects.
- Testers who report lots of defects are not considered "team players" and are held responsible for any resulting cost or schedule overruns.

Recommendations

- Prepare:
  - Explicitly state the goals of testing in the project test planning documentation:

- **Primary Goal:** To enable the system or software under test (SUT) to be improved by:
  - Exposing its defects so that they can be fixed
  - Finding these defects by "breaking" the SUT; that is, by causing faults and failures of the defective (already broken) SUT
- **Secondary Goal:** To provide objective evidence that determines the system's:
  - Quality
  - Fitness for purpose
  - Readiness for shipping, deployment, or operation

- **Enable:**
  - Provide test training that emphasizes:
    - Uncovering defects by causing faults or failures
    - Uncovering useful information (that is, information that can be used to improve the system) is much more important than simply determining if tests pass or fail
  - Provide sufficient time in the schedule for testing beyond the basic success paths.
  - Hire new testers who exhibit a strong "destructive" mindset (that is, those who try to make the system fail rather than to demonstrate that it never fails).

- **Perform:**
  - In addition to test cases that verify all normal behavior, emphasize looking for defects where they are most likely to hide (for example, boundary values, corner cases, and input type or range verification).[17]
  - Incentivize the test team based more on the percentage of significant defects they uncover than merely on the number of requirements "verified" or test cases run.[18]
  - Foster a *healthy* competition between developers (who seek to avoid inserting defects) and testers (who seek to find those defects).

- **Verify:**
  - Determine whether the goals of testing are documented in the test planning documentation.
  - Determine whether any test training covers the proper testing mindset.
  - Determine whether adequate time has been scheduled to enable testing beyond the basic success paths.

♦ Determine (for example, via conversation or questioning) whether testing goes beyond "demonstrate that the system works" (sunny-day path testing) to also include "demonstrate that the system does not work" (rainy-day path testing)

♦ Determine whether the testers exhibit the correct testing mindset.

Related Pitfalls   Inappropriate External Pressures (GEN-MGMT-2), Inadequate Communication Concerning Testing (GEN-COM-5)

Unrealistic Testing Expectations (GEN-SIC-2)

Description   Testing stakeholders (especially customer representatives and managers) have various unrealistic expectations with regard to testing.

Potential Applicability   This pitfall is always potentially applicable.

Characteristic Symptoms

■ Testing stakeholders (for example, managers and customer representatives) and some testers falsely believe that:

♦ Testing detects all (or even the majority of) defects.[19]

♦ Testing *proves* that there are no remaining defects and that the system therefore works as intended.

♦ Testing can be, for all practical purposes, exhaustive. (This is false because, for example, testing cannot test all input values under all conditions.)

♦ Automated testing can be exhaustive. (It is impractical to automate certain types of tests and exhaustive testing is almost always impossible, regardless of whether the tests are manual or automated.)

♦ Automated testing improves or even guarantees the quality of the tests. (It is quite possible to automate poor tests.)

♦ Automated testing will always decrease costs. (It may cost more, depending on how rapidly the system under test—especially its user interface—is iterated and how often regression testing must occur.)

♦ There is no need to provide additional resources to develop, verify, and maintain the automated test cases.

♦ Testing can be relied on for *all* verification, even though some requirements are better verified via analysis, demonstration, certification, and inspection.

Potential Negative Consequences

- Testing stakeholders (for example, customer representatives, managers, developers or testers) have a false sense of security (that is, unjustified and incorrect confidence) that the system will function properly when delivered and deployed.
- Non-testing forms of verification (for example, analysis, demonstration, inspection, and simulation) are not given adequate emphasis, thereby unnecessarily increasing cost and schedule.
- When the system inevitably fails, the testers are more likely to get "blamed" for causing the failure of the unrealistic expectation. Although this may happen even without the unrealistic expectation, the existence of the expectation increases the likelihood and severity of the blame.

Potential Causes

- Managers and other testing stakeholders did not understand that:
  - A passed test could result from a weak or incorrect test rather than from a lack of defects.
  - There are always defects to be revealed. A truly successful or useful test is one that uncovers one or more defects, whereas a passed test proves only that the system worked in that single, specific instance.[20]
  - Test automation requires specialized expertise and needs to be budgeted for the effort required to develop, verify, and maintain the automated tests. Testing stakeholders may get a false sense of security that there are no defects when the system passes all automated tests; these tests could be incomplete, contain incorrect data, or have defects in their scripting.
- Testing stakeholders and testers were not exposed to research results that document the relatively large percentage of residual defects that typically remain after testing.
- Testers and testing stakeholders were not trained in verification approaches (for example, analysis, demonstration, and inspection) other than testing and its relative pros and cons.
- Project testing metrics did not include estimates of residual defects.

Recommendations

- Prepare:
  - Collect information on the limitations of testing.

- ◆ Collect information on when and how to augment testing with other types of verification.
- ▪ **Enable:**
  - ◆ Provide basic training in verification methods, including their associated strengths and limitations.
- ▪ **Perform:**
  - ◆ Explain the limits of testing to managers, customer representatives, testers, and other testing stakeholders:
    - • Testing will not detect all (or even a majority of the) defects.
    - • *No* testing is truly exhaustive.
    - • Testing cannot *prove* (or demonstrate) that the system works under all combinations of preconditions and trigger events.
    - • A passed test could result from a weak test rather than from a lack of defects.
    - • A truly successful test is one that finds one or more defects.
  - ◆ Do not rely on testing for the verification of all requirements, but rather also incorporate other verification approaches, especially when verifying the architecturally significant quality requirements.
  - ◆ Collect, analyze, and report testing metrics that estimate the number of defects remaining after testing.
- ▪ **Verify:**
  - ◆ Determine whether testing stakeholders understand the limitations of testing.
  - ◆ Determine whether testing is the only type of verification being used.
  - ◆ Determine whether the number of defects remaining is being estimated and reported.

Related Pitfalls   Inappropriate External Pressures (GEN-MGMT-2), Inadequate Communication Concerning Testing (GEN-COM-5), Regression Testing Not Performed (TTS-REG-2)

LACK OF STAKEHOLDER COMMITMENT TO TESTING (GEN-SIC-3)

Description   Stakeholder commitment to the testing effort is inadequate.

Potential Applicability   This pitfall is always potentially applicable.

Characteristic Symptoms

- ▪ Stakeholders ignore the testers and their test results. For example, stakeholders stop:

- ◆ Reading reports summarizing test results
- ◆ Attending meetings where test program status and test results are presented and discussed
- ◆ Responding to testers' emails and phone calls, and, especially, their questions
- Stakeholders (especially customers and management) are not providing sufficient resources (for example, people, schedule, tools, funding) for the testing effort.
- Stakeholders and subject-matter experts (SMEs) are unavailable to review test assets, such as:
  - ◆ Test documents such as test plans, test procedures, and test reports
  - ◆ Test environments (also known as test beds), test tools, and test facilities
  - ◆ Test software such as test cases, test drivers or scripts, test stubs, and test tools
- Stakeholders do not exhibit a proper commitment to testing, giving testers the message that testing is unimportant, which causes:
  - ◆ Tester morale to suffer
  - ◆ Testers to stop trying hard to improve and do their best
  - ◆ Testers to become less productive (effective and efficient)
- Stakeholders view testers as not being team players when they report major defects.

Potential Negative Consequences

- Testing is less effective due to inadequate resources.
- Testing is provided inadequate resources at the beginning of the project.
- The testing effort loses needed resources every time resources must be cut (for example, due to schedule slippages and budget overruns).
- Testing assets retain defects that should have been found during stakeholder reviews.

Potential Causes

- Stakeholders did not understand the scope, complexity, and importance of testing.
- Stakeholders were not provided adequate estimates of the resources needed to properly perform testing.

- Stakeholders were extremely busy with other duties, even if those duties had a lower priority than testing.
- The overall project schedule and budget estimates were inadequate, thereby forcing cuts in testing.

Recommendations

- **Prepare:**
  - Convey the scope, complexity, and importance of testing to the testing stakeholders.
- **Enable:**
  - Provide stakeholders with solid estimates of the resources needed to properly perform sufficient testing to:
    - Uncover the system's important defects
    - Verify whether the system has adequate quality (that is, adequate levels of the quality characteristics and quality attributes), is fit for its purpose, and is ready for shipping, deployment, or being placed into operation
- **Perform:**
  - Officially request sufficient testing resources from the testing stakeholders.
  - Obtain commitments of support for authoritative stakeholders at the beginning of the project.
- **Verify:**
  - Determine whether the testing stakeholders are providing sufficient resources (for example, people, schedule, tools, and funding) for the testing effort.

Related Pitfalls   Inadequate Test Schedule (GEN-TPS-5), Inadequate Test Resources (GEN-MGMT-1), Inappropriate External Pressures (GEN-MGMT-2), Test Lessons Learned Ignored (GEN-MGMT-6), Inadequate Communication Concerning Testing (GEN-COM-5), Inadequate Support from Individual System Projects (TTS-SoS-6)

3.3.3   Management-Related Testing Pitfalls

The following testing pitfalls are related to stakeholder involvement in and commitment to the testing effort:

- Inadequate Test Resources (GEN-MGMT-1)
- Inappropriate External Pressures (GEN-MGMT-2)
- Inadequate Test-Related Risk Management (GEN-MGMT-3)
- Inadequate Test Metrics (GEN-MGMT-4)

- Inconvenient Test Results Ignored (GEN-MGMT-5)
- Test Lessons Learned Ignored (GEN-MGMT-6)

INADEQUATE TEST RESOURCES (GEN-MGMT-1)

Description   Management allocates an inadequate amount of resources to testing.

Potential Applicability   This pitfall is always potentially applicable.

Characteristic Symptoms

- Testers have to work an excessive number of hours per day and work on the weekends.
- There are insufficient testers with adequate expertise to perform adequate testing or to automate tests.
- There is insufficient time in the schedule to perform adequate testing or to automate tests.

Potential Negative Consequences

- The test planning documentation and schedules *failed* to state clearly what test resources were needed:
  - ◆ Test time in the schedule with adequate schedule reserves
  - ◆ Trained and experienced testers and reviewers
  - ◆ Funding
  - ◆ Test tools, environments (for example, integration test beds and repositories of test data), and test facilities, including office and laboratory space
- Insufficient budget and schedule are allocated to acquire, build, and verify the needed test tools, test hardware and software, test environments, repositories of test data, and the needed test facilities.
- Adequate testing is not performed within the limits of the provided test resources.
- Management gives testers the message that testing is unimportant, which causes:
  - ◆ Tester morale to suffer
  - ◆ Testers to stop trying to improve and do their best
  - ◆ Testers to become less productive (effective and efficient)

- There is an increase in the number of defects that make it through testing and into the deployed system.

Potential Causes

- Testing stakeholders did not understand the scope, complexity, and importance of testing, and thus did not understand its impact on the resources needed to properly perform testing.
- Estimates of needed testing resources were:
  - Not derived from any evidence-based cost/effort models
  - Informally made by management without eliciting or believing input from the testing organization, especially those testers who would be actually performing the testing tasks
  - Based on available resources rather than resource needs
- Management believed that the testers padded their estimates and therefore cut the testers' estimates.
- Testers and testing stakeholders were overly optimistic, so their informal estimates of needed resources were based on best-case scenarios rather than most-likely or worst-case scenarios.
- Management viewed testing as a cost center to be minimized, rather than as an investment, because they did not see the test cases, test environments, and test documents as valuable, reusable assets.
- Significant redundant testing was taking place due to unclear testing responsibilities or poor testing strategy (for example, user acceptance testing is merely a "quick and dirty" repeat of previously executed development system tests).

Recommendations

- **Prepare:**
  - Ensure that testing stakeholders understand the scope, complexity, and importance of testing.
  - Ensure that the testing stakeholders understand that investing adequately in testing more than pays for itself in both development and lifecycle cost and schedule savings.
- **Enable:**
  - Begin test planning at project inception (for example, at contract award or during proposal development).
  - Ensure that test planning includes all testing tasks such as test planning, test environment development, test case development, test case automation, executing tests, and recording and reporting test results.
  - Train testers and managers to use evidence-based cost/effort models to estimate the amount of testing resources needed.

- **Perform:**
  - ◆ Use evidenced-based cost/effort models to estimate the needed testing resources.
  - ◆ Officially request sufficient testing resources from the testing stakeholders.
  - ◆ Ensure that the test planning documentation, schedules, and project Work Breakdown Structure (WBS) provide for adequate levels of these test resources.
  - ◆ Obtain commitments of support from authoritative stakeholders at the beginning of the project.
- **Verify:**
  - ◆ Determine whether the testing stakeholders are providing sufficient resources for the testing effort.

Related Pitfalls   Lack of Stakeholder Commitment to Testing (GEN-SIC-3), Unclear Testing Responsibilities (GEN-STF-2), Inadequate Testing Expertise (GEN-STF-3)

INAPPROPRIATE EXTERNAL PRESSURES (GEN-MGMT-2)

Description   Managers or others in positions of authority subject testers to inappropriate external pressures.

Potential Applicability   This pitfall is potentially applicable anytime that:
- The project is sufficiently large to have different people assuming the manager and tester roles.
- There are budget and schedule pressures to complete and deliver the system or software under test.

Characteristic Symptoms
- Testers are not rewarded for finding defects.
  - ◆ Testers are not viewed as being team players.
  - ◆ Testers are blamed as the reason why:
    - • The project is behind schedule and over budget
    - • The system or software can't be released
- Managers (or developers) dictate to the testers what constitutes a bug or a defect *worth reporting*.
- Pressure is misapplied to force testers to:
  - ◆ Inappropriately cut corners (for example, only perform "sunny-day" testing in order to meet schedule deadlines)
  - ◆ Inappropriately lower the severity and priority of reported defects

- ◆ Avoid finding defects (for example, until after delivery because the project is so far behind schedule that there is no time to fix any defects found)
- ◆ Abstain from mentioning significant defects or risks in meetings (for example, with customers and other stakeholders), even if those are a major reason for the meetings in the first place
- Managers (or developers) dictate to the testers what constitutes a bug or a defect *worth reporting.*
- Project staff are discouraged from using certain "negative" terms such as defect, bug, and risk.

Potential Negative Consequences

- Testers are given contradictory direction concerning defect identification and reporting:
  - ◆ If the testers *yield* to this pressure, then the test metrics do not accurately reflect either the true state of the system (or software) or the status of the testing process.
  - ◆ If the testers *do not yield* to this pressure, then the pressure causes:
    - Stress and conflict in the work environment
    - Negative relationships to develop among the managers, developers, and testers
    - Time to be wasted on:
      - ‣ Communicating only through formal channels (for example, via email rather than by phone or in person)
      - ‣ Ego games that cause defects to be unjustly rejected and fixes to be delayed
- Tester morale suffers greatly.
- There is an increase in the number of defects that make it through testing and into the deployed system.

Potential Causes

- The project was significantly behind schedule or over budget.
- There was insufficient time prior to the delivery or release date to fix a significant number of defects that were found via testing.
- The project was in danger of being cancelled due to lack of performance.

- Management (at the project level or higher) was highly risk averse and therefore did not want to officially label any testing risk as a risk.
- Management had a strong "go to market" attitude.
- Management took the reporting of defects personally and feared that uncovering defects might lead others to have a lower opinion of the manager.

Recommendations

- **Prepare:**
  - ◆ Establish criteria for determining the priority and severity of reported defects.
- **Enable:**
  - ◆ Ensure that the testers and test manager report independently of the project manager—technically, managerially, and financially (for example, place the manager of the testing organization at the same or higher level as the project manager in the organizational hierarchy).[21]
  - ◆ Ensure that trained testers collaborate with customer or user representatives (if they are available) to determine what constitutes a defect *worth reporting*.
- **Perform:**
  - ◆ Support testers when they oppose any inappropriate external pressure that would have them violate their professional ethics.
  - ◆ Customer representatives must insist on proper testing.
- **Verify:**
  - ◆ Determine whether any of the listed inappropriate external pressures are being applied to the testers.
  - ◆ Determine whether tester morale is suffering from these inappropriate external pressures.
  - ◆ Determine whether any testers are succumbing to these inappropriate external pressures.
  - ◆ Determine whether the testers are the ones who decide what constitutes a reportable defect.
  - ◆ Determine whether the testers report independently of the project manager.

Related Pitfalls Wrong Testing Mindset (GEN-SIC-1), Lack of Independence (GEN-STF-1)

INADEQUATE TEST-RELATED RISK MANAGEMENT (GEN-MGMT-3)

Description   There are too few test-related risks identified in the project's official risk repository.[22]

Potential Applicability   This pitfall is potentially applicable anytime that the project has one or more testing-related risks.

Characteristic Symptoms

- Managers treat *risk* as a "four-letter word" and try to get everyone to substitute less negative terms such as *issue* or *concern*.
- Because adding risks to the risk repository is viewed as a symptom of management failure, risks (including testing risks) are mislabeled as issues or concerns so that they need not be reported as official risks.
- Test-team-level risks are not bubbled up to be project-level risks because they would then have to be:
  - Reported to acquisition personnel and executive management
  - Acted upon
- The number of test-related risks identified in the project's official risk repository is unrealistically low.
- The identified test-related risks have inappropriately low probabilities, low harm severities, and low priorities.
- The identified test risks have no:
  - Associated risk-mitigation approaches
  - Person assigned as responsible for tracking and mitigating the risk
- The test risks are never updated (for example, with additions or modifications) over the course of the project.
- Testing risks are not addressed in either the test planning documentation or the risk management plan.

Potential Negative Consequences

- Testing risks are not reported.
- Management and acquirer representatives are unaware of the existence of these testing risks.
- Testing risks are not managed nor are their potential consequences mitigated.
- Managing testing risks is not given sufficiently high priority.

Potential Causes

- Managers were highly risk averse.
- Managers strongly communicated their preference that only a small number of the most critical risks be entered into the project's risk repository.
- The people responsible for risk management and managing the risk repository were never trained or exposed to the many potential test-related risks (for example, those associated with the commonly occurring testing pitfalls addressed here).
- The risk management process strongly emphasized system-specific or system-level (as opposed to software-level) risks and tended not to address any development activity risks (such as those associated with testing).
- There were few, if any, evaluations of the testing process (quality assurance) or testing work products (quality control).
- There was little if any oversight of the testing process.

Recommendations

- **Prepare:**
  - Determine management's degree of risk aversion and attitude regarding the inclusion of testing risks in the project's risk repository.
- **Enable:**
  - Ensure that the people responsible for risk management and managing the risk repository are aware of the many potential test-related risks.
- **Perform:**
  - Identify these relevant test-related risks and incorporate them into the project's official risk repository.
  - Provide test-related risks with realistic probabilities, harm severities, and priorities.
- **Verify:**
  - Determine whether the risk repository contains an appropriate number of testing risks.
  - Determine whether there is sufficient management and quality assurance oversight and evaluation of the testing process.

Related Pitfalls   Unrealistic Testing Expectations (GEN-SIC-2)

INADEQUATE TEST METRICS (GEN-MGMT-4)

Description   Too few test metrics are produced, analyzed, reported, or acted upon, and those test metrics that are produced are not very useful.

Potential Applicability   This pitfall is potentially applicable anytime that:
- The test program is sufficiently large and complex to justify managing it
- One or more managers need visibility into the test program

Characteristic Symptoms
- Little or no test metrics are being produced, analyzed, reported, and used as a basis for making decisions.
- The primary test metrics (for example, the number of tests developed and executed[23], the number of tests needed to meet adequate or required test coverage levels, the number of tests passed or failed, and the number of defects found) show neither the productivity of the testers nor their group effectiveness at finding defects (for example, defects found per test or per tester-day).
  - Merely counting defects does not take into account the initial defect density (quality).
  - Merely recording cost per defect penalizes high initial quality because the cost per defect increases as the number of defects to uncover decreases [Jones 2013c].
- Merely counting the number of tests developed and passed does not take into account the size and complexity of the tests and the number of tests needed to achieve the planned level of code coverage. The effectiveness of testing is not being estimated:
  - The number of latent *undiscovered* defects remaining is not being estimated (for example, using a constructive quality model [COQUALMO][24]).
  - The number of defects that slipped through prior testing (thereby indicating a problem with that prior testing) such as:
    - Unit defects that should have been uncovered during unit testing but instead were uncovered during integration- and system-level testing
    - Interface defects that should have been uncovered during unit or integration testing but instead were uncovered during system testing
    - Defects causing failures to meet required levels of quality attributes, which should have been uncovered during specialty engineering testing, were instead discovered during system, acceptance, or operational testing

- ◆ The cost, cost savings, and return on investment associated with different types or levels of testing (for example, unit testing, integration testing, specialty engineering testing, and system testing)
- Management measures overall test program productivity strictly in terms of defects found per unit time, ignoring the importance or severity of the defects found.

Potential Negative Consequences

- Managers, testers, and other stakeholders in testing do not accurately know the quality of testing, the importance of the defects being found, or the number of residual defects in the delivered system.
- Managers do not know the productivity of the test team and their effectiveness at finding important defects, thereby making it difficult to improve the testing process.[25]
- Testers concentrate on finding lots of (unimportant) defects rather than finding critical defects (for example, those with mission-critical, safety-critical, or security-critical ramifications).
- Testing stakeholders (for example, customer representatives, managers, developers or testers) have a false sense of security that the system will function properly when delivered and deployed.

Potential Causes

- Project management (including the managers or leaders of test organizations or teams) is not familiar with the different types of testing metrics (for example, quality, status, and productivity) that could be useful.
- Metrics collection, analysis, and reporting is at such a high level that individual disciplines (such as testing) are rarely assigned more than one or two highly generic metrics (for example, "If the test environment is not completed in time, then testing will be delayed").
- Project management (and testers) are aware of only backward-looking metrics (for example, defects found and fixed) as opposed to forward-looking metrics (for example, residual defects remaining to be found).

Recommendations

- Prepare:
  - ◆ Provide testers and testing stakeholders with basic training in metrics with an emphasis on test metrics.

- Enable:
  - ◆ Incorporate a robust metrics program in the test plan that includes all relevant metrics.
  - ◆ Emphasize finding important defects.
- Perform:
  - ◆ Consider using some of the following representative examples of useful testing metrics:
    - The number of defects found during the initial test execution (test effectiveness metric)[26]
    - The number of defects that slip through each verification milestone or inch pebble (for example, reviews, inspections, tests)[27]
    - The estimated number of latent undiscovered defects remaining in the delivered system (for example, estimated using COQUALMO)
    - The estimated total percentage of residual defects found per unit time, weighted by defect severity (test program productivity metric)[28]
  - ◆ Regularly collect and analyze an appropriate set of progress, productivity, and quality test metrics.
  - ◆ Report these testing metrics to project management (and customer, if relevant).
- Verify:
  - ◆ Determine whether the as-performed testing process has become excessively metrics-driven.[29]
  - ◆ Determine whether the testers are worrying more about looking good (for example, by concentrating on only the defects that are easy to find) than on finding the most important defects.
  - ◆ Determine whether sufficient testing metrics are being collected, analyzed, and reported.

Related Pitfalls   None

INCONVENIENT TEST RESULTS IGNORED (GEN-MGMT-5)

Description   Management ignores or treats lightly inconvenient negative test results.

Potential Applicability   This risk is always potentially applicable.

Characteristic Symptoms

- Management ignores, treats lightly, and consistently fails to act when faced with poor test results, especially those having significant negative ramifications for the schedule, budget, functionality, or system quality.[30]

- Management consistently values meeting schedule, budget, and functionality targets over system quality even when the lack of quality is likely to have major negative consequences on the:
  - Program (for example, it could get cancelled)
  - System's stakeholders (for example, the system might not be accepted and might even have significant safety and security ramifications)
- Managers say they do not believe the system is as bad as the test results indicate.
- Usability defects are relabeled as enhancements to be allocated to some future release that may never come.

Potential Negative Consequences

- If management ignores test results, they give testers the message that testing is unimportant, which causes:
  - Tester morale to suffer
  - Testers to stop trying as hard
  - Testers to become less productive (effective and efficient)
- Defects do not get fixed when initially found but only:
  - When they can no longer be ignored
  - After delivery
- Usability defects are ignored and never fixed.
- Defects have negative ramifications for users and other stakeholders.
- There is not sufficient time before delivery to fix the defects, so the system is unnecessarily delivered or fielded with known defects.
- Management looks for scapegoats for their own failure. For example, management blames the testers (that is, kill the messenger) because "The test team should have been more forceful or vocal about their negative results if they really thought it was going to be a problem."

Potential Causes

- Management did not want to extend the schedule and potentially delay completion and delivery.
- Management could not or would not find extra funding to cover the additional work of fixing the defects and regression testing the changes.

- Management did not want to believe that the quality was as bad as the test results indicate.
- When budget, schedule, functionality, and quality compete, it is usually the quality and functionality that suffer.
- Management had a conflict of interest: (1) bring in the project on budget and schedule and (2) deliver a quality product.
- The developers incorrectly argued that the system was actually okay and that the negative test results were really due to tester misunderstandings and mistakes (for example, defects in the test environment or in the test cases).
- The project's original budget and schedule were inadequate to properly address defects found during testing.
- The manager was scheduled to rotate out of the position before poor quality could no longer be ignored, thereby making it the replacement manager's problem. Note that this cause tends to be most common on military acquisitions where the five- to fifteen-year-long projects are managed by program office staff who rotate in and out every two to three years.

Recommendations

- **Prepare:**
  - Project management should ensure that the project schedule and budget are adequate for fixing defects found by testing and for subsequent regression testing.
- **Enable:**
  - Properly use an appropriate cost model and historical data to determine the needed budget, staffing, and schedule.
  - Executive management should have the independent test team (and quality-assurance or -control engineers) report independently of the project manager and technical lead.
- **Perform:**
  - If necessary, testers should raise the issue of the failed tests to the appropriate management level.
- **Verify:**
  - Determine whether testers or quality engineers complain that managers or other authoritative stakeholders are ignoring important negative test results.
  - Determine whether an appropriate cost model and historical data are being used to determine whether the budget, staffing, and schedule are reasonable.
  - Determine whether testing reports independently to management.

Related Pitfalls   Test Assets Not Delivered (GEN-TTE-8)

TEST LESSONS LEARNED IGNORED (GEN-MGMT-6)

Description Lessons that are (or should have been) learned from testing on previous projects are not placed into practice.

Potential Applicability This pitfall is always potentially applicable.

Characteristic Symptoms

- Lessons learned from previous testing are never documented.
- Management, the test teams, or customer representatives ignore lessons learned during previous projects or during the testing of previous increments of the system or software under test.

Potential Negative Consequences

- The test processes are not being continually improved.
- The same problems continue to occur and the testing stakeholders continue to fall into the same old pitfalls.
- Testing stakeholders (for example, customer representatives, managers, developers or testers) have a false sense of security that the system will function properly when delivered and deployed.

Potential Causes

- Lessons were not learned in the first place.
- The "wrong" lessons were learned:
  - Low testing effectiveness and productivity were assigned to the wrong cause.
  - Ineffective mitigation measures were chosen.
- Capturing lessons as they are learned was *not* an explicit (or even implicit) part of the testing process.
  - Capturing the lessons learned was postponed until after the project was over, when the people who learned the lessons were no longer available, having scattered to new projects.
  - Lessons learned were not documented.
- There was no tool or repository in which to easily store lessons learned.

- Lessons learned from previous projects were not reviewed before starting new projects.
- The only usage of lessons learned was informal and was solely based on the experience that individual developers and testers bring to new projects.

Recommendations

- **Prepare:**
  - Make documenting lessons learned an explicit part of the testing process.
  - Review previous lessons learned as an initial step in determining the testing process.
- **Enable:**
  - Incorporate previously learned testing lessons into the current testing process and test plans.
- **Perform:**
  - As lessons are learned:
    - Capture them.
    - Instill them into the project or organizational culture.
    - Put them into practice.
  - Do not wait to capture lessons learned until a project postmortem when project staff members' memories are fading and they are moving (or have moved) on to their next project.
  - Put testing lessons learned into practice.
- **Verify:**
  - Determine whether testing lessons learned are captured (and implemented) as they are learned.
  - Determine whether previously learned testing lessons have been incorporated into the current testing process and test planning documentation.
  - Determine whether lessons learned are put into practice.

Related Pitfalls   Lack of Stakeholder Commitment to Testing (GEN-SIC-3)

3.3.4   Staffing Pitfalls

The following testing pitfalls are related to the staffing problems:

- Lack of Independence (GEN-STF-1)
- Unclear Testing Responsibilities (GEN-STF-2)
- Inadequate Testing Expertise (GEN-STF-3)
- Developers Responsible for All Testing (GEN-STF-4)
- Testers Responsible for All Testing (GEN-STF-5)

GEN-MGMT-6   Test Lessons Learned Ignored

LACK OF INDEPENDENCE (GEN-STF-1)

Description The test organization or project test team lacks adequate technical, managerial, and financial independence to enable them to withstand inappropriate pressure from the development (administrative and technical) management to cut corners.

Potential Applicability This pitfall is potentially applicable anytime that the:

- The business-, mission-, safety-, or security-critical nature of the system or software under test (SUT) justifies independent testing as part of an *independent* verification and validation (IV&V) program
- The project is under significant budget and schedule pressures to cut corners

Characteristic Symptoms

- The manager of the test organization reports to the development manager.
- The lead of the project test team reports to the project manager.
- The test organization manager or project test team leader does not have sufficient authority to raise and manage testing-related risks.

Potential Negative Consequences

- Technical leaders and other authoritative stakeholders unintentionally exploit the test team's lack of sufficient independence to force the test organization or team to select and use an inappropriate test process or tool.
- Members of the test organization or team are intimidated into withholding objective and timely information from the testing stakeholders.
- The test organization or team has insufficient budget and schedule to be effective.
- Project manager(s) inappropriately overrule or pressure the testers to violate their principles.

Potential Causes

- The test team and testers reported to:
  - The wrong management chain (that is, the project development manager):
    - When the test team and testers report to project management, it typically creates a conflict of interest with regard to quality versus schedule, budget, and functionality.
  - Two potentially opposing management chains in a matrix organization:

- The test team and testers receive inconsistent direction from project management and from testing or quality engineering.
- Management did not see the value or need for independent reporting.
- Although managers were familiar with the idea that the quality-assurance function should be independent of the development organization, they did not understand that some level of testing needs the same kind of independence for many of the same reasons.

Recommendations

- **Prepare:**
  - Determine reporting structures.
  - Identify potential independence problems.
- **Enable:**
  - Clarify to testing stakeholders (especially project management) the value of independent reporting for the test organization manager and project test team leader.
- **Perform:**
  - Ensure that the test organization or team has:
    - *Technical* independence so that they can select the most appropriate test process and tools for the job
    - *Managerial* independence so that they can provide objective and timely information about the test program and results without fear of intimidation due to business considerations or project-internal politics
    - *Financial* independence so that their budget (and schedule) will not be sacrificed if setbacks in other parts of the project cause those parts to exceed their budgets.
  - The test organization manager reports at the same or higher level as the development organization manager.
  - The project test team leader reports independently of the project manager to the test organization manager or equivalent (for example, the quality-assurance manager).
  - Use an independent verification and validation (IV&V) organization to perform certain types of testing, especially of subsystems or software that is mission, safety, or security critical.
- **Verify:**
  - Determine whether the test organization manager reports at the same or higher level as the development organization manager.
  - Determine whether the project test team leader reports independently of the project manager to the test organization manager or equivalent (for example, quality-assurance manager).

Related Pitfalls   Inappropriate External Pressures (GEN-MGMT-2)

GEN-STF-1   Lack of Independence

UNCLEAR TESTING RESPONSIBILITIES (GEN-STF-2)

Description   The testing responsibilities are unclear and do not adequately address which organizations, teams, and people are responsible for and will perform the different types of testing.

Potential Applicability   This pitfall is potentially applicable anytime that the size and complexity of the system or software under test justifies having more than one person responsible for testing.

Characteristic Symptoms

- The test planning documentation does not adequately address testing responsibilities in terms of which organizations, teams, and roles:
    - Will perform which types of testing on what (types of) components
    - Are responsible for procuring, building, configuring, and maintaining the test tools, test environments, test facilities, and test data.
    - Are the ultimate decision makers regarding testing risks, test-completion criteria, test completion, and the status or priority of defects

Potential Negative Consequences

- Certain tests are not performed, while other tests are performed redundantly by multiple organizations or by people playing multiple roles.
- Incomplete testing enables excessive defects to make it through testing and into the deployed system.
- Redundant testing wastes test resources and causes testing and other deadlines to slip.

Potential Causes

- The test plan template did not clearly address responsibilities.
- The types of testing were not clearly identified and so were not easily able to be allocated to specific developer or tester roles.

Recommendations

- Prepare:
    - Obtain documents describing current testing responsibilities.
    - Identify potential testing responsibility problems (for example, missing or vague responsibilities).

- **Enable:**
  - ◆ Obtain organizational agreement about the testing responsibilities.
- **Perform:**
  - ◆ Clearly and completely document the responsibilities for testing in the test planning documentation as well as in the charters of the teams who will be performing the tests.
  - ◆ Clearly communicate the testing responsibilities to the relevant organizations and people.
  - ◆ Regardless of which teams and roles are responsible for which testing, make it clear that quality is everyone's shared responsibility.
- **Verify:**
  - ◆ Determine whether the testing responsibilities are clearly and completely documented in the:
    - • Test planning documentation
    - • High-level overviews of testing in the System Engineering Management Plan (SEMP) and system development plan (SDP)
    - • Charters of the teams who will be performing the tests

Related Pitfalls   Incomplete Test Planning (GEN-TPS-2), Too Immature for Testing (GEN-PRO-7), Inadequate Test Documentation (GEN-COM-3), Unclear SoS Testing Responsibilities (TTS-SoS-2)

INADEQUATE TESTING EXPERTISE (GEN-STF-3)

Description   Some testers and testing stakeholders have inadequate testing-related understanding, expertise, experience, or training.

Potential Applicability   This pitfall is potentially applicable anytime that:
- The size, complexity, and criticality of the system necessitate a nontrivial testing program.
- The system is in an application domain that is new to the testers.
- New testing tool(s), including new scripting languages, are being used.
- A new testing environment is being used.
- Testing is outsourced to a foreign country where test training and experience is limited and the native language differs from that of others on the project.

Characteristic Symptoms
- Testers have inadequate expertise, experience, or training in one or more of the following areas:
  - ◆ Testing (for example, testing methods, types of testing, and testing techniques)

- The application domain of the system being developed or maintained
- Test tools and environments, including test automation and associated scripting languages
- The native language spoken by most of the stakeholders, developers, and managers

- Testing stakeholders (for example, managers and developers) have inadequate understanding of the:
  - Purpose and limitations of testing
  - Importance of testing
  - Basic testing types and methods
- Developers who are not professional testers have been tasked to perform testing.
- Testers have had little or no classroom or on-the-job training.
- Testers are not certified in testing (for example, by the International Software Certifications Board [ISCB] and the International Software Testing Qualifications Board [ISTQB])
- Testing is ad hoc without any proper process.
- Industry best practices are not followed.

Potential Negative Consequences

- Testing is not effective at detecting defects, especially the less obvious ones.
- There are unusually large numbers of false-positive and false-negative test results.
- The testers' productivity is needlessly low.
- Test automation will be slow, difficult, and error prone if the tester responsible for automating tests does not have the specialized expertise and experience needed to perform that task.
- Miscommunication occurs between the testers and the testing stakeholders.
- There is a high probability that the system will be delivered late, with an unacceptably large number of residual defects.
- Testing stakeholders (for example, customer representatives, managers, developers or testers) have a false sense of security that the system will function properly when delivered and deployed.[31]

Potential Causes
- Management did not understand the scope and complexity of testing.
- Management did not understand the required qualifications of a professional tester.

- There was insufficient funding to hire fully qualified professional testers.
- Many of the testers and developers did not have the specialized skills required for test automation.
- The project team was very small, with everyone wearing multiple hats; therefore, they were performing testing on an as-available or as-needed basis.
- An agile development method that emphasizes cross-functional development teams was being followed.
- The less-experienced developers are tasked to perform testing.
- To meet schedule constraints when the project is late or over budget, the more-experienced testers are tasked to perform development and bug fixes instead of testing.

Recommendations

- **Prepare:**
  - Provide proper test processes, including procedures, standards, guidelines, and templates, to use during On-the-Job Training (OJT).
  - Ensure that the required qualifications of a professional tester are documented in the tester job description.
- **Enable:**
  - Convey the required qualifications of the different types of testers to those technically evaluating prospective testers (for example, during résumé evaluation and job interviews).
  - Provide appropriate amounts of both classroom and on-the-job test training for both testers and those overseeing testing.
  - Ensure that the testers who will be automating testing have the necessary specialized expertise and training.[32]
- **Perform:**
  - Hire full-time (that is, professional) testers who have sufficient expertise and experience in testing.
  - Use an independent test organization staffed with experienced, trained testers for system or acceptance testing.
- **Verify:**
  - Determine whether those technically evaluating prospective testers understand the required qualifications of the different types of testers.
  - Determine whether the testers have adequate testing expertise, experience, and training.

Related Pitfalls   Inadequate Test Resources (GEN-MGMT-1), Inadequate Testing Expertise (GEN-STF-3)

GEN-STF-3   Inadequate Testing Expertise

DEVELOPERS RESPONSIBLE FOR ALL TESTING (GEN-STF-4)

Description There is no separate full-time tester role.

Potential Applicability This pitfall is always potentially applicable. In fact, it is becoming increasingly common due to the popularity of agile development that largely (and incorrectly) implicitly depends on all developers on the team having adequate testing expertise.

Characteristic Symptoms

- There is no separate tester role.
- The members of each development team share responsibility for testing what the team has developed:
  - Not just individual programmers performing unit testing of their own code, but also integration testing, system testing, specialty engineering testing, and so on.
- Individual development team members are responsible for testing:
  - The software that they personally developed
  - The software developed by other members of their team (that is, peer testing)

Potential Negative Consequences

- Testing is incomplete and inefficient due to lack of expertise and experience, thereby permitting excessive numbers of residual defects to remain in the delivered system.
- The developers performing testing are neither objective nor unbiased because they have a major conflict of interest: As designers and implementers, they must ensure that the system works properly; as testers, they must determine why the system does not work correctly.
- When the developers performing testing make false assumptions concerning how the system under test is supposed to behave, their false assumptions:
  - Will not be spotted by the testers
  - Will influence the test cases such that the test cases do not spot the false assumptions
- Because they don't report independently, developers performing testing are intimidated into withholding information about negative test results in order to meet schedule deadlines.

Potential Causes

- According to Capers Jones, individual programmers typically find less than one-half of the defects when they test their own software [Jones 2012].
- Testing stakeholders (especially acquisition and development management) were unaware of the levels of expertise and experience needed to be an effective professional tester.
- The developers performing testing did not have adequate training, expertise, and experience to perform testing, especially higher-level testing such as integration, system, and acceptance testing.
- An agile development process and philosophy were used, whereby everyone performs the same tasks. Therefore, some testing is being performed by non-testers who do not have adequate training, expertise, or experience in testing.
- Management did not see the value of or understand the need for professional testers (that is, people who specialize in and are responsible for testing).
- Management was not able to hire a sufficient number of testers with the appropriate training, expertise, and experience.

Recommendations

- **Prepare:**
  - Ensure that the test planning documentation includes the use of full-time, professional testers.
- **Enable:**
  - Clarify to testing stakeholders (especially project management) the value of and need for professional, full-time testers.
  - Staff the project with full-time, professional testers.
  - Give the testers the resources they need to properly perform testing.
- **Perform:**
  - Ensure that the testers perform high-level (for example, integration and system) testing.
- **Verify:**
  - Determine whether the test planning documentation specifies using full-time, professional testers.
  - Determine whether full-time, professional testers are performing the more sophisticated, higher-level testing while developers do the lowest-level testing.

Related Pitfalls   Inappropriate External Pressures (GEN-MGMT-2), Inadequate Testing Expertise (GEN-STF-3), Testers Responsible for All Testing (GEN-STF-5)

TESTERS RESPONSIBLE FOR ALL TESTING (GEN-STF-5)

Description   Testers are responsible for all of the testing during system development.

Potential Applicability   This pitfall is potentially applicable anytime that tester is a role or job title of one or more persons or teams during development.

Characteristic Symptoms
- Developers are not performing unit testing (either of their own software or that of their peers).
- Developers have essentially no testing training, expertise, or experience.

Potential Negative Consequences

- Testers must develop a deep understanding of the internals of everyone's units and low-level components.
- There needs to be a greater number of testers than is typical.
- Testers rarely have sufficient resources to perform integration and higher-level testing.
- Testing becomes a significant bottleneck that lowers developers' productivity.

Potential Causes
- There was a misunderstanding that testers were the only ones responsible for quality.
- There was a misunderstanding about the need for independent testing of units and small components.
- The developers did not know enough about how to perform unit and low-level integration testing.
- There was not sufficient time in the schedule or funding to provide the developers with any training in testing.
- Because the testers had to perform the lowest-level testing, there were too few testers to perform all of the other testing within schedule and funding constraints.

Recommendations
- Prepare:
  - Ensure that the test planning documentation includes the testing responsibilities of developers who are not professional testers.

- **Enable:**
  - ◆ Provide training in low-level testing to the developers.
  - ◆ Hire developers who have sufficient training, expertise, and experience performing low-level testing.
  - ◆ Provide developers with sufficient resources (time, funds, and tools) to perform unit and low-level integration testing.
- **Perform:**
  - ◆ Ensure that the developers perform unit testing and, potentially, integration testing.
- **Verify:**
  - ◆ Determine whether the test planning documentation includes the developers' responsibilities with regard to testing.
  - ◆ Determine whether developers are performing their assigned testing.

Related Pitfalls   Developers Responsible for All Testing (GEN-STF-4)

3.3.5   Test Process Pitfalls

The following testing pitfalls are related to the processes and techniques being used to perform testing:

- Testing and Engineering Process Not Integrated (GEN-PRO-1)
- One-Size-Fits-All Testing (GEN-PRO-2)
- Inadequate Test Prioritization (GEN-PRO-3)
- Functionality Testing Overemphasized (GEN-PRO-4)
- Black-Box System Testing Overemphasized (GEN-PRO-5)
- Black-Box System Testing Underemphasized (GEN-PRO-6)
- Too Immature for Testing (GEN-PRO-7)
- Inadequate Evaluations of Test Assets (GEN-PRO-8)
- Inadequate Maintenance of Test Assets (GEN-PRO-9)
- Testing as a Phase (GEN-PRO-10)
- Testers Not Involved Early (GEN-PRO-11)
- Incomplete Testing (GEN-PRO-12)
- No Operational Testing (GEN-PRO-13)
- Inadequate Test Data (GEN-PRO-14)
- Test-Type Confusion (GEN-PRO-15)

TESTING AND ENGINEERING PROCESSES NOT INTEGRATED (GEN-PRO-1)

Description   The testing process is not adequately integrated into the overall system engineering process.

Potential Applicability   This pitfall is potentially applicable anytime that engineering and testing processes both exist.

Characteristic Symptoms

- There is little or no discussion of testing in the system engineering documentation: System Engineering Management Plan (SEMP), Software Development Plan (SDP), Work Breakdown Structure (WBS), Project Master Schedule (PMS), or System Development Cycle (SDC).
- All or most of the testing is done as a completely independent activity performed by staff members who are not part of the project engineering team.
- Testing is treated as a separate specialty engineering activity with only limited interfaces with the primary engineering activities.
- Testers are not included in the requirements teams, architecture teams, or any cross-functional engineering teams.

Potential Negative Consequences

- There is inadequate communication between testers and other system or software engineers (for example, requirements engineers, architects, designers, and implementers).
- Few nontesters understand the scope, complexity, and importance of testing.
- Testers do not understand the work being performed by other engineers.
- Testing is less effective and takes longer than necessary.

Potential Causes

- Testers were not involved in determining and documenting the overall engineering process.
- The people determining and documenting the overall engineering process did not have significant testing expertise, training, or experience.
- Testing was outsourced.

Recommendations

- **Prepare:**
  - ◆ Include testers in the initial staffing of the project.
- **Enable:**
  - ◆ Provide a top-level briefing or training in testing to the chief system engineer, system architect, and process engineer.
- **Perform:**
  - ◆ Subject-matter experts and project testers collaborate closely with the project chief engineer or technical lead and process engineer when they develop the engineering process descriptions and associated process documents.
  - ◆ Provide high-level overviews of testing in the SEMP(s) and SDP(s).
  - ◆ Document how testing is integrated into the system development or life cycle, regardless of whether it is traditional waterfall, evolutionary (iterative, incremental, and parallel), or anything in between.
    - • For example, document handover points in the development cycle when testing input and output work products are delivered from one project organization or group to another.
  - ◆ Incorporate testing into the Project Master Schedule.
  - ◆ Incorporate testing into the project's Work Breakdown Structure (WBS).
- **Verify:**
  - ◆ Determine whether testers were involved in planning the project's system or software development process.
  - ◆ Determine whether testing is incorporated into the project's:
    - • System engineering process
    - • System development cycle
    - • System Engineering Master Plan and System Development Plan
    - • Work Breakdown Structure
    - • Master Schedule

Related Pitfalls   Inadequate Communication Concerning Testing (GEN-COM-5)

ONE-SIZE-FITS-ALL TESTING (GEN-PRO-2)

Description   All testing is performed the same way, to the same level of rigor, regardless of its criticality.

Potential Applicability   This pitfall is always potentially applicable.

Characteristic Symptoms

- The test planning documents contain only generic, boilerplate testing guidelines rather than appropriate, system-specific information.
- All testing is performed the same way, regardless of the types of requirements or the types of system or software components being verified.
- Mission-, safety-, and security-critical system or software components are not required to be tested more completely and rigorously than other, less-critical components.
- Only general techniques suitable for testing functional requirements or behavior are documented; for example, there is no description of the specialized types of testing used to verify quality requirements (for example, availability, capacity, performance, reliability, robustness, safety, security, and usability requirements).

Potential Negative Consequences

- Mission-, safety-, and security-critical software are not adequately tested.
- There is no specialized testing to verify that the system or software has sufficient levels of the important quality characteristics and attributes. For example, there is no penetration testing (for security) or usability testing.
- When there are insufficient resources to test all of the software adequately, some of these limited resources are misapplied to lower-priority software instead of concentrating on testing more critical capabilities.
- Some defects are not uncovered, and therefore make it through testing and into the deployed system.
- The system does not meet its non-functional requirements (that is, its data, interface, and quality requirements, as well as any architectural, design, implementation, or configuration constraints).
- The system is not sufficiently safe or secure.

Potential Causes

- There were no process requirements to test critical components differently than non-critical components.
- Test plan templates and content or format standards were incomplete and did not address the impact of mission, safety, or security criticality on testing.
- No quality requirements (including safety and security) were engineered.

- Test engineers were not familiar with the impact of safety and security on testing (for example, the high level of testing rigor required to achieve accreditation and certification).
  - ◆ This might have been due to poor communication between the testers and the safety and security engineers.
- No human factors, reliability, safety, or security engineers had input into the test planning process.

Recommendations

- **Prepare:**
  - ◆ Provide training to those performing system or software development and test planning concerning the need to include project-specific, specialized testing information.
  - ◆ Tailor the templates for test plans and development process documents (for example, procedures and guidelines) to address the need for project- and system-specific information.
- **Enable:**
  - ◆ Update (if necessary) the templates or content and format standards for development, testing, and process documents to address the type, completeness, and rigor of testing needed.
- **Perform:**
  - ◆ Address in the system development and test planning documentation:
    - Differences in testing types or degrees of completeness and rigor as a function of mission, safety, or security criticality.
    - Specialty engineering testing methods and techniques for testing the quality requirements (for example, penetration testing for security requirements).
  - ◆ Test mission-, safety-, and security-critical software more completely and rigorously than other less-critical software.
- **Verify:**
  - ◆ Determine whether the completeness, type, and rigor of testing are:
    - Addressed in the system development and test planning documentation
    - A function of the criticality of the system or subsystem being tested
    - Sufficient, based on the degree of criticality of the system or subsystem being tested

Related Pitfalls   Inadequate Test Prioritization (GEN-PRO-3), Inadequate Communication Concerning Testing (GEN-COM-5)

GEN-PRO-2   One-Size-Fits-All Testing

INADEQUATE TEST PRIORITIZATION (GEN-PRO-3)

Description   Testing is not adequately prioritized (for example, all types of testing have the same priority).

Potential Applicability   This pitfall is potentially applicable anytime there are insufficient resources (for example, schedule, budget, staffing, and test environments) to perform sufficient:

- Testing of all types of tests
- Regression testing of all defects

Characteristic Symptoms

- All types of testing (and all test cases of a given type of testing) have the same priority, regardless of:
  - The criticality of the subsystem being tested
  - The risks associated with the subsystem being tested (for example, difficult testing, or testing of high-risk functionality or components, is postponed until late in the schedule)
  - The natural order of integration and delivery (for example, unit testing before integration; integration before system testing; and testing the functionality of the current increment before testing the future increments)[33]
- Regression testing of iterated components is not prioritized by defects fixed:
  - High priority defects are not fixed and regression tested first.
  - Low priority defects never get fixed, thereby forcing the testing team to constantly report the same defects over and over again.
- Testers concentrate heavily on the easy tests (that is, "low-hanging fruit").

Potential Negative Consequences

- Limited testing resources are wasted or ineffectively used.
- On the other hand, users get frustrated when the same defects are reported over and over again without ever getting fixed.
- Some of the most critical defects (in terms of failure consequences) are not discovered until after the system is delivered and placed into operation.
- Specifically, defects with mission, safety, and security ramifications are not found.

Potential Causes

- The system test plans and the testing sections of the system development plans did not address prioritizing testing.
- Test prioritization was too granular to properly allocate test resources.
- Those who planned and performed the testing did not understand the need to prioritize testing.
- Any prioritization of testing that was specified was not used to schedule testing.
- Evaluations of the individual testers and test teams drive the priority and selection of test cases:
    - They were evaluated on the number of tests performed per unit time.
    - They were not evaluated on the importance or risk of the defects potentially uncovered by the tests (for example, severity of harm and frequency of faults and failures caused).

Recommendations

- **Prepare:**
    - Update the following documents to address the prioritization of testing:
        - System test plans
        - Testing sections of the system development plans
    - Define the different types and levels or categories of criticality.
- **Enable:**
    - Perform a mission analysis to determine the mission criticality of the different capabilities and subsystems.
    - Perform a safety (hazard) analysis to determine the safety criticality of the different capabilities and subsystems.
    - Perform a security (threat) analysis to determine the security criticality of the different capabilities and subsystems.
    - Identify which low-priority defects are never getting fixed but rather are constantly passed on from one release to the next.
- **Perform:**
    - Work with the developers, management, and stakeholders to prioritize testing according to the:
        - Criticality (for example, mission, safety, and security) of the system or subsystem being tested
        - Potential level of risk incurred if the defects are not uncovered
        - Potential importance of the defects uncovered via test failure
        - Probability that the test is likely to elicit important failures
        - Relative frequency with which the component under test will execute (be used), given the concept of operations (that is, operational profile)

- Delivery schedules
- Integration or dependency order
- Length of time
- Use prioritization of testing to schedule testing so that the highest priority tests are tested first.
- Collect test metrics based on the number and importance of the defects found.
- Base the performance evaluations of the individual testers and test teams on the test effectiveness (for example, the number and importance of defects found normalized by the number of defects to be uncovered) rather than merely on the number of tests written and performed (assuming that the testers have the authority to determine test prioritization).
- Verify:
  - Determine whether the system test planning documentation and the testing sections of the system or software development plans properly address test prioritization.
  - Determine whether mission, safety, and security analysis have been performed and whether the results are used to prioritize testing.
  - Determine whether testing is properly prioritized.
  - Determine whether testing is in fact performed in accordance with the prioritization.
  - Determine whether testing metrics address test prioritization.
  - Determine whether relevant performance evaluations are based on successful testing.

Related Pitfalls One-Size-Fits-All Testing (GEN-PRO-2)

FUNCTIONALITY TESTING OVEREMPHASIZED (GEN-PRO-4)

Description There is an overemphasis on testing functionality, as opposed to testing quality, data, and interface requirements and testing architectural, design, and implementation constraints.[34]

Potential Applicability This pitfall is potentially applicable anytime that significant nonfunctional (for example, data, interface, quality, and constraints) requirements exist.

Characteristic Symptoms
- The vast majority of testing is concerned with verifying functional behavior.

- Little or no testing is performed to verify adequate levels of the quality characteristics (for example, availability, reliability, robustness, safety, security, and usability).

- Testers, reliability engineers, security engineers, human factors engineers, and other specialized engineers are not performing their associated specialized types of testing (for example, there is no penetration testing taking place).

- Inadequate levels of various quality characteristics and their attributes are recognized only after the system has been delivered and placed into operation.

Potential Negative Consequences

- Testing fails to verify whether the system has adequate levels of important quality characteristics and their attributes and thereby whether it meets all of its associated quality requirements.

- Failures to meet data and interface requirements (for example, due to a lack of verification of input data and message contents) are not recognized until late during integration or after delivery.

- The system is delivered late and fails to meet an unacceptably large number of nonfunctional requirements.

Potential Causes

- The test planning and process documentation did not adequately address testing nonfunctional requirements.

- There were no process requirements (for example, in the development contract) mandating specialized testing of nonfunctional requirements.

- Managers, developers, or testers believed:

  - Testing other types of requirements (that is, data, interface, and quality, and architecture, design, implementation, or configuration constraints) was too difficult.

  - Quality requirements should be verified by methods other than testing (for example, analysis, inspection, and review).

  - Testing these nonfunctional requirements would take too long because of their cross-cutting nature.[35]

  - The nonfunctional requirements were not as important as the functional requirements.

- The nonfunctional testing would naturally occur as a byproduct of testing the functional requirements.[36]
- The other types of requirements (especially quality requirements) were:
  - Poorly specified (for example, "The system shall be secure." Or "The system shall be easy to use.")
  - Not specified
  - Therefore not testable (nor verifiable, for that matter)
- Functional testing was the only testing mandated by the development contract; therefore, testing the nonfunctional requirements was out of scope or believed to be unimportant to the acquisition organization.

Recommendations

- **Prepare:**
  - Adequately address testing nonfunctional requirements in the test planning and process documentation.
  - Include process requirements mandating specialized testing of nonfunctional requirements in the contract.
- **Enable:**
  - Ensure that managers, developers, and testers understand the importance of testing nonfunctional requirements as well as conformance to the architecture and design (for example, via white-box testing).
- **Perform:**
  - Adequately perform the other types of testing.
- **Verify:**
  - Determine whether the managers, developers, and or testers understand the importance of testing nonfunctional requirements and conformance to the architecture, design, implementation, and configuration constraints.
  - Determine whether quality engineers verify that the testers are testing the nonfunctional requirements and constraints.
  - Determine whether the test plans and process documents adequately address testing nonfunctional behavior.
  - Determine whether all types of nonfunctional defects are being measured, analyzed, and reported.
  - Determine whether nonfunctional defects are being detected.

Related Pitfalls None

BLACK-BOX SYSTEM TESTING OVEREMPHASIZED (GEN-PRO-5)

Description   Black-box system testing is overemphasized, resulting in inadequate white-box unit and integration testing.[37]

Potential Applicability   This pitfall is always potentially applicable.

Characteristic Symptoms

- The vast majority of testing is at the system level for purposes of verifying conformance to requirements.
- There is very little white-box unit and integration testing to verify architecture, design, implementation, and configuration constraints.
- System testing is detecting many defects that could have been more easily uncovered during unit or integration testing.
- Similar residual defects are causing faults and failures after the system has been delivered and placed into operation.

Potential Negative Consequences

- Defects that could have been found during unit or integration testing are harder to detect, localize, analyze, and fix.
- System testing is unlikely to be completed on schedule because excess time is used addressing these defects.
- The system is delivered late with an unacceptably large number of residual defects that are only rarely executed and thereby only rarely cause faults or failures.

Potential Causes

- The test plans and process documents did not adequately address unit and integration testing.
- There were no process requirements (for example, in the development contract) mandating unit and integration testing.
- Management believed that black-box system testing was all that was necessary to detect the defects.
- Developers believed that the independent test team was responsible for all testing, whereas the test team was only planning on performing system-level testing.
- The schedule did not contain adequate time for unit and integration testing.

Recommendations

- **Prepare:**
  - ◆ Adequately address in the test planning documentation, test process documents, and contract (if any):
    - • White-box and gray-box testing
    - • Unit and integration testing
- **Enable:**
  - ◆ Ensure that managers, developers, and testers understand the importance of these lower-level types of testing.
  - ◆ Use a test plan template or content and format standard that addresses these lower-level types of testing.
- **Perform:**
  - ◆ Increase the amount and effectiveness of these lower-level types of testing.
- **Verify:**
  - ◆ Determine whether the test planning documentation and process documents adequately address lower-level—such as white-box and gray-box—types of tests.
  - ◆ Determine whether the managers, developers, and or testers understand the importance of these lower-level types of testing.
  - ◆ Determine whether the developers are actually performing these lower-level types of testing and whether they are an appropriate percentage of the total tests.
  - ◆ Determine whether the test planning documentation and process documents adequately address the developers' responsibilities with regard to lower-level testing.
  - ◆ Determine whether the number of defects slipping past unit and integration testing are measured or estimated and whether they are excessive.

Related Pitfalls   Black-Box System Testing Underemphasized (GEN-PRO-6)

BLACK-BOX SYSTEM TESTING UNDEREMPHASIZED *(GEN-PRO-6)*

Description   Black-box system testing to determine whether the system meets requirements is underemphasized in favor of white-box unit and integration testing.

Potential Applicability   This pitfall is always potentially applicable.

Characteristic Symptoms

- The vast majority of testing occurs at the unit and integration level to verify the architecture, design, and implementation.

- Very little time is spent on black-box system testing to verify conformance to the requirements.
- People are stating that significant system testing is not necessary (for example, because "lower-level tests have already verified the system requirements" or "there is insufficient time left to perform significant system testing.")
- There is little or no testing of quality requirements (for example, because the associated quality characteristics and attributes strongly tend to be system-level characteristics).

Potential Negative Consequences

- The delivered system fails to meet some of its system requirements, especially quality requirements and those functional requirements that require collaboration of the integrated subsystems.

Potential Causes

- The test planning documentation and process documents did not adequately address black-box system testing.
- There were no process requirements (for example, in the development contract) mandating black-box system testing.
- The managers or developers mistakenly believed that if the system's components worked properly, then the system would work properly once these components were integrated.
- No black-box testing metrics were collected, analyzed, or reported.
- The schedule did not contain adequate time for black-box system testing (for example, due to schedule slippages coupled with a firm release date).
- Developers, rather than independent testers, performed much or most of the testing.
- The developers were using an agile development method, with its very strong emphasis on testing what is currently being developed and integrated (that is, unit testing and integration testing).

Recommendations

- Prepare:
  - Address black-box system testing in the test planning documentation.
  - Review the test planning documentation and process documents to ensure that they adequately address black-box system testing.

- Enable:
  - ◆ When appropriate, improve the test planning documentation and process documents with regard to system testing.
  - ◆ Train those who will be performing testing in system-level testing.
  - ◆ Provide sufficient time in the overall project's master schedule for system-level testing.
- Perform:
  - ◆ Increase the amount and effectiveness of system testing.
- Verify:
  - ◆ Determine whether the test planning documentation and process documents adequately address system-level testing.
  - ◆ Determine whether the number of requirements that have been verified by system testing is being measured, analyzed, and reported (for example, as part of a metrics program).
  - ◆ Determine whether adequate resources were provided to support adequate system-level testing.

Related Pitfalls   Black-Box System Testing Overemphasized (GEN-PRO-5)

TOO IMMATURE FOR TESTING (GEN-PRO-7)

Description   Products are delivered for testing before they are ready to be tested.

Potential Applicability   This pitfall is always potentially applicable.

Characteristic Symptoms
- Some of the products being tested are excessively immature.
- Products contain an inappropriately large number of requirements, architecture, design, and implementation defects that should have been discovered (for example, during inspections, reviews, and earlier tests) and fixed prior to the current testing.

Potential Negative Consequences

- It is difficult to perform and complete planned testing because the large number of system and test failures makes it difficult to successfully run through the planned test cases.

- Testing is not completed on schedule.
- Testers must work long hours dealing with the unexpected defects.
- Developers pass their units on to integration testers when they still have large amounts of defects that should have been found during unit testing.
  - Encapsulation due to integration makes it unnecessarily difficult to localize the defects that caused the test failure.

Potential Causes

- Managers, customer or user representatives, and developers did not understand the impact of product immaturity on testing.
- Schedule pressures caused corners to be cut:
  - There was insufficient time to properly evaluate the architecture, design, and implementation prior to testing.
  - There was insufficient time to properly perform lower-level testing prior to higher-level testing.
- There were insufficient resources (for example, staffing, budget, schedule, and testing tools or environments) for proper design, implementation, and low-level testing.
- There were no completion criteria for design, implementation, and lower-level testing.
- Test readiness criteria did not exist or were not enforced.
- Lower-level testing was either not performed or not properly performed.

Recommendations

- **Prepare:**
  - Improve the effectiveness of architecture engineering, design, implementation, and lower-level testing (for example, by improving methods and providing training).
  - Set reasonable completion criteria for design, implementation, and low-level testing.
- **Enable:**
  - Enforce standards of test readiness-criteria.
  - Set reasonable criteria for test readiness.
- **Perform:**
  - Increase the amount of testing for earlier verification of the requirements, architecture, and design (for example, with peer-level reviews and inspections).
  - Increase the amount of lower-level testing prior to higher-level testing.
- **Verify:**
  - Determine whether managers, customer or user representatives, and developers understand the impact of product immaturity on testing.

GEN-PRO-7   Too Immature for Testing

- Determine whether adequate resources (for example, staffing, budget, schedule, and testing tools or environments) were provided for architecture engineering, design, implementation, and their associated types of testing.
- Determine whether test completion criteria exist for lower-level types of testing and whether these completion criteria are being enforced and followed.
- Determine whether the number of defects slipping through multiple disciplines and types of testing are being measured and reported (for example, where the defect was introduced and where it was found).

Related Pitfalls   Unclear Testing Responsibilities (GEN-STF-2)

INADEQUATE EVALUATIONS OF TEST ASSETS (GEN-PRO-8)

Description   The quality of the test assets is not adequately evaluated prior to using them.

Potential Applicability   This pitfall is potentially applicable anytime that test assets are being produced (that is, almost always).

Characteristic Symptoms
- There is little or no verification, validation, accreditation, or certification of the test tools, test environments or test beds, and test laboratories or facilities.
- Little or no (peer-level) inspections, walk-throughs, or reviews of the test cases (for example, test input data, including large test data sets, preconditions, trigger events, expected test outputs and postconditions) are being performed prior to actual testing.
- Test cases are not verified by subject-matter experts who understand the requirements that the software under test is intended to implement.

Potential Negative Consequences

- Test planning documentation, procedures, test cases, and other testing work products contain defects that could have been found during these evaluations.
- There is an increase in false-positive and false-negative test results.

- Unnecessary effort is wasted identifying and fixing defects in test assets after the associated tests have been run.
- Some defects are not found, and an unnecessary number of these defects make it through testing and into the deployed system.

Potential Causes

- Evaluating the test assets was not addressed in the:
  - Test planning documentation
  - Quality-engineering or quality-assurance plans
  - Master project schedule
  - Work Breakdown Structure (WBS)
- There were insufficient time and staff to evaluate the deliverable system and the test assets.
- The test assets were not deemed to be sufficiently important to evaluate.
- The management, developers, or testers believed that the test assets would automatically be verified during the actual testing.

Recommendations

- Prepare:
  - Incorporate test evaluations into the:
    - System development plans and processes
    - System test planning documentation
    - Quality engineering plans and processes
    - Project schedules (master and team)
    - Project Work Breakdown Structure (WBS)
  - Ensure that the following test assets are reviewed prior to actual testing: test inputs, preconditions (pre-test state), and test oracle, including expected test outputs and postconditions.
- Enable:
  - Where appropriate and to the extent practical, ensure that the team(s) evaluating testing include:
    - Process engineers, technical managers, and other testers when evaluating test planning and test process documentation
    - Requirements engineers, user representatives, subject-matter experts, quality engineers, and other testers when evaluating black-box tests
    - Architects, designers, programmers, and other testers when evaluating white-box tests
- Perform:
  - Quality control evaluations of testing work products:[38]
    - Evaluate the test planning and test process documentation.

- Perform technical evaluations of the major testing work products (for example, test inputs, preconditions (pretest state), and test oracle, including expected test outputs and postconditions, test tools, test environments or test beds, test laboratories or facilities, and tracings between requirements and tests) prior to their use.
- Quality assurance evaluations of the as-performed testing process:
    - Evaluate the performance of the testing process (for example, for efficiency, effectiveness, and conformance to the as-planned process).
- Present the results of these technical evaluations at major project status meetings and major formal reviews.
- Verify:
    - Determine whether these evaluations do in fact occur and if they are properly performed.
    - Determine whether these evaluations are effective at identifying problems and opportunities for improvement.
    - Determine whether the results of these evaluations are reported to the proper stakeholders.
    - Determine whether problems discovered are assigned for fixing and are in fact being fixed.

Related Pitfalls   Incomplete Test Planning (GEN-TPS-2), Unclear Testing Responsibilities (GEN-STF-2)

INADEQUATE MAINTENANCE OF TEST ASSETS (GEN-PRO-9)

Description   Test assets are not properly maintained.

Potential Applicability   This pitfall is potentially applicable anytime that test assets need to be maintained (that is, almost always).

Characteristic Symptoms

- Test assets (for example, test inputs, preconditions (pretest state), and test oracle, including expected test outputs and postconditions, test tools, test environments or test beds, test laboratories or facilities, and tracings between requirements and tests) are not adequately updated and iterated as defects are found and the system or software under test is changed (for example, due to refactoring, change requests, or the use of an evolutionary—that is, incremental and iterative—development cycle).
- Requirements are not traced to test assets so that these assets can be updated as the requirements change.[39]

Potential Negative Consequences

- Test assets are no longer consistent with the current requirements, architecture, design, and implementation.
- Test productivity decreases as the number of false-negative test results increases (that is, as tests fail due to test defects).
- The amount of productive regression testing decreases as effort is redirected to identifying and fixing test defects.
- If test data is not migrated to new versions of the database (for example, SQL Server, Oracle, Sybase, IMS), then the test data in the database tables becomes inaccessible.

Potential Causes

- Maintenance of the test assets was not an explicit part of the testing process.
- Maintenance of the test assets was not explicitly documented in the test planning documentation.
- The test resources (for example, schedule and staffing) provided by management were insufficient to properly maintain the test assets.
- The project's master schedule did not included (sufficient) time for test asset maintenance.
- Testing stakeholders did not understand the importance of maintaining the test assets.
- There was no tool support, such as requirements management, test management, or configuration management, for maintaining the test assets.

Recommendations

- **Prepare:**
  - Explicitly address maintaining the test assets in the:
    - Test planning documentation
    - Testing process documents (for example, procedures and guidelines)
    - Project Work Breakdown Structure (WBS)
  - Include adequate time for test asset maintenance in the project's master schedule.
  - Clearly communicate the importance of maintaining the test assets to the testing stakeholders.

- ◆ Ensure that the maintenance testers are adequately trained and experienced.[40]
- ■ **Enable:**
  - ◆ Provide sufficient test resources (for example, schedule and staffing) to properly maintain the test assets.
  - ◆ Provide tool support (for example, via a requirements management, test management, or configuration management tool) for maintaining the tracing between requirements and tests.[41]
  - ◆ Update the databases holding large amounts of test data as new versions of the database are released and determined to be sufficiently mature to use.
- ■ **Perform:**
  - ◆ Keep the test assets consistent with the current requirements, architecture, design, and implementation.[42]
  - ◆ Properly maintain the test assets as defects are found and system changes are introduced.
- ■ **Verify:**
  - ◆ Determine whether the test plans address maintaining test assets.
  - ◆ Determine whether the project's master schedule includes time for maintaining test assets.
  - ◆ Determine (for example, via quality assurance and control) whether the test assets are in fact being maintained.

Related Pitfalls   No Separate Test Planning Documentation (GEN-TPS-1), Incomplete Test Planning (GEN-TPS-2), Unclear Testing Responsibilities (GEN-STF-2)

TESTING AS A PHASE (GEN-PRO-10)

Description   Testing (primarily integration and system testing) is treated largely as a phase that takes place late in a sequential (such as waterfall) development cycle instead of as an ongoing activity that takes place continuously in an iterative, incremental, and concurrent (that is, an evolutionary, or agile) development cycle.

Potential Applicability   This pitfall is potentially applicable anytime that sequential development cycles are being used.

Characteristic Symptoms
- ■ A waterfall development cycle is being used.
- ■ Testing is documented as a phase in the:
  - ◆ Test planning documentation
  - ◆ Project master schedule

- The majority of defects are identified late in the development cycle (that is, right before system delivery).

Potential Negative Consequences

- System-level defects are harder to localize because the entire system has been integrated. If unit and integration testing had occurred, then any defects found would have been in the individual units or in the integrated subsystem.
- System-level defects are found when they take longer and are more expensive to fix than if system testing were an ongoing activity.
- System-level defects are found so late that there is insufficient time in which to fix them prior to delivery.

Potential Causes

- Management decided to use a traditional, sequential development cycle because they:
  - Are used to managing a waterfall development cycle
  - Think that a sequential development cycle is easier to manage
  - Do not understand an evolutionary development cycle and do not know how to manage a project that uses one
  - Think that an evolutionary development cycle is higher risk than a sequential development cycle
- The developers did not have experience or expertise in evolutionary development cycles.

Recommendations

- **Prepare:**
  - Include incremental, iterative, and concurrent testing beginning early in the project in the test planning documentation, project planning documents, and project master schedule.
- **Enable:**
  - Provide training and consulting support in evolutionary, or agile, development process, including testing.
- **Perform:**
  - Perform testing in a continuous, incremental, iterative, and concurrent manner, beginning as soon as is practical (that is, as soon as any units or components are stable enough to test).

- **Verify:**
  - Determine whether evolutionary, or agile, testing has been included in the test planning documentation, project planning documents, and schedule.
  - Determine whether the testers and other developers who will be performing some level of testing (typically unit testing) have adequate expertise, experience, or training to perform evolutionary testing.
  - Determine whether managers have adequate expertise, experience, or training to manage an evolutionary development cycle, including evolutionary testing.
  - Determine whether evolutionary testing is being performed.
  - Determine whether the benefits of evolutionary testing are being realized.

Related Pitfalls   Testing at the End (GEN-TPS-6), Inadequate Testing Expertise (GEN-STF-3)

TESTERS NOT INVOLVED EARLY (GEN-PRO-11)

Description   Testers are not involved at the beginning of the project, but rather only once an implementation exists to test.

Potential Applicability   This pitfall is potentially applicable on every project.

Characteristic Symptoms

- Early involvement of the testers is not documented in the planning and scheduling documents:
  - System or software planning documentation
  - Test planning documentation
  - Project Master Schedule
- Testers are not involved with engineering and evaluating the requirements.
- No executable architecture or design models are tested, possibly because none exist.
- Developers develop all test cases (including those for integration and system testing), which the testers merely execute without determining whether the developer-implemented tests are adequate to verify the requirements and meet appropriate test-case-selection and test-completion-criteria.

Potential Negative Consequences

- Many of the requirements are not testable.

- Executable architecture and design models contain defects that could have been caught via testing.
- Test cases developed by developers do not test how well the system meets its requirements (that is, how well it does what it must), but rather only how well the system implements its design (that is, how well it does what the developers thought it should).
- Testers and the test environments or laboratories are not ready for testing to begin until relatively late in the development cycle.

Potential Causes

- Sufficient testers were not part of the initial project staffing.
- Testers could not help ensure that the requirements were testable, at least those that were not intended to be verified by other means (for example, analysis, demonstration, and inspection).
- Managers viewed testing as one or more phases that occur late in the lifecycle, once software has been developed (for example, because they think "How can you test something that doesn't exist yet?").

Recommendations

- **Prepare:**
  - Document early involvement of testers in the planning and scheduling documentation
- **Enable:**
  - Add a sufficient number of testers at the beginning of the project to perform early testing activities.
- **Perform:**
  - Don't wait for the implementation to start testing.
    - Involve the testers in the requirements engineering activity.
    - Develop test cases (including test data) once the requirements are at least semi-stable.
    - Test executable architecture and design models as they are created.
- **Verify:**
  - Determine whether early involvement of the testers is documented in the planning documentation and the project's master schedule.
  - Determine whether the testers are involved from the beginning of the development cycle.
  - Determine whether one or more testers are involved with the requirements engineering team.
  - Determine whether executable architecture or design models (if any) are being tested.

Related Pitfalls   Inadequate Test Schedule (GEN-TPS-5), Testing at the End (GEN-TPS-6), Testing and Engineering Processes Not Integrated (GEN-PRO-1), Testing as a Phase (GEN-PRO-10)

INCOMPLETE TESTING (GEN-PRO-12)

Description   The testers inappropriately fail to test certain testable behaviors, characteristics, or components of the system.[43]

Potential Applicability   This pitfall is always potentially applicable, especially when testing resources are limited.

Characteristic Symptoms
- Some of the system's testable requirements (especially quality requirements) are not tested prior to delivery of the completed system.
- Some of the system's features, capabilities, or functions are not tested prior to delivery.
- Some system components (subsystems, software components, or devices) are not tested prior to delivery.
- Some of the system's software is not tested (that is, one or more appropriate measures of code coverage are not completely achieved).[44]
- Certain relevant types of testing are not performed.

Potential Negative Consequences

- The system is delivered with an unnecessarily large number of unknown defects.
- An unnecessarily large number of system defects will be uncovered during operational usage.
- Such defects will cost a great deal more than if they had been discovered by testing earlier during development.

Potential Causes
- The testers did not have the expertise, test environments or tools, or time to perform any additional testing. Note that this is especially true with regard to testing the quality requirements and their associated specialty engineering features, capabilities, and functions.

- Some features, capabilities, or functions were not considered sufficiently important to verify, given the project's limited testing resources.
- Certain types of testing were postponed until so late in the development process that there was insufficient time and funding to perform them prior to delivery.
- Commercial, off-the-shelf (COTS) components were assumed not to have any significant defects and, therefore, to work correctly and not need testing.
- Test-completion criteria were not determined, were not stated in any test planning documentation, or were not mandatory.
- Changes were being made to the system under test at such a high rate that the testers could not keep up with them.
- Test coverage levels (for example, types of code coverage) were not determined, were not stated in any test planning documentation, or were not mandatory.
- Test planning documentation did not specify the types of tests that needed to be performed.
- Those performing the tests made decisions regarding the appropriate amount of testing on the fly, with little thought of the overall testing process.[45]

Recommendations

- **Prepare:**
  - Include sufficient types of testing, test-case-selection criteria, and test-completion criteria—including mandatory levels of test coverage—in the test planning documentation.
  - Ensure that testing stakeholders (especially management) understand what constitutes adequate testing and what the negative consequences of inadequate testing might be.
- **Enable:**
  - Provide sufficient resources (for example, time, budget, environments, or tools) to adequately perform testing.
  - Ensure that the people performing testing have sufficient testing expertise and understand all relevant testing types, test-case-selection criteria, and test-completion criteria, including mandatory code coverage levels.
- **Perform:**
  - Perform all needed testing, including adequate testing of requirements, capabilities and functions, components and subsystems, and software.
- **Verify:**
  - Determine whether test-completion criteria and test-case-selection criteria, including code coverage, has been documented and mandated.
  - Determine whether testing stakeholders understand the selected test-completion criteria.

- Determine whether sufficient testing resources ('for example, personnel, funding, schedule, and testing tools, environments, and facilities) are provided.
- Determine whether the testers are competent to perform all needed testing.
- Determine the degree to which the actual performance of testing is complete and conforms to the documented test-completion criteria.

Related Pitfalls   Incomplete Test Planning (GEN-TPS-2), Inadequate Test Schedule (GEN-TPS-5), Testing at the End (GEN-TPS-6), Inadequate Test Resources (GEN-MGMT-1), Inadequate Testing Expertise (GEN-STF-3), Inadequate Test Prioritization (GEN-PRO-3), Inadequate Architecture or Design Documentation (GEN-COM-1), Missing Requirements (GEN-REQ-3), Unavailable Components (TTS-INT-3), Inadequate End-to-End Testing (TTS-SYS-3), Regression Testing Not Performed (TTS-REG-2), Test Resources Not Delivered for Maintenance (TTS-REG-5)

No Operational Testing (GEN-PRO-13)

Description   Representative users are not performing any operational testing of the "completed" system under actual operational conditions.

Potential Applicability   This pitfall is potentially applicable once the system is placed into operation.

Characteristic Symptoms

- All testing occurs in the developer organization's development and test facilities.
- The test planning documentation and master project schedule do not address operational testing.
- There is no alpha testing or beta testing.

Potential Negative Consequences

- Residual defects, which should be uncovered by operational testing, cause faults and failures during operational usage.
- The negative impact of defect execution and system failure is higher once the system is declared finished and placed into production and operation.

Potential Causes

- Project managers, technical leaders, and test managers were unaware of the benefits of operational testing.
- There is no funding for operational testing.
- The system release date does not allow time for operational testing.
- Management has the attitude that the initial operational use by the initial users automatically provides adequate operational testing without the costs associated with producing and executing actual operational tests.
- Management considered operational testing an unjustifiable expense or risk because it:
  - Increases the effort and schedule required for initial development
  - Raises the potential for unwanted early publication of system capabilities and readiness for release
  - Is not under management's control to the same degree as organization-internal testing

Recommendations

- **Prepare:**
  - Educate testing stakeholders about the costs and benefits of operational testing.
- **Enable:**
  - Include operational testing in the project's:
    - Test planning documentation
    - Master schedule
    - Work Breakdown Structure (WBS)
  - Include funding for operational testing in the project budget.
  - Consider the pros and cons of beta testing and crowdsource testing if there will be insufficient organization-internal testers and test environments to provide adequate testing.
- **Perform:**
  - Perform appropriate amount(s) of the appropriate type(s) of operational testing.
- **Verify:**
  - Determine whether authoritative testing stakeholders understand the pros and cons of operational testing.
  - Determine whether operational testing is included in the project's test planning documentation, master schedule, WBS, and budget.
  - Determine whether operational testing is taking place.

GEN-PRO-13   No Operational Testing

- If operational testing is not taking place, determine whether it was properly considered and rejected for sufficient reasons.

Related Pitfalls Incomplete Test Planning (GEN-TPS-2), Inadequate Test Resources (GEN-MGMT-1), Developers Responsible for All Testing (GEN-STF-4), Inadequate Test Environments (GEN-TTE-5)

INADEQUATE TEST DATA (GEN-PRO-14)

Description The test data is incomplete, incorrect, or invalid.

Potential Applicability This pitfall is potentially applicable anytime, but is especially likely when the system under test is required to handle large amounts and many types of data.

Characteristic Symptoms
- Individual test inputs (for example, records) are:
  - Missing components (for example, fields or attributes)
  - Of the wrong data type
  - Using incorrect units of measure
  - Out of their valid ranges
  - In the wrong language or character set (for textual data)
- An entire test data set (for example, a test file) does not:
  - Have a large enough number of test inputs (for example, records) to properly perform capacity and stress testing
  - Have enough valid test inputs to verify the desired level of code coverage
  - Have enough valid test inputs to verify mandatory precision of numerical values
  - Include data in a mandatory language, character set, or units of measure

Potential Negative Consequences

- Data and interface requirements will not be properly verified.
- Testing will be incomplete.
- The delivered system is likely to incorporate residual defects that would have been uncovered if the test data were more complete.

Potential Causes

- There were no project-wide or test-team-wide test-case-selection criteria.
- There were no test-completion criteria.
- The testers were not using a testing method (for example, boundary-value testing) that implies selecting test cases based on equivalent classes of test data.
- The testers did not base their test case selection on a:
    - Requirements analysis method that implies test cases (for example, use case modeling with at least one test case for each path)
    - Design method that implies test cases, such as design by contract (DBC), with its reliance on using assumptions (for example, preconditions, invariants, and postconditions)

Recommendations

- Prepare:
    - Include criteria in the project's test planning documentation:
        - Test-coverage criteria (for example, branch, condition, or statement coverage)
        - Test-case-selection criteria (for example, boundary-value testing)
        - Test-completion criteria
- Enable:
    - Ensure that the testers have sufficient training, experience, and expertise in generating test data.
    - Ensure that the testers have test tools that will help with generating adequate amounts of test data.
- Perform:
    - Develop test data that exercises:
        - All normal (primary and alternative) use case paths (also known as "sunny-day paths," "happy paths," and "golden paths")
        - Credible exceptional (error-, fault-, and failure-tolerant) use case paths (also known as "rainy-day paths")
        - Boundary values and edge cases
    - Develop sufficient test data to meet any relevant test-coverage criteria, test-completion criteria, and test-case-selection criteria.
    - Develop sufficient test data to justify sufficient confidence that there are adequate levels of relevant quality requirements (for example, availability, reliability, robustness, safety, and security).
- Verify:
    - Determine whether test-coverage criteria, test-case-selection criteria, and test-completion criteria have been determined and documented.

GEN-PRO-14   Inadequate Test Data

- Determine whether the testers have sufficient training, experience, and expertise in generating test data.
- Determine whether the testers have test tools that will help with generating test data.
- Determine whether the test data adequately exercise the system's normal and exceptional behavior.
- Determine whether the test data meet the test-coverage criteria, test-case-selection criteria, and test-completion criteria.
- Determine whether sufficient test data have been developed to justify sufficient confidence that there are adequate levels of relevant quality requirements.
- Determine the correctness or validity of the test data.

Related Pitfalls   Incomplete Test Planning (GEN-TPS-2), Inadequate Testing Expertise (GEN-STF-3), One-Size-Fits-All Testing (GEN-PRO-2), Functionality Testing Overemphasized (GEN-PRO-4), Over-Reliance on Testing Tools (GEN-TTE-2), Inadequate Reliability Testing (TTS-SPC-6), Inadequate Robustness Testing (TTS-SPC-7), Inadequate Safety Testing (TTS-SPC-8), Inadequate Security Testing (TTS-SPC-9)

TEST-TYPE CONFUSION (GEN-PRO-15)

Description   Test cases from one type of testing are redundantly repeated as part of another type of testing, even though the testing types have quite different purposes and scopes. This pitfall is also called *Accidental* or *Unintentional Regression Testing*.

Potential Applicability   This pitfall is potentially applicable whenever there are multiple types of testing being performed (that is, it is for all practical purposes universally applicable).

Characteristic Symptoms
- Integration testing repeats unit-level tests rather than tests designed specifically to uncover integration defects.
- System testing repeats white-box tests developed for unit and integration testing rather than black-box, system-level tests designed specifically to uncover defects causing failure to meet the system's specified requirements.
- Acceptance testing (also known as user acceptance testing), end-user testing, and operational acceptance testing merely reuses tests developed for system-level developer testing rather than those designed specifically to uncover defects that:
  - Prevent the system from meeting business or mission or user needs
  - Make the system unacceptable to the acquirer or customer

Potential Negative Consequences

- Redundantly repeating tests (especially reusing system tests as acceptance tests) wastes limited testing resources repeating tests that are relatively unlikely to uncover new defects.
- This pitfall prevents the acceptance tests (user needs in an operational environment) from serving as an independent double check on the system tests (system requirements in the development environment).
- Developers, testers, and managers believe that reusing test cases is an "industry best practice" because it:
  - Saves time spent developing test cases, which is true for regression testing
  - Is an effective way to uncover additional defects, even though it is untrue for other types of testing

Potential Causes

- The testers were unaware of the:
  - Many different types of testing
  - Different purposes and scopes of these different types of testing
  - Impact that the test type's purpose and scope have on the associated test cases
- There were insufficient resources to develop and run all relevant types of tests.

Recommendations

- **Prepare:**
  - Address the purpose, scope, test-case-selection criteria, and test-completion criteria of each type of testing in the test planning documentation.
- **Enable:**
  - Provide sufficient resources (for example, schedule, budget, and staffing) to create new test-type-specific test cases.
  - If appropriate, provide training that covers developing different types of test cases for different types of testing.
- **Perform:**
  - For each type of testing, create test cases that are appropriate, given the testing type's purpose and scope.

- Verify:
  - ◆ Determine whether the test planning documentation documents the purpose, scope, test-case-selection criteria, and test-completion criteria for each of the different types of tests.
  - ◆ Determine whether there are sufficient resources to develop different, mostly disjointed sets of test cases for the different types of testing.
  - ◆ Determine whether different types of testing are reusing unreasonably large percentages of the same test cases.

Related Pitfalls   Incomplete Test Planning (GEN-TPS-2), Inadequate Test Schedule (GEN-TPS-5), Inadequate Testing Expertise (GEN-STF-3), Incomplete Testing (GEN-PRO-12)

3.3.6   Test Tools and Environments Pitfalls

The following testing pitfalls are related to the test tools and environments:

- Over-Reliance on Manual Testing (GEN-TTE-1)
- Over-Reliance on Testing Tools (GEN-TTE-2)
- Too Many Target Platforms (GEN-TTE-3)
- Target Platform Difficult to Access (GEN-TTE-4)
- Inadequate Test Environments (GEN-TTE-5)
- Poor Fidelity of Test Environments (GEN-TTE-6)
- Inadequate Test Environment Quality (GEN-TTE-7)
- Test Assets Not Delivered (GEN-TTE-8)
- Inadequate Test Configuration Management (GEN-TTE-9)
- Developers Ignore Testability (GEN-TTE-10)

OVER-RELIANCE ON MANUAL TESTING (GEN-TTE-1)

Description   Testers place too much reliance on manual testing such that the majority of testing is performed manually, without adequate support of test tools or test scripts.

Potential Applicability   This pitfall is always potentially applicable.

Characteristic Symptoms
- All, or the majority of, testing is performed manually without adequate support of test tools or test scripts.[46]

Potential Negative Consequences

- Testing is very labor intensive.
- Testing includes *manual*:
  - Developing test cases
  - Developing test scripts and test data
  - Executing tests
  - Documenting test results
- Any nontrivial amount of regression testing is likely to be impractical.
- Testing is likely subject to significant human error, especially with regard to test inputs and interpreting and recording test outputs.
- Several types of quality requirements (for example, availability, capacity, reliability, robustness, and safety requirements) are not adequately tested, thereby leaving these requirements unverified.
- Testing is neither consistent nor repeatable because different testers often approach the same manual test case differently.
- Manual testing is not scalable.
- The costs (time and effort) of manual testing rapidly increase to infeasible levels as the size and complexity of the system grows.

Potential Causes

- Test automation was not addressed in the test planning documentation.
- Test automation was not included in the project's Work Breakdown Structure (WBS).
- Time for test automation was not included in the project's master schedule and test team schedules, including time for a:
  - Determination of tests and associated test cases to automate
  - Development of test software (for example, test scripts)
  - Development of test data
  - Proof of Concept study of test automation
  - Return on investment (ROI) study of test automation
- Testers did not have adequate training and experience in test automation.
- It was not feasible to manually test many of the quality requirements.

Recommendations

- **Prepare:**
  - ◆ Address test automation in the test planning documentation.
  - ◆ Address test automation in the project's WBS.
  - ◆ Include time for test automation in the project's master schedule and test team schedules.
  - ◆ Provide sufficient funding to evaluate, select, purchase, and maintain test tools, test environments or test beds, and test laboratories or facilities.
  - ◆ Provide sufficient staff and funding to automate testing.
- **Enable:**
  - ◆ Evaluate, select, purchase, and maintain test tools.
  - ◆ Where needed, provide training in automated testing.
- **Perform:**
  - ◆ Limit manual testing to only the testing for which is most appropriate.
  - ◆ Automate regression testing.
  - ◆ Maintain regression tests (for example, scripts, inputs, and expected outputs).
  - ◆ Use test tools and scripts to automate appropriate parts of the testing process (for example, to ensure that testing provides adequate code coverage).
- **Verify:**
  - ◆ Determine whether the test planning documentation includes automated testing.
  - ◆ Determine whether the schedules include sufficient time to automate testing.
  - ◆ Determine whether sufficient tests are being automated and maintained.

Related Pitfalls   Over-Reliance on Testing Tools (GEN-TTE-2), Inadequate Regression Test Automation (TTS-REG-1)

OVER-RELIANCE ON TESTING TOOLS (GEN-TTE-2)

Description   Testers and other testing stakeholders are relying too heavily on automated testing.[47]

Potential Applicability   This pitfall is potentially applicable anytime that testing tools are being used.

Characteristic Symptoms

- Testers and other testing stakeholders rely very heavily on Commercial-off-the-Shelf (COTS), open source, Government-off-the-Shelf (GOTS), Military-off-the-Shelf (MOTS), or home-grown or proprietary test tools:
  - To do far more than merely generate sufficient white-box test cases to ensure code coverage
  - To automate creating test cases, including test-case-selection and completion ("coverage") criteria
  - As their test oracle (to determine the expected—correct—test result)
- Testers let the tool drive the test method or process and techniques rather than the other way around.

Potential Negative Consequences

- Testing emphasizes white-box (design-driven) testing and includes inadequate black-box (requirements-driven) testing.
- Many design defects are not found during testing and thus remain in the delivered system.

Potential Causes

- The tool vendor's marketing information:
  - Was overly optimistic (for example, promised that it covers everything)
  - Equated the tool with the test method or process.
- Managers, developers, or testers equated the test tools with the test method or process and therefore believed that no additional test process needed to be addressed.
- The testers were sufficiently inexperienced in testing not to recognize what the tool did not cover.
- Testers were using tools to automate for the sake of automation.

Recommendations

- Prepare:
  - Ensure that manual testing, including its scope (when and for what), is documented in the test planning and test process documentation.
- Enable:
  - Provide sufficient resources to perform the tests that should or must be performed manually.

- ♦ Ensure that testers understand (for example, via training and test planning) the limits of testing tools and of automating test-case creation.
- Perform:
  - ♦ Let testing needs drive the testing method or process, and let this method drive test tool selection.
  - ♦ Determine what tests need to be run first, and only then determine which of these tests should be automated and which should be performed manually.
  - ♦ Ensure that testers use the requirements, architecture, and design (when appropriate) as the test oracle (to determine the correct test result).
- Verify:
  - ♦ Determine whether the testers are relying 100% on test tools to:
    - • Automate test-case selection
    - • Set the test-completion ("coverage") criteria

Related Pitfalls   Over-Reliance on Manual Testing (GEN-TTE-1)

TOO MANY TARGET PLATFORMS (GEN-TTE-3)

Description   The test team and testers are not adequately prepared for testing applications that will execute on numerous target platforms (for example, mobile devices such as smart phones and tablet computers).

Potential Applicability   This pitfall is potentially applicable anytime there are multiple target platforms.

Characteristic Symptoms
- There are many target platforms including hardware (such as processor and memory), operating systems, and middleware.
- The software application is not being tested on some target platforms (for example, manufacturer, vendor, model, and version) prior to delivery.

Potential Negative Consequences

- Certain platform-specific defects are not uncovered because testing is not performed on the associated platform.

- Either (1) many different platform-specific test tools need to be acquired and used, or else (2) the test tools are limited because they are highly generic and largely platform-independent.
- Residual defects will be discovered after the software is placed into operation, causing greatly increased maintenance costs and user dissatisfaction.

Potential Causes

- The software was developed to execute on so many target platforms that exhaustive testing (in terms of platform, not test cases) was infeasible.[48]
- Software needed to be tested on test environments using software simulators and hardware emulators, which did not completely match the target platforms.
- Different intended target platforms had different:
  - Form factors (for example, laptop versus tablet versus smart phone; keyboard versus touch screen; and varying screen resolutions)
  - Configurations (for example, number of processors, single- versus multicore, amount of random access memory, storage)
  - Vendors and types (Intel versus Samsung versus Toshiba versus Texas Instruments, and so on and on)
  - Operating systems (for example, Windows versus Linux versus Android versus Apple iOS and real-time versus non-real-time)
  - Middleware such as message-oriented middleware (MOM) and object request brokers (ORBS)
  - Versions of hardware and software
  - Graphical user interface technologies (potentially including touch-sensitive displays)
- The target platforms were rapidly evolving (with, for example, new features, bug fixes, and security patches).

Recommendations

- Prepare:
  - Determine how the multiple target platforms will be tested.
  - Document how testing multiple target platforms will be addressed in the test planning documentation.
- Enable:
  - Determine on which *different platforms* the operational software is intended to run.

- ◆ Determine the *most important* platforms on which the operational software is intended to run, including the:
  - • Most common platforms
  - • Highest risk platforms
- ◆ Determine the different types of platforms on which the operational software is intended to run.
- ▪ **Perform:**
  - ◆ Select as many of the most important target platforms of as many types as is practical, given limited testing resources (for example, staffing, schedule, budget, available testing environments, and accessibility to platforms).
  - ◆ Obtain more test resources so that the software can be tested on more target environments, if feasible within technical, financial, and schedule constraints.
- ▪ **Verify:**
  - ◆ Determine whether the test platforms are being selected wisely in terms of importance, risk, and wide applicability.
  - ◆ Determine whether the software is being tested on as many target platforms as is feasible.

Related Pitfalls   Incomplete Test Planning (GEN-TPS-2), Inadequate Test Resources (GEN-MGMT-1), Inadequate Test Prioritization (GEN-PRO-3), Inadequate Test Environments (GEN-TTE-5), Poor Fidelity of Test Environments (GEN-TTE-6)

TARGET PLATFORM DIFFICULT TO ACCESS (GEN-TTE-4)

Description   The testers are not prepared to perform adequate testing when the target platform is not designed to enable access for testing.

Potential Applicability   This pitfall is potentially applicable anytime that the target platform(s) are not designed for testing.

Characteristic Symptoms

- ▪ The completed system does not have any general-purpose hardware access ports. For example, the iPad and iPhone do not have USB ports.
- ▪ The target platform vendor has made it difficult to access the software internals of the target platform. For example, the vendor might have locked down the operating system and middleware, making it difficult to access them for testing purposes.
- ▪ Running tests requires significant modification of the target platform, potentially using hacker tools (for example, root kits and jailbreaking).

Potential Negative Consequences

- The system is less testable because it is less controllable (for example, to place the system in the appropriate pretest state, to stimulate the system with inputs, and to stimulate the system with exceptions) and less observable (for example, it is difficult to observe the system's pretest and posttest states).
- Certain types of system tests requiring easy access are impractical to perform.
- Automated regression testing is very difficult.
- Testing takes more time and effort.

Potential Causes

- The system under test is a software application that must coexist with other applications produced by other vendors on a single platform.
- The system has significant security requirements.
- The platform was designed to limit arbitrary access to its internals.
  - The platform vendor wanted to control the platform (for example, the operating system, middleware, and supplied applications) to ensure that applications and users would not inadvertently change the platform's core software so that it no longer worked.
  - The system customer, integrator, or prime contractor limited access to make the system more secure by making it more tamper resistant and less vulnerable to attack.

Recommendations

- **Prepare:**
  - Evaluate potential target platforms for testability (controllability and observability).
  - Evaluate potential target platforms for physical access.
- **Enable:**
  - Develop software simulators or hardware emulators for test environments that mimic the target platforms.
  - To the extent practical, ensure that lower-level test cases verify the same functionality and capabilities as black-box system-level tests would have verified were they practical, in spite of the operational system's lack of easy access.
- **Perform:**
  - Rely on software simulation and hardware emulation for testing prior to porting to the target environment.

- ◆ Perform as much testing as is practical in a relatively open test environment before porting the operational software to the target environment.
- ▪ Verify:
  - ◆ Determine whether potential target platforms are being evaluated for testability.
  - ◆ Determine whether any simulators or emulators needed as components of test environments are planned, developed, tested, and, if necessary, approved.
  - ◆ Determine whether lower-level testing verifies as much of the system's functionality and capabilities as is practical.

Related Pitfalls   Poor Fidelity of Test Environments (GEN-TTE-6), Lack of Test Hooks (TTS-SYS-1)

INADEQUATE TEST ENVIRONMENTS (GEN-TTE-5)

Description   There are insufficient test tools, test environments or test beds, and test laboratories or facilities, so adequate testing cannot be performed within the schedule and personnel limitations.

Potential Applicability   This pitfall is potentially applicable anytime that one or more test environments are needed.

Characteristic Symptoms
- ▪ There are inadequate test environments or test beds of one or more types (listed in order of increasing fidelity) such as:
  - ◆ Software-only test environments hosted on basic, general-purpose platforms such as desktop and laptop computers
  - ◆ Software-only test environments on appropriate computational environments (for example, correct processors, busses, operating systems, middleware, and databases)
  - ◆ Software with prototype hardware (for example, sensors and actuators)
  - ◆ Software with an early or previous version of the actual hardware
  - ◆ Initial integrated test system with partial functionality (for example, initial test aircraft for ground testing or flight testing of existing functionality)
  - ◆ Integrated test system with full functionality (for example, operational aircraft for flight testing or operational evaluation testing)
  - ◆ Deliverable system for operational testing in the target environment
- ▪ There are insufficient test laboratories and facilities to support testing.

- Developmental testers, developers, Independent Verification and Validation (IV&V) testers, and even users are sharing (and competing for time on) the same test environments.
- To be certified (for example, as being sufficiently safe or secure to operate), the following three conditions hold:
  - The system must undergo accreditation testing by an independent accreditation organization in an independently managed testing facility.
  - One or more other systems must also undergo accreditation testing.
  - The independent accreditation organization's test facility can test only a limited number of systems, thereby causing the different systems to compete for a limited amount of test time.
- There is an excessive amount of competition between and among the integration testers and other testers for time on the test environments.

Potential Negative Consequences

- The types of test environments needed are not adequately or completely addressed in the test planning documentation.
- It is difficult to optimally schedule the allocation of test teams to test environments, resulting in scheduling conflicts.
- Too much time is wasted reconfiguring the test environments for the next team's use.
- Testing is incomplete or is behind schedule because test environments and facilities are being shared:
  - Developer testing is incomplete because the test environment(s) are being used for IV&V and certification testing.
  - IV&V testing is incomplete because the test environment(s) are being used for development and certification testing.
  - Certification testing is incomplete because the test environment(s) are being used for development and IV&V testing.
  - Testing is delayed because the testers are waiting for their turn to use the environment(s).
  - Developers, end users, and others may inadvertently delete or corrupt test data.
- Certain types of testing can not be adequately performed.

- Defects that should be found during testing on earlier test environments are not found until later test environments, when it becomes more difficult to cause and reproduce test failures and localize defects.

Potential Causes

- There was inadequate planning (for example, test environments were missing from test plans).
- There was insufficient experience with the different types of test environments.
- There was insufficient funding for creating, testing, and maintaining test environments.
- The amount of testing to be performed was underestimated.
- Development testers, IV&V testers, and certification testers had to share the same test environments and facilities.
- There was inadequate hardware for test environments because, for example:
  - Hardware was needed for:
    - Initial prototype systems
    - Initial systems during Low Rate of Initial Production (LRIP)
  - The deliverable software was intended to run on a great number of target environments (for example, all popular mobile devices, including laptops, tablets, and smart phones).
- The lack of sufficient test tools, test environments or test beds, or test laboratories or facilities prevented adequate testing from being performed within schedule and personnel limitations.

Recommendations

- **Prepare:**
  - Ensure that the test team and especially the test managers understand the different types of test tools, test environments, and test laboratories as well as their uses, their costs, and their benefits.
  - Determine or estimate the amount and types of tests needed.
  - Determine the number of testers needed.
  - Determine the test environment requirements in terms of types of test environments and numbers of each type.
- **Enable:**
  - Address all of the types of test tools, environments, and laboratories needed in the test planning documentation.
  - Include the development of the test environments in the project's master schedule (and the schedules of individual test teams) and ensure that it is consistent with the test schedule.

- Include the development and maintenance of the test environments and facilities in the project Work Breakdown Structure (WBS).
- Record all test configurations (for example, system, subsystem, hardware, software or data versions, and configuration for system under test and test environments) so that everything can be restored to its proper configuration after another organization has used the shared test environment.
- Ensure that the necessary software (for example, test tools and software simulators) is available when needed.
- Ensure that sufficient hardware (for example, computers, networks, hardware emulators) or subsystems to build or support the test environments are available when needed.
- Do not transfer the hardware or subsystems needed for the test environments to other uses, leaving insufficient hardware for the test environments.
- Create and use a process for scheduling the test teams' use of the test environments.
- Consider using the cloud (servers and testing tools) to provide Testing as a Service (TaaS). However, beware of beginning cloud-based testing too early because it often makes defect location and defect root-cause analysis more difficult.

- **Perform:**
  - To the extent practical, develop and maintain all of the needed test environments.
  - Prioritize the needed test environments in terms of importance and risk, and then test on as many of the high-priority test environments as is practical.

- **Verify:**
  - Determine whether the development of the test environments and laboratories is properly addressed in the test planning documentation, schedules, and WBS.
  - Determine whether sufficient test environments and laboratories are available and sufficiently reliable (for example, via testing metrics).
  - Determine whether the hardware components needed for software or hardware integration testing are available when needed.

Related Pitfalls   Inadequate Test Environment Quality (GEN-TTE-7), Inadequate Test Configuration Management (GEN-TTE-10)

GEN-TTE-5   Inadequate Test Environments

POOR FIDELITY OF TEST ENVIRONMENTS (GEN-TTE-6)

Description   The testers build and use test environments or test beds that have poor fidelity to the operational environment of the system or software under test (SUT), and this causes inconclusive or incorrect test results (false-positive and false-negative test results).

Potential Applicability   This pitfall is potentially applicable anytime that test environments are being used, especially if they were developed in-house.

Characteristic Symptoms

- Parts of certain test environments poorly emulate or simulate parts of the operational environment:
  - Test tools play the role of system-external actors (for example, human operators or external systems), whereby the behavior of the test tool does not exactly match that of the system-external actors.
  - The test tools communicate with the SUT via a different network than the one that actors will eventually use to communicate with the SUT, such as a public (or private) network substituting for a private (or public) network, or an unclassified network (such as the Internet or Non-classified Internet Protocol Router Network [NIPRNet]) substituting for a classified network (such as the Secure Internet Protocol Router Network [SIPRNet]), whereby the test network's behavior (for example, bandwidth or reliability) does not exactly match that of the actual network.
  - Test drivers or test stubs substitute for the actual clients or servers of the SUT.
  - The test environment contains prototype subsystems, hardware, or software that substitute for actual subsystems, hardware, or software.
  - The test environment contains test software that imperfectly simulates actual software or test hardware that imperfectly emulates actual hardware.
  - The test data (or database) is an imperfect replica of the actual data (or database)[49]:
    - The size of the data or database differs.
    - The type or vendor of the database differs (for example, relational versus object or Oracle versus IBM versus Microsoft)
    - The format of the data differs.
- Cloud-based testing is being used.

Potential Negative Consequences

- The low fidelity of a testing environment causes too many tests to yield inconclusive or incorrect results:
  - Testing produces false-positive test results (that is, the system passes the test even though it will not work in the actual operational environment).
  - Testing produces false-negative test results (that is, the system fails the test even though it will work properly in the actual operational environment).[50]
- It is more difficult to localize and fix defects.
- Test cases need to be repeated when the fidelity problems are solved by:
  - Using a different test environment that better conforms to the operational system and its environment (for example, by replacing software simulation by hardware or by replacing prototype hardware with actual operational hardware)
  - Fixing defects in the test environment

Potential Causes

- **Forms of poor fidelity**. Testing was performed using test environments consisting of components or versions of components that are different from the operational environment(s):
  - **Different software platform**. The software test platform significantly differed from the one(s) that were used to execute the delivered software:
    - Compiler or programming language class library
    - Operating system(s) such as:
      - Android, Apple iOS, Windows (for example, an application that must run on all popular mobile devices), LINUX, UNIX
      - Non-real-time instead of real-time operating system
    - Middleware
    - Database(s)
    - Network software
    - Competing programs and applications (apps)[51]
  - **Different hardware platform**. The hardware test platform significantly differed from the one(s) that were used to execute the delivered software:[52]
    - Processor(s)
    - Memory
    - Motherboard(s)

- Graphic cards
- Network devices (for example, routers and firewalls)
- Disc or tape libraries
- Sensors and actuators
- Battery age[53]

- **Different data.** The data stored by the test platform significantly differed from the data that was used with the delivered software:
  - Amount of data
  - Validity of the data

- **Different computing environment:**
  - Apps intended for mobile devices were tested using a brand new, out-of-the-box device. However, the apps run on users' devices that contain other apps competing for the device's resources (for example, processing power, memory, and bandwidth) and often have a battery that no longer stores a full charge.
  - When using the cloud to provide Testing as a Service (TaaS), the cloud servers had different amounts of utilization by other users and the Internet provided different bandwidth depending on Internet usage.
  - The integration environment includes sensors, which were subject to sensor drift (that is, an increase in sensor output error due to a slow degradation of sensor properties).

- **Different physical environment.** The test physical environment significantly differed from real-world conditions of the physical environment surrounding the operational system. For example, the actual physical environment has different extremes of:
  - Acceleration (whether relatively constant or rapidly changing)
  - Ionizing radiation (for example, in outer space, nuclear reactors, or particle accelerators)
  - Network connectivity (for example, via radio, microwave, or Wi-Fi) that is intermittent, noisy, does not have sufficient power[54], or is not permitted to be used for security reasons
  - Poor electrical power (for example, spikes, surges, sags (or brownouts), blackouts, noise, and EMI)
  - Temperature (high, low, or variable)
  - Vacuum (for example, of space)
  - Vibration

- **Causes of poor fidelity.** The lack of adequate test environment fidelity can be due to:
  - Lack of funding
  - Inadequate tester expertise

- Difficulty in recreating the potentially huge number of device-internal configurations (for example, existence of unrelated software and data running on the same platform as the SUT[55])
- Poor configuration management of the hardware or software
- Lack of availability of the correct software, hardware, or data
- Lack of availability of sufficient computing resources to match the production system
- Resource contention between SUT and other software executing on the same platform
- The high cost of replicating the physical environment
- Prohibited access to classified networks, such as the US Department of Defense Global Information Grid (GIG) and, more specifically, the SIPRNet, for testing systems or software that has not yet been accredited and certified as being sufficiently secure to operate.[56]

Recommendations

- **Prepare:**
  - Determine how the testers are going to address test-environment fidelity.
  - Document how the testers are going to address test-environment fidelity in the test planning documentation.
  - For testing mobile devices, consider using a commercial company that specializes in testing:
    - On many devices
    - Networks
- **Enable:**
  - Provide the test labs with sufficient numbers of COTS, prototype, or Low Rate of Initial Production (LRIP) system components (subsystems, software, and hardware).
  - Provide sufficient funding to recreate the physical operational environment in the physical test environment(s). Test using a shielded room but realize that operational testing (OT) will still need to be performed.
  - Provide good configuration management of components under test and test environments.
  - Provide tools to evaluate the fidelity of the test environment's behavior.
  - Evaluate commercial companies that specialize in on-device testing and network simulation and testing.
- **Perform:**
  - To the extent practical, use the operational versions of development tools (for example, the compiler and software class libraries).

- ◆ To the extent practical, test the software executing on the actual operational platforms, including software, hardware, and data.
- ◆ Test on used hardware as well as new, just out-of-the-box devices.
- ◆ To the extent practical, test the system in the operational physical environment.
- ◆ Perform operationally relevant testing using the actual operational software, hardware, data, and physical environments.[57]
- ◆ Recalibrate sensors to compensate for **sensor drift.**
- ▪ Verify:
  - ◆ To the extent practical, determine whether test simulators, emulators, stubs, and drivers have the same characteristics as the eventual components they are replacing during testing.

Related Pitfalls Inadequate Test Environment Quality (GEN-TTE-7), Unavailable Components (TTS-INT-3)

INADEQUATE TEST ENVIRONMENT QUALITY *(GEN-TTE-7)*

Description The quality of one or more test environments is inadequate due to an excessive number of defects.[58]

Potential Applicability This pitfall is potentially applicable anytime that one or more test environments are being used.

Characteristic Symptoms
- ▪ An excessive number of false-positive or false-negative test results are traced back to the poor quality of one or more test environments.
- ▪ The test environment often crashes during testing.
- ▪ Subsystem or hardware components of an integration test environment are not certified (for example, flight certified, safety certified, security certified) even though the actual subsystem or hardware components must be certified prior to incorporating them into a deliverable system.

Potential Negative Consequences

- ▪ There are numerous false-positive or false-negative test results.

- Test results are invalidated due to the test environment crashing.
- Testing is interrupted because defects are traced to the test environment or the test environment crashes.
- It is more difficult to determine whether test failures are due to the system or software under test (SUT) or the test environments.
- Testing takes a needlessly long time to perform.
- The system is delivered late and with an unacceptably large number of residual defects.
- The quality of the test environment is not adequate, in spite of being used to test mission-, safety-, or security-critical software.

Potential Causes

- The test environments were home grown using resources, such as Independent Research and Development (IRAD) funding, that were insufficient to result in high quality.
- Development and verification of the system or software under test and the test environments competed for the same limited resources (for example, funding, schedule, or staff).
- Insufficient resources were allocated to developing and verifying the test environments.
- One or more test environments were not adequately verified (for example, by testing).
- One or more test environments were not accredited and certified.
- One or more test environments were not properly configured.
- The architectures, designs, and implementations of the test environments were not adequately documented (for example, in test environment installation and user manuals).
- The integration and system test environments or test beds were not under configuration control, thereby permitting one or more test environments to contain the wrong versions of operating environments, middleware, test tools, software simulators, hardware emulators, actual deliverable software components, or actual hardware components (such as sensors and actuators).

Recommendations

- Prepare:
  - Address the testing and evaluation of the test environments in the test planning documentation.
- Enable:
  - Provide adequate funding and time in the schedule to select, purchase, develop, and test the test environments.

- ◆ Provide adequate staffing for the development, integration, verification, and configuration control of the test environments.
- ◆ Place the test environments under configuration control.
- ▪ Perform:
  - ◆ Use good development practices, including proper testing, when developing the test environments.
  - ◆ Include the evaluation of test environments when selecting test tools.
  - ◆ To the extent practical, use COTS testing tools that have been properly tested and widely used successfully.
- ▪ Verify:
  - ◆ Determine whether testing and evaluating the test environments are adequately addressed in the test planning documentation.
  - ◆ Determine whether adequate resources (for example, funding, time, and staff) have been provided to select, purchase, develop, and test the test environments. Determine whether the test environments are under configuration control.
  - ◆ Determine whether any COTS testing tools have been widely and successfully used on similar projects.
  - ◆ Determine whether the test environments have sufficient quality.

Related Pitfalls   Poor Fidelity of Test Environments (GEN-TTE-6), Inadequate Test Configuration Management (GEN-TTE-10)

TEST ASSETS NOT DELIVERED (GEN-TTE-8)

Description   Developers deliver the system or software to the sustainers without the associated test assets.[59]

Potential Applicability   This pitfall is potentially applicable anytime that:
- ▪ The system is delivered
- ▪ Test assets exist

Characteristic Symptoms
- ▪ The delivery of test assets (for example, test planning documentation, test reports, test cases, test oracles, test drivers or scripts, test stubs, and test environments) is neither required nor planned.
- ▪ Non-testing assets needed by the regression testers (for example, the System Installation Manual or System Reference Manual) are also not delivered.
- ▪ Test assets are not delivered along with the system or software.

Potential Negative Consequences

- It is unnecessarily difficult to perform testing during sustainment and maintenance.
- There is inadequate regression testing as the delivered system is updated.
- Residual and new defects are not uncovered and fixed.

Potential Causes

- The development contract and statement of work (SOW) did not require delivery of the test assets.
- The test planning documentation and development plans did not mention delivery of the test assets.
- The testing process did not explicitly include delivery of the test assets.

Recommendations

- Prepare:
  - Include delivery of the test assets in the:
    - Development contract or SOW
    - Test planning documentation
    - Development plans and processes
  - Include the test assets in the deliverables list.
- Enable:
  - Provide sufficient funding, schedule, and staffing to enable the test assets to be delivered to the acquisition and sustainment organizations.
- Perform:
  - The development organization delivers all test assets created or used during development to the acquisition organization.
  - The acquisition organization delivers all test assets to the maintenance organization.
- Verify:
  - Determine whether delivery of the test assets is in the:
    - Development contract or SOW
    - Test planning documentation
    - Development plans and processes
    - Deliverables list

- Determine whether the development organization delivers the test assets to the acquisition organization.
- Determine whether the development organization also delivers the documentation needed to install and configure the system for testing.
- Determine whether the development organization provides licenses and data rights to the acquisition organization for all test assets.
- Determine whether the acquisition organization delivers the test assets to the sustainment organization.

Related Pitfalls   Incomplete Test Planning (GEN-TPS-2), Unclear Testing Responsibilities (GEN-STF-2), Test Resources Not Delivered for Maintenance (TTS-REG-5)

INADEQUATE TEST CONFIGURATION MANAGEMENT (GEN-TTE-9)

Description   Testing work products are not under configuration management (CM).

Potential Applicability   This pitfall is potentially applicable anytime that configuration management is needed (that is, almost always).

Characteristic Symptoms

- Significant test configurations of target platforms (for example, mobile devices, plus operating systems and middleware) are not identified.
- Configurations of the test environments are not identified.
- Test environments, test cases, and other testing work products are *not* under configuration control.
- Inconsistencies are found between the current versions of the system or software under test (SUT) and the test cases and test environments.
- Different testers or test teams are simultaneously testing different updated variants or versions of parts of the software under test (SUT) where these variants or versions are part of different parallel baselines (for example, test baselines that have branched off of the primary baseline).

Potential Negative Consequences

- Test environments, test cases, and other testing work products cease to be consistent with the system being tested and with each other.[60]

- It becomes impossible to reproduce tests (that is, get the same test results given the same preconditions and test stimuli) if changes are not properly managed.
- It is much more difficult to know if the correct versions of the system, test environment, and tests are being used when testing.
- The software is not tested on all important target platforms (that is, some combinations of hardware, operating system, and middleware accidentally fall through the cracks).
- There is an increase in false-positive and false-negative test results.
- False-positive test results due to incorrect versioning leads to incorrect fixes and results in inserting defects into the system.
- Unnecessary effort is wasted identifying and fixing CM problems.
- Some defects are not found, and an unnecessary number of these defects make it through testing and into the deployed system.
- The different parallel baselines become out of sync with each other, incorporating different increments of new functionality, different patches, and so on. Eventually, a configuration management nightmare occurs when someone tries to merge these different, inconsistent parallel baselines into a single build.

Potential Causes

- Placing the test assets under configuration management was not an explicit part of either the CM or testing process.
- The CM of test assets was not mentioned in the test planning documentation.
- There were so many test configurations that identifying and managing them all was overwhelming. For example, consider a software application that is intended to run on all major mobile platforms such as smart phones and tablet computers. There are many devices, including multiple versions of numerous hardware models from many vendors. These mobile devices could be running multiple versions of multiple operating systems (for example, Android, Apple iOS, and Windows) with multiple releases for bug fixes and patches for security vulnerabilities.
- Final testing occurred when the SUT was almost—but not quite—finished. Because the version of the SUT delivered was not the version last tested, final incremental and iterative updates were not tested and may include defects that were delivered and placed into operation.
- A defect was inadvertently introduced when one or more last little defects were "fixed" after testing was officially completed. Note that this is also a CM problem because the version of the SUT was not the same version as the last version tested.
- A parallel (for example, agile) development process was being used in which different developers and testers were simultaneously creating, updating, and testing new software components. Sometimes, they were not aware that once

their component passed its component test, it would fail integration testing because of merging inconsistent partial baselines.

Recommendations

- Prepare:
  - Include configuration management of test assets in the test planning documentation and configuration management plan.
  - Make configuration management of test assets an explicit part of the configuration management and testing processes.
- Enable:
  - Baseline the test assets, including configuration identification and configuration control.
- Perform:
  - Identify all significant configurations of test environments and target platforms. Note that there may well be insufficient test resources (for example, staff, schedule, and budget) to test using every configuration, such that only the most important ones can be identified and managed. This is especially true for applications intended to run on all popular mobile devices.
  - Place all test planning documentation, procedures, test cases, test environments, and other testing work products under configuration control before they are used.
  - Improve configuration management so that the last version of the SUT that passes testing is the one that is delivered.
  - If appropriate, restore the test environments to the correct baseline before each new testing cycle.
- Verify:
  - Determine whether the last version of the SUT that passed testing is the one that is delivered.
  - To the extent practical, determine whether all test configurations of the SUT and the test environments are identified and managed.
  - Determine whether the right versions of test environment components are being used.

Related Pitfalls   Incomplete Test Planning (GEN-TPS-2), Inadequate Test Resources (GEN-MGMT-1), Inadequate Test Prioritization (GEN-PRO-3), Inadequate Test Environments (GEN-TTE-5), Inadequate Test Documentation (GEN-COM-3)

DEVELOPERS IGNORE TESTABILITY (GEN-TTE-10)

Description   It is unnecessarily difficult to develop automated tests because the developers do not consider testing when designing and implementing their system or software.

Potential Applicability   This pitfall is always potentially applicable.

Characteristic Symptoms

- Software units are large and have a high McCabe's complexity.
- Units and subsystems have unnecessary interfaces and dependencies.
- It is difficult to control the unit, subsystem, system, or software under test (for example, to set preconditions and provide test inputs, including data, messages, and exceptions or error codes).
- It is difficult to observe the internal intermediate and final state of the class under test (for example, to observe postconditions).
- It is difficult to test a unit in isolation from other units (for example, via using stubs and drivers).
- Individual tests are unnecessarily large and complex.

Potential Negative Consequences

- It takes significantly longer than necessary to develop the tests.
- The tests are less effective than they need to be.
- The testers are frustrated and team morale or cohesion is lowered because it is difficult to perform the desired tests.

Potential Causes

- Developers did not understand the importance of testability, including controllability and observability.
- Developers did not know how to write testable software.
- The design guidelines and coding standards did not adequately promote testability.
- If developers did not provide unique object names for GUI elements, the functional test automation tool might not have been able to recognize those test objects.

- Integration inherently made testing the internals of a subsystem, system, or software less testable.
- Safety and security requirements necessitated the removal of all test hooks and interfaces from the delivered system or software.

Recommendations

- **Prepare:**
  - Search the web for testability guidelines (there are many) that are appropriate for the programming language (for example, Java or C++) and design paradigm (for example, object-oriented development).
  - Incorporate testability guidelines into the design guidelines and coding standards.
- **Enable:**
  - Ensure that the developers understand the importance of testability.
  - Ensure that the developers have adequate training, expertise, and experience in developing testable software, hardware, subsystems, and systems.
- **Perform:**
  - Follow the design guidelines and coding standards.
  - Incorporate built-in-tests, prognostics, and health-maintenance subsystems into the system or software.
- **Verify:**
  - Determine whether the design guidelines and coding standards promote testability.
  - Determine whether the developers know how to develop testable systems or software.
  - Determine whether the software conforms to the testability-related parts of the design guidelines and coding standards.
  - Determine whether testing hooks and interfaces have been removed prior to delivery.

Related Pitfalls   Lack of Stakeholder Commitment to Testing (GEN-SIC-3), whereby the stakeholders are the developers who ignore testability; Unclear Testing Responsibilities (GEN-STF-2); Testers Responsible for All Testing (GEN-STF-5); Too Immature for Testing (GEN-PRO-7), because software needs to be refactored to be more testable; Inadequate Communication Concerning Testing (GEN-COM-5); Testing Does *Not* Drive Design and Implementation (TTS-UNT-1); Integration Decreases Testability Ignored (TTS-INT-1)

3.3.7 Test Communication Pitfalls

The following testing pitfalls are related to communication, including documentation and reporting:

- Inadequate Architecture or Design Documentation (GEN-COM-1)
- Inadequate Defect Reports (GEN-COM-2)
- Inadequate Test Documentation (GEN-COM-3)
- Source Documents Not Maintained (GEN-COM-4)
- Inadequate Communication Concerning Testing (GEN-COM-5)

INADEQUATE ARCHITECTURE OR DESIGN DOCUMENTATION (GEN-COM-1)

Description Architects and designers produce insufficient architecture or design documentation (for example, models and documents) to support white-box (structural) unit and integration testing.

Potential Applicability This pitfall is always potentially applicable.

Characteristic Symptoms
- There are few or no architectural or design models.
- There is little or no architecture or design documentation, such as:
  - System architecture document
  - Subsystem design documents
  - System-internal interface documents
- Testers do not have adequate timely access to architectural and design documentation (for example, when testing is outsourced to a foreign test organization).
- Architecture and design documentation:
  - Is in draft form and has not been approved
  - Is not under configuration control
  - Has not been updated in a long time
- It is difficult to understand the architecture and design.
- It is difficult to determine the set of white-box test cases that:
  - Support white-box (structural) unit testing of individual units,
  - Support integration testing of subsystems and systems
  - Ensure adequate code coverage during unit and integration testing

Potential Negative Consequences

- The set of test cases:
  - Do not achieve adequate:
    - Requirements coverage (for example, all functional requirements, all data requirements, all interface requirements, and all quality requirements)
    - Requirements model coverage (for example, all normal and all credible exceptional mission threads and use case paths)
    - Architecture coverage (for example, all subsystems and the interfaces between them)
    - Design coverage (for example, all units and unit interfaces)
    - Code coverage; for example, statement, path, branch, and condition coverage
  - Therefore, fail to find certain defects
  - Provide a false sense of security that testing has detected all defects
- Unit and integration testing fails to include sufficient white-box and gray-box test cases.
- Unit and integration tests take an unnecessarily long time to develop and iterate once defects have been uncovered.
- Unit and integration test cases are difficult to maintain, especially during maintenance by someone other than the original developer or tester.

Potential Causes

- The architecture engineering and design processes did not require sufficient architecture and design information to drive unit and integration testing.
- The contract, statement of work (SOW), or list of deliverables did not include delivery of architectural and design models and documentation to the acquisition organization so that those could be provided to the sustainment organization to support regression testing.
- The set of unit and integration test cases were based on false assumptions and misunderstandings concerning the architecture and design.

- An agile mindset prevailed, which excessively denigrates documentation in favor of verbal communication, which resulted in insufficient architecture and design information to support testing, especially during maintenance.
- A false belief that the software is self-documenting led to inadequate documentation of the architecture and design.[61]
- Testers (especially maintenance testers) were not considered as important stakeholders in the architecture and design documentation.

Recommendations

- **Prepare:**
  - Ensure that the architecture and design documentation identifies testers (especially maintenance testers) as important stakeholders.
  - When using software as a design language, use a coding standard that results in highly readable source code.
- **Enable:**
  - Ensure that the complexity of the architecture, design, and code are sufficiently low (for example, low McCabe's Complexity score) so as to be easy to understand and make it easy to develop test cases.
- **Perform:**
  - Ensure that the architects, designers, and programmers provide sufficient, well-written documentation to drive the unit and integration testing:
    - System architecture document
    - Subsystem design documents
    - System-internal interface documents
  - Ensure that the software is written to be self-documenting:
    - In a high-level, highly readable programming language that can also be used as a program design language (PDL)
    - With adequate readable comments
- **Verify:**
  - Determine whether adequate architecture and design documentation (models and documents) was developed to support unit and integration testing prior to developing the associated white-box test cases.
  - Determine whether the architecture and design documentation were delivered to the test, acquisition, and sustainment organizations.

Related Pitfalls Wrong Testing Mindset (GEN-SIC-1), Source Documents Not Maintained (GEN-COM-4)

INADEQUATE DEFECT REPORTS (GEN-COM-2)

Description Testers and others create defect reports (also known as bug and trouble reports) that are incomplete, contain incorrect information, or are difficult to read.[62]

Potential Applicability This pitfall is always potentially applicable.

Characteristic Symptoms

- Too many defect reports are incomplete (for example, they do not contain some of the following information):
  - Summary—a one-sentence summary of the fault or failure
  - Detailed description—a relatively comprehensive detailed description of the failure
  - Author—the name and contact information of the person reporting the defect
  - System—the version (build) or variant of the system
  - Environment—the software infrastructure such as the operating system, middleware, and database types and versions
  - Test environment—the name, version, and content of the test environment used, if any
  - Location—the author's assessment of the subsystem, line replaceable unit (LRU), or software module that contains the defect that caused the fault or failure
  - Priority and severity—the author's assessment of the priority and severity of the defect
  - Steps—the steps to follow to replicate the fault or failure (if reproducible by the report's author) including:
    - Preconditions (for example, the system mode or state and stored data values)
    - Trigger events, such as input data, message, and exception or error code
  - Actual behavior, including fault or failure warnings, cautions, or advisories
  - Expected behavior
  - Comments
  - Attachments (for example, screen shots or logs)
- Defect reports are written in a different native language from the one spoken by the testers or developers
- Defect reports are illegibly hand-written.
- Some defect reports contain incorrect information.
- Defect reports are returned to their authors with comments such as "not clear" and "need more information."

- Developers or testers contact the defect report author requesting more information.
- Different individuals or teams use different defect report templates, content or format standards, or test management tools.[63]

Potential Negative Consequences

- Testers are unable to reproduce faults or failures, and thereby are unable to identify the underlying defects.
- It takes longer for developers or testers to identify and diagnose the underlying defects.

Potential Causes

- Testing was outsourced to a foreign company whose employees do not have adequate fluency in the native language in which the defect report was written.
- The defect report content and format standard or template did not exist.
- The defect report content and format standard or template was incomplete.
- The defect report content and format standard or template was not used.
- There was no verification that submitted defect reports were complete or correct.
- There was no negative consequence if submitted defect reports were incomplete or incorrect.
- No test management tool was being used to input and manage defect reports.

Recommendations

- **Prepare:**
  - Create or reuse a defect report content and format standard and template.
- **Enable:**
  - Train testers to create and use defect reports.
  - Obtain a test management tool that incorporates defect reporting and enforces completion of defect reports.
- **Perform:**
  - Use the project test management tool to enter and manage the defect reports.
  - To the extent practical, completely fill out all defect reports with all relevant known information.

- Verify:
    - ◆ To the extent practical,[64] determine whether all defect reports are reviewed for completeness, duplication, and scope by the test manager or the change control board (CCB) before being assigned to:
        - Individual testers for testing and analysis (for defect reports not authored by testers)
        - Developers for analysis and fixing (for defect or test reports authored by testers)

Related Pitfalls   None

INADEQUATE TEST DOCUMENTATION (GEN-COM-3)

Description   Testers create test documentation that is incomplete or contains incorrect information.

Potential Applicability   This pitfall is always potentially applicable.

Characteristic Symptoms

- Some test documentation is inadequate for defect identification and analysis, regression testing, test automation, reuse, and quality assurance of the testing process.
- Some test documentation templates or format and content standards are either missing or incomplete.
- Test scripts or cases do not completely describe test preconditions, test trigger events, test input data, expected or mandatory test outputs (data and commands), and expected or mandatory test postconditions.
- The architecture and design of the test environments are not documented.
- An agile approach is being used by developers with insufficient testing expertise and experience to know what testing documentation is not needed for the current project and can therefore be dispensed with.
- Testing documents are not maintained or placed under configuration management.

Potential Negative Consequences

- Test assets (for example, test documentation, environments, and test cases) are not sufficiently documented to be used by:

- ✦ Testers, to drive test automation
- ✦ Testers, to perform regression testing, either during initial development or during maintenance
- ✦ Quality-assurance personnel and customer representatives, during evaluation and oversight of the testing process
- ✦ Testers, other than the original test developer, who:
  - • Must automate and maintain the prior testers' tests
  - • Performs integration testing, system testing, and system of system testing
- ✦ Maintainers, who must maintain, reproduce, or iterate the test environments
- ✦ Safety and security accreditors, to determine whether the system is sufficiently safe and secure to be placed into operation and therefore to be certified as adequately safe and secure
- ✦ Test teams from other projects developing or maintaining related systems within a product family or product line

- Tests are not reproducible.
- It takes too long to identify and fix some of the underlying defects, thereby causing some test deadlines to be missed.
- Maintenance costs are needlessly high.
- Insufficient regression testing is performed.
- The reuse of test assets is needlessly low, thereby unacceptably increasing the costs, schedule, and effort that will be spent recreating test assets.

Potential Causes

- Managers or testers attempted to decrease the testing effort and thereby meet schedule deadlines by decreasing test documentation.
- Testers did not appreciate the need for good test documentation, which tends to occur if an agile development method is used (for example, because of the emphasis on minimizing documentation and on having each development team determine its own documentation needs on a case-by-case basis).
- People who did not have adequate testing training and experience developed the testing process.
- The content (and format) of test documentation was not an explicit part of the testing process and thus not adequately addressed (for example, in document templates or content and format standards).

Recommendations

- Prepare:
  - ✦ Ensure that the testing stakeholders understand the importance of complete and correct test documentation.

- **Enable:**
  - ◆ Use the contract, test planning documentation, test training, test process documents, and test standards to specify the required test documents and ensure that test work products are adequately documented.
  - ◆ Create common standard templates for test documents (for example, test plans, test cases, test procedures, and test reports).
- **Perform:**
  - ◆ Use common standard templates for test documents (for example, test plans, test cases, test procedures, and test reports).
  - ◆ Ensure that test cases completely describe test preconditions, test trigger events, test input data, mandatory or expected test outputs (data and commands), and mandatory or expected system postconditions.
  - ◆ Use a test documentation tool or test repository to record test documentation (for example, test cases and reports).
  - ◆ Set up the schema of the test documentation tool or test repository so that it supports easy searching.
  - ◆ To the extent practical, make the executable testing work products self-documenting (rather than using separate testing documentation) so that the components and their testing work products are more likely to be changed together and thereby remain consistent with each other.
  - ◆ Ensure that the requirements, architecture, design, and configuration of the various test environments are adequately documented.
  - ◆ Ensure consistency by clearly identifying the versions of the software, test environment, test cases, and so on.
- **Verify:**
  - ◆ Determine whether common standard templates exist for test documentation (for example, test plans, test cases, test procedures, and test reports).
  - ◆ Determine whether the test cases completely describe test preconditions, test trigger events, test input data, mandatory or expected test outputs (data and commands), and mandatory or expected system postconditions.
  - ◆ Determine whether the test documentation tool or database is being consistently and correctly used to record test documents (for example, test cases and test reports).
  - ◆ Determine whether the schema of the test documentation tool or test repository supports easy searching.

Related Pitfalls   Unclear Testing Responsibilities (GEN-STF-2), Inadequate Maintenance of Test Assets (GEN-PRO-9), Inadequate Test Configuration Management (GEN-TTE-10)

SOURCE DOCUMENTS NOT MAINTAINED (GEN-COM-4)

Description   Developers do not properly maintain the requirements specifications, architecture documents, design documents, and associated models that are needed as inputs to the development of tests.[65]

Potential Applicability   This pitfall is potentially applicable anytime that source documentation exists.

Characteristic Symptoms

- The requirements specifications, architecture documents, design documents, and developmental documents or models are obsolete.
- The test drivers and software are drifting out of sync with each other as the software evolves.

Potential Negative Consequences

- The regression tests run during maintenance begin to produce large numbers of false-negative results.[66]
- The effort running these tests is wasted.
- Testing takes too long because the testers must determine the true current state of the requirements, architecture, design, and implementation.

Potential Causes

- The testers were unaware that their tests have become obsolete by undocumented changes to the requirements, architecture, design, and implementation.
- Testing stakeholders (especially management) did not see the value of maintaining the source documents driving testing.
- The source documents were not placed under configuration control.
- Testers (correctly) believed that maintaining these documents and models was not their responsibility.[67]
- Testers falsely believed that these documents were being maintained.

Recommendations

- Prepare:
  - A maintenance plan should exist, and it should include maintaining the requirements, architecture, and design.

- Maintaining the requirements, architecture, and design should be in the maintenance master schedule and Work Breakdown Structure (WBS).

- **Enable:**
  - Management should ensure that the requirements, architecture, and design documents and models are properly maintained.
  - Place these documents and associated models under configuration control. [68]
  - Notify the testers when relevant updates to these documents and models occur.
  - Management should provide sufficient resources (that is, staffing, budget, and schedule) to enable these documents and associated models to be maintained.
  - During development and maintenance, at least one tester (not necessarily the same one) should be part of both the requirements team and the architecture team.

- **Perform:**
  - The requirements team should properly maintain the requirements models and specifications.
  - The architecture team should properly maintain the architecture models and documents.
  - The developers should properly maintain the design models and documents.

- **Verify:**
  - Determine whether the maintenance plan, master schedule, and WBS address maintaining the requirements specifications, architecture documents, and design documents with associated models.
  - Determine whether sufficient resources exist to maintain this documentation.

Related Pitfalls   Inadequate Test Configuration Management (GEN-TTE-10), Inadequate Architecture or Design Documentation (GEN-COM-1)

INADEQUATE COMMUNICATION CONCERNING TESTING (GEN-COM-5)

Description   There is inadequate verbal and written communication concerning testing among testers and other testing stakeholders.

Potential Applicability   This pitfall is always potentially applicable.

Characteristic Symptoms

- There is inadequate testing-related communication between:
  - Teams within large or geographically distributed programs
  - Contractually separated teams such as:
    - Development, acquisition, and sustainment or maintenance organizations
    - Prime contractor versus subcontractors
    - System of systems versus systems versus subsystems developers
    - System integrator versus product line component developers
  - Between testers and:
    - Other developers (requirements engineers, architects, designers, and implementers)
    - Other testers (especially when they are members of different test teams)
    - Customer representatives, user representatives, and subject-matter experts (SMEs)
- Testers produce incomplete documentation of test cases, such as:
  - Trigger events
  - Preconditions
  - Mandatory quantitative thresholds
  - Mandatory postconditions
  - Mandatory behaviors (for example, returning data, issuing a command or message, and raising an exception)
- The developers fail to notify the testers of bug fixes and their consequences.
- Testers fail to notify other testers of test environment changes (for example, configurations and usage of different versions of hardware and software).

Potential Negative Consequences

- Some architectural decisions make certain types of testing difficult or impossible.
- Safety and security concerns do not influence the level of testing of safety- and security-critical functionality.
- Failure to notify the test team of changes to the system under test greatly slows down regression testing because the testers often learn of changes that necessitate new or modified test cases only when they rerun the unchanged test cases. This also postpones developing or modifying test cases.

- As requirements are postponed to future releases when schedules overrun, the testers continue to create, execute, and maintain tests for these deferred requirements unless notified that they are being allocated to future releases.
- Different test teams have difficulty:
  - Coordinating their testing:
    - None of the teams develop, execute, and maintain certain tests because each thinks it is another team's responsibility.
    - Multiple teams redundantly develop, execute, and maintain the same tests because each thinks it is their own responsibility.
  - Scheduling their use of common test environments

Potential Causes

- Teams were geographically distributed.
  - Testers in different locations had different native languages, cultures, and training.
- Different types of testers did not communicate their different testing goals and mindsets.
- There were contractual barriers between people in different organizations.
- No standard lines of communication were documented or communicated.
- Testers were not notified of relevant changes, such as:
  - Requirements engineers did not notify the testers when requirements were changed (for example, new ones added, existing ones modified or deleted), which thereby necessitated changes to existing tests.
  - Architects and designers did not notify the testers when the architecture or design was changed, which thereby necessitated changes to existing tests.
  - Testers were not involved in analyzing proposed changes to requirements, architecture, design, and implementations under configuration management change control.
- No common communications technologies (for example, instant messaging, audio- and video-conferencing, document repository and management tool, web teleconferencing, wiki, or blog) were selected and made available to the testing stakeholders.
- Testing stakeholders were not interested in testing and therefore felt that communication with testers was unimportant or insufficiently important to spend time on.

Recommendations

- Prepare:
  - Include communications and reporting in the test planning documentation and system development plans.

- **Enable:**
  - ◆ Provide tool support for collaboration (for example, wiki, document repository, audio-, video-, or web-based teleconferencing, and so on).
  - ◆ Provide document templates or content and format standards.
- **Perform:**
  - ◆ Place one or more testers on the requirements team, development team(s), or integrated product teams (IPTs), where they can ensure that requirements are testable, that developers understand testing and how to perform it, and to act as liaison to the potentially independent test team(s).
  - ◆ Place one or more requirements engineer(s) onto the test team(s).
  - ◆ Involve testers in change control.
    - • Require that testers determine the impact of proposed changes on testing.
    - • Notify the testers of the results of all change requests.
  - ◆ Hold regular communication and technical interchange meetings (TIMs) involving testers and members of other organizations.
  - ◆ Include testers in cross-functional integrated product teams (IPTs).
- **Verify:**
  - ◆ Determine whether the test planning documentation includes communication with management, the technical leader, other teams, and, potentially, customer representatives.
  - ◆ Determine whether collaboration tools to improve communication exist and are being used.
  - ◆ Determine whether any testers are members of other teams and whether members of other teams are also members of the test team.
  - ◆ Determine whether testers are involved in analyzing the testing ramifications of change requests.
  - ◆ Determine whether sufficient testing-related communication is occurring between and among the testers and the stakeholders in testing.

Related Pitfalls   Testing and Engineering Processes Not Integrated (GEN-PRO-1), Inadequate Test Documentation (GEN-COM-3)

3.3.8   Requirements-Related Testing Pitfalls

Although many testing pitfalls result from poor decisions or incorrect assumptions by testers and managers, some pitfalls are caused by requirements engineers. Testers need good requirements if they are going to be able to properly verify them. Among other characteristics, good requirements are complete, consistent, correct, feasible, mandatory,[69] testable, and unambiguous.[70] Requirements that are deficient in any of these characteristics decrease the testability of systems and software. Given poor requirements, black-box testing is relatively inefficient and ineffective, so testers may rely on higher-risk strategies, including overreliance on white-box testing (for example, structural testing such as path testing for code coverage).[71]

The following testing pitfalls are directly related to requirements:[72]

- Ambiguous Requirements (GEN-REQ-1)
- Obsolete Requirements (GEN-REQ-2)
- Missing Requirements (GEN-REQ-3)
- Incomplete Requirements (GEN-REQ-4)
- Incorrect Requirements (GEN-REQ-5)
- Requirements Churn (GEN-REQ-6)
- Improperly Derived Requirements (GEN-REQ-7)
- Verification Methods Not Specified (GEN-REQ-8)
- Lack of Requirements Trace (GEN-REQ-9)

AMBIGUOUS REQUIREMENTS (GEN-REQ-1)

Description   Testers misinterpret a great many ambiguous requirements and therefore base their testing on incorrect interpretations of those requirements.

Potential Applicability   This pitfall is potentially applicable anytime requirements exist.

Characteristic Symptoms
- Some of the requirements are ambiguous due to:
  - Using inherently ambiguous words
  - Using undefined technical jargon (for example, application domain-specific terminology) and acronyms
  - Misuses of contractual words such as "shall," "should," "may," "recommended," and "optional"
  - Specifying required quantities without associated units of measure
  - Using unclear synonyms, near synonyms, and false synonyms
- Requirements engineers and testers interpret the same requirement differently.

Potential Negative Consequences

- Testers misinterpret the requirements, leading to incorrect black-box testing.
- Numerous false-positive and false-negative test results are observed because the tests are developed in accordance with the testers', rather than the requirements engineers', interpretation of the associated requirements.
- Ambiguous requirements often give rise to incorrect test inputs and incorrect expected outputs (that is, the test oracle is incorrect).
- Testers must spend significant time meeting with requirements engineers, customer or user representatives, and subject-matter experts to clarify ambiguities so that testing can proceed.

Potential Causes

- The people (for example, requirements engineers and business analysts) who engineered the requirements were not adequately trained in how to recognize and avoid ambiguous requirements.
- Requirements engineers did not properly update the requirements repository and specification(s) in a timely manner as ambiguous requirements were identified.
- The requirements team did not include anyone with testing expertise.
- The requirements were not reviewed for ambiguity. Specifically, the testers did not review the requirements for ambiguity.
- The requirements reviewers did not use a requirements-review checklist, or the checklist they used did not address ambiguous requirements.
- The textual requirements were not analyzed by a tool that checks for inherently ambiguous words.
- The requirements engineers were rushed because insufficient resources (for example, time and staffing) were allocated to properly engineer the requirements.
- There was no project- or domain-specific glossary or acronym list that defined technical jargon and acronyms.
- There were stakeholder or manager pressures to keep the requirements ambiguous in order to reduce accountability, increase flexibility, or achieve "apparent" consensus.
- Stakeholders, especially acquisition organizations, demanded that very high-level policies be specified as requirements (that is, policies masquerading as requirements).

Recommendations

- Prepare:
  - Improve the requirements engineering process and associated training with regard to preventing, identifying, and fixing ambiguous requirements.
- Enable:
  - Consider adding a senior test engineer to the requirements engineering team to ensure that the requirements are unambiguous.[73]
  - Ensure that one or more testers review the requirements specifications (or requirements in the requirements repository) and each requirement for verifiability (especially testability) before it is approved for use.
  - Encourage testers to request clarification for all ambiguous requirements, and encourage that the requirements be updated based on the clarification given.
  - Ensure that (1) the project has both a glossary and acronym list; and (2) the requirements include technical jargon and acronyms only if they are defined therein.
  - Ensure that the master test schedule includes sufficient time to address the requirements found during testing to be ambiguous.
- Perform:
  - Run the textual requirements through a static analyzer to identify words and phrases that are inherently ambiguous (if this is not already done during requirements analysis or quality control of the requirements).
  - Request requirements models (for example, use cases and mission threads) as well as the actual textual requirements.
  - Work with the requirements team(s) to make the requirements clear and unambiguous and therefore more testable.
  - Have one or more system stakeholders (for example, customer representatives, user representatives, and testers) and subject-matter experts (SMEs) review the requirements documents and the requirements repository contents for ambiguous requirements before they are accepted and approved for use.
  - Do not accept the requirements for generating black-box test cases until they have been reviewed for ambiguous requirements.
  - Notify the requirements engineers (and, if possible, the system stakeholders and SMEs) of any ambiguous requirements that are found during testing.
- Verify:
  - Determine whether a project- or domain-specific glossary and acronyms list, which define relevant technical jargon and acronyms, exist, and whether the requirements engineers and the testers are both using them.

- ◆ Determine whether the requirements are ambiguous by ensuring they are:
  - Reviewed by stakeholders and SMEs
  - Statically analyzed by a tool to determine whether the requirements contain any inherently ambiguous words or phrases
- ◆ Determine whether the requirements include words that are inherently ambiguous, undefined technical terms and acronyms, quantities without associated units of measure, or synonyms.
- ◆ Determine whether the requirements have been reviewed by one or more requirements engineers, system stakeholders, and SMEs for ambiguity.
- ◆ Have requirements engineers determine whether the testers have interpreted correctly the test cases and test results associated with complex or potentially ambiguous requirements.
- ◆ Determine whether any requirements were not implemented or tested by having one or more system stakeholders review the black-box system test results.
- ◆ Determine whether black-box test cases were developed from requirements that have not been reviewed for ambiguity.
- ◆ Determine whether the requirements engineers have been notified of all requirements found to be ambiguous during testing.

Related Pitfalls   Testing at the End (GEN-TPS-6), Inadequate Communication Concerning Testing (GEN-COM-5), Incomplete Requirements (GEN-REQ-4), Inadequate SoS Requirements (TTS-SoS-5)

OBSOLETE REQUIREMENTS (GEN-REQ-2)

Description   Testers waste effort and time testing whether the system or software under test (SUT) correctly implements a great many obsolete requirements.

Potential Applicability   This pitfall is potentially applicable anytime requirements can change.

Characteristic Symptoms
- The set of requirements has not been updated for a long while, possibly since it was initially developed or approved.
- Requirements changes occur informally and are not:
  - ◆ Officially approved
  - ◆ Stored in the requirements repository or management tool
  - ◆ Published in official requirements specifications.

Potential Negative Consequences

- Tests for new requirements are not developed and run.
- Tests developed for changed requirements are not changed, and thus are obsolete.
- Tests developed for deleted requirements are not deleted.
- Testers have to spend a sizable amount of time meeting with requirements engineers, customer or user representatives, and subject-matter experts (SMEs) to determine what the actual requirements are.
- Tests developed at different levels (for example, unit testing, integration testing, and system testing) by different testers become inconsistent as testers informally learn of different unofficial changes.

Potential Causes

- The people (for example, requirements engineers and business analysts) who engineered the requirements were not adequately trained in how to recognize and avoid obsolete requirements.
- Requirements engineers did not properly update the requirements repository and specification(s) in a timely manner as obsolete requirements were identified.
- Requirements naturally change over time due to:
  - New or changed customer or user needs
  - Advances in available technology
  - New or changed competing products (systems or software applications)
  - Newly discovered safety hazards, security threats, and survivability threats
- Official changes to the requirements necessitated unacceptable changes to the development contract, schedule, or budget.
- Requirements engineers did not notify the testers of changes to the requirements.

Recommendations

- Prepare:
  - Improve the requirements engineering process and associated training with regard to preventing, identifying, and fixing obsolete requirements.
- Enable:
  - Provide training to the members of the requirements team(s) on techniques for dealing with changing requirements.

- ◆ Ensure that the master test schedule includes sufficient time to address obsolete requirements found during testing.
- ◆ Ensure that there is a process and associated tool(s) for notifying stakeholders (including testers) of requirements changes.
- ■ **Perform:**
  - ◆ Regularly have stakeholder representatives validate the requirements-level tests by:
    - • Reviewing the current requirements
    - • Observing the system behavior
    - • Observing test execution or the results of testing
  - ◆ Use an evolutionary (that is, an iterative, incremental, and concurrent) development cycle in which requirements are rapidly implemented and tested in small, iterative increments.
  - ◆ Ensure that one or more system stakeholders (for example, customer representatives, user representatives, and testers) and subject-matter experts (SMEs) review the requirements documents and requirements repository contents for obsolete requirements before they are accepted and approved for use.
  - ◆ Do not accept the requirements for generating black-box test cases until they have been reviewed for obsolete requirements.
  - ◆ Notify the requirements engineers (and, if possible, the system stakeholders and SMEs) of any obsolete requirements that were found during testing.
- ■ **Verify:**
  - ◆ Determine whether stakeholder representatives are regularly validating the requirements.
  - ◆ Determine whether one or more system stakeholders and SMEs have reviewed the requirements for obsolescence.
  - ◆ Determine whether the obsolete requirements are being deleted or modified.
  - ◆ Determine whether any requirements are obsolete by having one or more system stakeholders review the black-box system test results.
  - ◆ Determine whether black-box test cases have been developed from requirements that have not been reviewed for obsolescence.
  - ◆ Determine whether the requirements engineers have been notified of all requirements found to be obsolete during testing.

Related Pitfalls   Inadequate Communication Concerning Testing (GEN-COM-5), Missing Requirements (GEN-REQ-3), Incomplete Requirements (GEN-REQ-4), Incorrect Requirements (GEN-REQ-5), Requirements Churn (GEN-REQ-6), Inadequate SoS Requirements (TTS-SoS-5)

GEN-REQ-3 Missing Requirements

MISSING REQUIREMENTS (GEN-REQ-3)

Description Testers overlook many undocumented requirements and therefore do not plan for, develop, or run the associated overlooked test cases.

Potential Applicability This pitfall is potentially applicable anytime requirements exist.

Characteristic Symptoms

- Some requirements are missing, such as:
  - ◆ Quality requirements (for example, availability, interoperability, maintainability, performance, portability, reliability, robustness, safety, security, and usability)
  - ◆ Data requirements
  - ◆ Interface requirements to external systems that are:
    - So obvious as to be "not worth writing down"
    - So minor as to be overlooked
  - ◆ Requirements specifying mandatory responses to abnormal conditions (for example, error, fault, and failure detection and reaction)[74]
  - ◆ Requirements specifying system behavior during non-operational modes (for example, start-up, degraded mode, training, and shut-down)

Potential Negative Consequences

- Tests cannot be efficiently developed for the missing requirements.[75]
- Requirements-based testing will not reveal missing behavior and characteristics.
- Testing stakeholders (for example, customer representatives, managers, developers, or testers) have a false sense of security that the system will function properly when delivered and deployed.
- Testers have to spend a sizable amount of time meeting with requirements engineers and customer or user representatives in order to identify missing requirements, the existence of which was implied by failed tests.
- Defects associated with missing requirements are not uncovered and therefore make it through testing and into the deployed system.
- The absence of the missing requirements causes inadequate design or implementation decisions that make finding and fixing the associated defects more difficult.

Potential Causes

- The people (for example, requirements engineers and business analysts) who engineered the requirements were not adequately trained in how to recognize and avoid missing requirements.
- The requirements engineers were not trained in:
  - Quality models, which define the relevant quality characteristics and attributes
  - The engineering of the associated quality requirements
- There was no project quality model, so for each requirement the writer had to rely on his or her own informal personal understanding of what quality characteristics and attributes were relevant and how they were defined.
- Requirements engineers did not properly update the requirements repository and specification(s) in a timely manner as missing requirements were identified.
- Use cases defined only normal (primary and alternative) use case paths and not exceptional (error-, fault-, and failure-tolerant) use case paths.[76]
- The stakeholders did not review the set of requirements for missing requirements.
- The requirements were not reviewed to ensure that they contained robustness requirements that mandate the detection and proper reaction to input errors, system faults (for example, incorrect system-internal modes, states, or data), and system failures.
- The requirements engineers were rushed because insufficient resources (for example, time and staffing) were allocated to properly engineer the requirements.

Recommendations

- **Prepare:**
  - Improve the requirements engineering process and associated training with regard to identifying and engineering missing requirements.
- **Enable:**
  - Provide training to the members of the requirements team(s) on techniques for identifying missing requirements.
  - Ensure that the master test schedule includes sufficient time to address missing requirements that will be identified during testing.
- **Perform:**
  - The requirements engineers identify missing requirements by using:
    - Context modeling to identify potentially missing interface, interoperability, and associated functional requirements

- End-to-end mission thread modeling to identify missing use cases.
- Use case modeling to address error-, fault-, and failure-tolerant (that is, rainy-day) paths as well as normal (sunny-day, or golden) paths
- A quality model to identify potentially missing quality requirements
- ◆ Consider adding a tester to the requirements engineering team to ensure that the requirements specify rainy-day situations that must be addressed to achieve error, fault, and failure tolerance.
- ◆ Have one or more system stakeholders (for example, customer representatives, user representatives, and testers) and subject-matter experts (SMEs) review the requirements documents and requirements repository contents for missing requirements before they are accepted and approved for use.
- ◆ Do not accept the requirements for generating black-box test cases until they have been reviewed for missing requirements.
- ◆ Notify the requirements engineers (and, if possible, the system stakeholders and SMEs) of any missing requirements that were found during testing.
- ▪ Verify:
  - ◆ Determine whether adequate requirements modeling (analysis) is being done.
  - ◆ Determine whether the functional requirements sufficiently address error-, fault-, and failure-tolerance.
  - ◆ Determine whether the requirements repository includes an appropriate number of quality and data requirements.
  - ◆ Determine whether the requirements have been reviewed by a sufficient number of system stakeholders and SMEs for missing requirements.
  - ◆ Determine whether the requirements engineers have been notified of all missing requirements that were identified during testing.

Related Pitfalls Inadequate Communication Concerning Testing (GEN-COM-5), Inadequate SoS Requirements (TTS-SoS-5)

INCOMPLETE REQUIREMENTS (GEN-REQ-4)

Description Testers fail to detect that many requirements are incomplete; therefore they develop and run correspondingly incomplete or incorrect test cases.

Potential Applicability This pitfall is potentially applicable anytime requirements exist.

Characteristic Symptoms

- ▪ Individual requirements are incomplete, for example, because they lack (where appropriate) some of the following components:[77]

- Trigger events
- Preconditions (for example, system state, valid range of input data, and valid types of input data)
- Mandatory quantitative thresholds
- Mandatory postconditions
- Mandatory behaviors (for example, returning data, issuing a command or message, and raising an exception)

Potential Negative Consequences

- Testing is incomplete in the sense that the missing parts of the requirements are not verified.
- Testing returns incorrect (that is, false-negative and false-positive) results.
- Some defects associated with incomplete requirements are not uncovered and therefore make it through testing and into the deployed system.

Potential Causes

- The people (for example, requirements engineers and business analysts) who engineered the requirements were not adequately trained in how to recognize and avoid incomplete requirements.
- Requirements engineers did not properly update the requirements repository and specifications in a timely manner as incomplete requirements were identified.
- The requirement team did not include anyone with testing expertise.
- The individual requirements were not reviewed for completeness.
- The testers did not review each requirement for completeness.
- The requirements reviewers did not use a requirements-review checklist or the checklist they used did not address incomplete requirements.
- The requirements engineers were rushed because insufficient resources (for example, time and staffing) were allocated to properly engineer the requirements.

Recommendations

- Prepare:
  - Improve the requirements engineering process and associated training.
  - Provide requirements guidelines or templates.

- **Enable:**
  - Provide members of the requirements team with training on whatever gaps they might have regarding requirements engineering and on how to spot and fix incomplete requirements.
  - Ensure that the master test schedule includes sufficient time to address the completion of requirements found during testing to be incomplete.
- **Perform:**
  - Consider adding a tester to the requirements engineering team to ensure that the requirements are sufficiently complete to enable testers to develop test inputs and determine correct associated outputs.
  - Have one or more system stakeholders (for example, customer representatives, user representatives, and testers) and subject-matter experts (SMEs) review the requirements documents and requirements repository contents for incomplete requirements.
  - Do not accept any requirements for generating black-box test cases until they have been reviewed for incomplete requirements.
  - Notify the requirements engineers (and, if possible, the system stakeholders and SMEs) of any requirements that were found to be incomplete during testing.
- **Verify:**
  - Determine whether one or more system stakeholders and SMEs have reviewed the requirements for completeness.
  - Determine whether black-box test cases have been developed from requirements that have not been reviewed for completeness.
  - Determine whether the requirements engineers have been notified of all requirements found to be incomplete during testing.

Related Pitfalls   Inadequate Communication Concerning Testing (GEN-COM-5), Ambiguous Requirements (GEN-REQ-1)

INCORRECT REQUIREMENTS (GEN-REQ-5)

Description   Testers fail to detect that many requirements are incorrect and therefore develop and run correspondingly incorrect test cases that produce false-positive and false-negative test results.[78]

Potential Applicability   This pitfall is potentially applicable anytime requirements exist.

Characteristic Symptoms

- Requirements are determined to be incorrect after the associated black-box tests have been developed, executed, and "passed."

Potential Negative Consequences

- Testing suffers from many false-positive and false-negative results.
- The tests associated with incorrect requirements must be modified or replaced and then rerun, potentially from scratch.
- Some defects caused by incorrect requirements are not found and therefore make it through testing and into the deployed system.

Potential Causes

- The people (for example, requirements engineers and business analysts) who engineered the requirements were not adequately trained in how to recognize and avoid incorrect requirements.
- Requirements engineers did not properly update the requirements repository and specifications in a timely manner as incorrect requirements were identified.
- Too few of the stakeholders (for example, customer representatives, user representatives, or subject-matter experts [SMEs]) from too few areas of expertise were available to validate the requirements as correct.
- Insufficient stakeholders or stakeholders were available to validate the requirements.
- Management did not allocate sufficient resources (for example, staffing, funding, or schedule) to properly engineer the requirements.
- There were contractual barriers separating the requirements stakeholders from the lower-level derived requirements.

Recommendations

- Prepare:
  - Improve the requirements engineering process with regard to increasing input from the system's authoritative stakeholders (both during requirements elicitation and requirements reviews).
  - Include stakeholder validation in the requirements engineering process.

GEN-REQ-5   Incorrect Requirements

- **Enable:**
  - ◆ Provide sufficient resources to properly engineer and validate the requirements.
  - ◆ Ensure that the master test schedule includes sufficient time to address any incorrect requirements found during testing.
- **Perform:**
  - ◆ Have a sufficient number of stakeholders properly validate the requirements.
  - ◆ Testers should not accept the requirements if they haven't been properly validated.
  - ◆ Testers should not develop many associated test cases based on the requirements until they know those requirements have been properly validated.
  - ◆ Require that one or more system stakeholders (for example, customer representatives, user representatives, and testers) and SMEs review the requirements documents and requirements repository contents for incorrect requirements.
  - ◆ Do not accept any requirements for generating black-box test cases until they have been reviewed for correctness.
  - ◆ Notify the requirements engineers (and, if possible, the system stakeholders and SMEs) of any incorrect requirements found during testing.
- **Verify:**
  - ◆ Determine whether management has allocated sufficient resources to properly validate the requirements.
  - ◆ Determine whether one or more system stakeholders and SMEs who have sufficient breadth and depth of expertise have reviewed the requirements for correctness.
  - ◆ Determine whether black-box test cases have been developed from requirements that have not been reviewed for correctness.
  - ◆ Determine whether the requirements engineers have been notified of all requirements found to be incorrect during testing.

Related Pitfalls Lack of Stakeholder Commitment to Testing (GEN-SIC-3), Inadequate SoS Requirements (TTS-SoS-5)

REQUIREMENTS CHURN (GEN-REQ-6)

Description Testers waste an excessive amount of time and effort developing and running test cases based on many requirements that are not sufficiently stable and that therefore change one or more times prior to delivery.[79]

Potential Applicability This pitfall is potentially applicable anytime requirements can change.

Characteristic Symptoms

- The requirements are continually changing at an unusually high rate: New requirements are being added and existing requirements are being modified and deleted.

- The requirements currently selected for implementation are not frozen, especially during a short-duration increment (for example, a Scrum sprint) when using an evolutionary (that is, incremental, iterative, and parallel) development cycle.[80]

Potential Negative Consequences

- The requirements are not being maintained, so they become obsolete when requirements changes occur.

- Test cases (test inputs, preconditions, and expected test outputs) and automated regression tests are continually becoming obsolete because of requirements changes.

- Significant time originally scheduled for developing and running new tests is spent in testing churn (fixing and rerunning tests that have become obsolete due to requirements changes).

- As the testing schedules get further behind, regression tests are not maintained and rerun.

- Broken tests are being abandoned rather than maintained.

Potential Causes

- The requirements were not well understood by the requirements stakeholders.

- Many of the requirements were being rapidly iterated because they did not exhibit the characteristics of good requirements.

- The effects of these potential causes were increased due to the use of a development cycle with many short-duration, iterative increments.

- The requirements engineers were rushed because insufficient resources (for example, time and staffing) were allocated to properly engineer the requirements.

- The requirements were frequently and unnecessarily changed in the middle of the current increment or release instead of postponing the requirements changes until the next increment or release.[81]

Recommendations

- **Prepare:**
  - Where needed, educate the requirements stakeholders about the need to minimize unnecessary requirements churn because of its negative impact on the testers (as well as on the architects, designers, and implementers).

- **Enable:**
  - Provide the requirements team with adequate resources to properly engineer the requirements.
  - Add a tester to the requirements engineering team as a liaison to the testers so that the testers know which requirements are most likely to be sufficiently stable as to enable them to begin developing and executing the associated tests.

- **Perform:**
  - Have the requirements team and stakeholders work to stabilize the requirements.
  - As soon as is practical, place the requirements under configuration control so that the impact of changing a requirement is estimated before the requirement is changed.
  - Iterate the requirements in a controlled manner based on developmental increments; postpone changes to requirements already approved for the current increment until a later increment.
  - Collect, analyze, and report metrics on requirements volatility and the resulting negative impact on testing productivity.
  - Where practical, postpone development of test cases (test scripts, test inputs, preconditions, and expected test outputs) and automating regression tests until the associated requirements are reasonably mature and stable.[82]
  - Especially postpone developing detailed test cases that require significant maintenance until the requirements stabilize.

- **Verify:**
  - Determine whether an inordinately high number of requirements have been added, modified, or deleted after the associated testing has been completed.
  - Determine whether requirements churn is causing significant wasted testing effort and schedule slippages.

Related Pitfalls   Inadequate Communication Concerning Testing (GEN-COM-5)

IMPROPERLY DERIVED REQUIREMENTS (GEN-REQ-7)

Description Testers base their testing on improperly derived requirements, resulting in missing test cases, test cases at the wrong level of abstraction, or incorrect test cases based on crosscutting requirements that are allocated without modification to multiple architectural components.

Potential Applicability This pitfall is potentially applicable anytime lower-level requirements are derived.

Characteristic Symptoms

- Derived requirements merely restate their associated parent requirements.
- Newly derived requirements are not at the proper level of abstraction (for example, subsystem requirements are at the same level of abstraction as the system requirements from which they were derived). Note that the first symptom is often an example of this second symptom.
- The set of lower-level requirements derived from a higher requirement is incomplete (that is, meeting the lower-level requirements does not imply meeting the higher-level requirement).[83]
- A derived requirement is not actually implied by its "source" requirement.
- Restrictions implied by architecture and design decisions are not being used to derive requirements in the form of derived architecture or design constraints.

Potential Negative Consequences

- Some test cases associated with derived requirements are not developed.
- Some test cases are at the wrong level of abstraction.
- It is difficult to produce tests at the correct level of abstraction.
- Some test cases are incorrect based on crosscutting requirements that are allocated without modification to multiple architectural components.
- Testing at the unit- and subsystem-level for derived requirements is incomplete.
- Associated lower-level defects are not detected during testing.

Potential Causes

- The people (for example, requirements engineers and business analysts) who engineered the requirements were not adequately trained in how to derive new requirements at the appropriate level of abstraction.
- Requirements engineers did not properly update the requirements repository and specifications in a timely manner as incorrect requirements were identified.
- The requirements engineers were rushed because insufficient resources (for example, time and staffing) were allocated to properly engineer the requirements.

Recommendations

- **Prepare:**
  - Make the requirements derivation an explicit part of requirements engineering (derivation of lower-level derived requirements) and architecture engineering (allocation of derived requirements to architectural components).
- **Enable:**
  - Train the members of the requirements and architecture teams in how to properly derive requirements to be allocated to lower-level architectural elements (for example, subsystems).
  - Provide sufficient time and staffing to derive lower-level requirements and allocate them to lower-level architectural elements.
- **Perform:**
  - Derive appropriate lower-level requirements for allocation to lower-level architectural components rather than merely allocating the higher-level requirements without modifying the architectural components.
- **Verify:**
  - Determine whether the derived and allocated requirements:
    - Are at the proper level of abstraction
    - Exhibit all of the standard characteristics of good requirements (for example, they are complete, consistent, correct, feasible, mandatory, testable, and unambiguous)
    - Are properly allocated to the correct architectural component(s)

Related Pitfalls   Lack of Requirements Trace (GEN-REQ-9)

VERIFICATION METHODS NOT PROPERLY SPECIFIED (GEN-REQ-8)

Description　Testers (or other developers, such as requirements engineers) fail to properly specify the verification method(s) for each requirement, thereby causing requirements to be verified using unnecessarily inefficient or ineffective verification method(s).[84]

Potential Applicability　This pitfall is always potentially applicable.

Characteristic Symptoms

- The requirements specifications do not specify the verification method (for example, analysis, demonstration, inspection, simulation, or testing) for its associated requirements.
- The requirements repository does not include verification method(s) as requirements metadata.[85]

Potential Negative Consequences

- Testers and testing stakeholders incorrectly assume that all requirements must be verified via testing, even though other verification methods may be adequate or more appropriate and require less time or effort.
- Time is spent testing requirements that should have been verified using another, more appropriate verification method.
- Requirements stakeholders incorrectly assume that if a requirement is not testable, then it is also not verifiable.

Potential Causes

- Specifying verification methods for each requirement or set of similar requirements was not an explicit part of the requirements engineering process.
- The requirements repository (or requirements management tool) schema did not include metadata for specifying verification methods.
- The requirements engineers were rushed because insufficient resources (for example, time and staffing) were allocated to engineer the requirements properly.

Recommendations

- Prepare:
  - ◆ Make specifying verification methods for each requirement (or set of similar requirements) an explicit part of the requirements engineering process, both as a task and as part of the contents in the requirements specification document(s).
- Enable:
  - ◆ Provide adequate staffing and time in the schedule to enable specifying the requirements verification method a part of the requirements engineering process.
  - ◆ Add a tester to the requirements engineering team to ensure that the requirements verification methods are properly specified.
  - ◆ Include metadata for documenting verification methods in the schema of the requirements repository (or requirements management tool).
- Perform:
  - ◆ Specify one or more verification methods for each requirement or set of similar requirements in the requirements repository.
  - ◆ Publish these verification methods in any associated requirements specifications.
- Verify:
  - ◆ Determine whether each requirement (or set of similar requirements) has one or more appropriate verification methods assigned to it or them.
  - ◆ Determine whether specified verification methods are appropriate.
  - ◆ Determine whether the actual verification methods used are consistent with the specified requirements verification methods and update the requirements specifications and repositories when necessary.

Related Pitfalls   Inadequate Communication Concerning Testing (GEN-COM-5)

LACK OF REQUIREMENTS TRACE (GEN-REQ-9)

Description   The testers do not trace requirements to the individual tests or test cases, thereby making it unnecessarily difficult to determine whether the tests are inadequate or excessive.

Potential Applicability   This pitfall is always potentially applicable.

Characteristic Symptoms

- There is no documented tracing from individual requirements to their associated test cases.
- The mapping from the requirements to the test cases is not stored in any project repository (for example, requirements management, test management, or configuration tool).
- There is only a backward trace from the individual test cases to the requirement(s) they test.
- Any tracing that was originally created is not maintained as the requirements change.

Potential Negative Consequences

- Testing is inadequate.
- Testing is excessive.
- There is no easy way to plan testing tasks, determine if all requirements have been tested, or determine what needs to be regression tested after changes occur.
- If requirements change, there is no way of knowing which test cases will need to be created, modified, or deleted.

Potential Causes

- The requirements repository (or requirements management tool) schema did not include metadata for specifying the requirements trace to test cases.
- Specifying the requirements trace to testing was not:
  - Addressed in the relevant planning documents, such as the:
    - Requirements Engineering Plan (REP)
    - Requirements section of the System Engineering Management Plan (SEMP) or System Development Plan (SDP)
    - Test planning documentation
  - An explicit part of the requirements engineering or testing processes
- There were insufficient staffing and time allocated to tracing requirements.
- The tool support for tracing requirements was inadequate or nonexistent.

Recommendations

- **Prepare:**
  - ◆ Include generating and maintaining the tracing from requirements to test cases in the test planning documentation.
- **Enable:**
  - ◆ Train the testers in how to trace from the requirements to the test cases.
  - ◆ Allocate time in the project's master schedule to perform this tracing.
  - ◆ Obtain a requirements management tool to automate recording and maintenance of the requirements traces.
- **Perform:**
  - ◆ Ensure that higher-level requirements are traced to lower-level (derived) requirements so that it is possible to verify that the lower-level requirements, if met, are sufficient to meet the higher-level requirements.
  - ◆ Create a tracing between the requirements and test cases.
  - ◆ Include the tracing from requirements to tests as a test asset in the appropriate repository.
- **Verify:**
  - ◆ Determine whether traces from requirements through architecture, design, and implementation to tests exist, are correct, and are being maintained.

Related Pitfalls   Inadequate Maintenance of Test Assets (GEN-PRO-9), Inadequate Architecture or Design Documentation (GEN-COM-1)

3.4   Test-Type-Specific Pitfalls

The following types of testing pitfalls are related to the type of testing being performed:

- Unit Testing Pitfalls
- Integration Testing Pitfalls
- Specialty Engineering Testing Pitfalls
- System Testing Pitfalls
- System of Systems (SoS) Testing Pitfalls
- Regression Testing Pitfalls

3.4.1   Unit Testing Pitfalls

The following testing pitfalls are related to software unit testing:

- Testing Does *Not* Drive Design and Implementation (TTS-UNT-1)
- Conflict of Interest (TTS-UNT-2)

Testing Does Not Drive Design and Implementation (TTS-UNT-1)

Description Software developers and testers do not develop their tests first and then use these tests to drive development of the associated architecture, design, and implementation.

Potential Applicability This pitfall is almost always potentially applicable to the software in the system under test. This pitfall is less appropriate for the integration and system testing of systems containing hardware, where simultaneous development of the system and its tests is often more appropriate.

Characteristic Symptoms

- Testing is not considered during unit-level design and implementation.
- Software units are designed and implemented before the development of any associated unit test cases.
- The software developers and testers are unfamiliar with Test Driven Development (TDD).

Potential Negative Consequences

- When unit tests are designed immediately after the units are implemented, the tests tend to verify that the units behave in the way they were implemented rather than in the way they should have been implemented.
- Unit-level designs and implementations are:
  - Less testable because decisions that could have increased unit testability were not made until after the units were already designed and implemented
  - More likely to contain defects that could have been avoided if the developer had considered testing from the beginning
- Existing test cases, test scripts, test drivers, and test stubs are less likely to be iterated and kept consistent as the unit design and implementation are iterated.
- This inconsistency between unit design, unit implementation, and unit testing results in excessive numbers of false-positive and false-negative test results.

Potential Causes

- The developers performing unit testing were unaware of and untrained in TDD.
- Software developers did not test the units that they developed (either personally or as part of a pair-programming team).

- Software developers were used to following a traditional, build-test-fix cycle.
- Most software developers prefer developing units over developing test cases (that is, they prefer design and programming over testing).
- Software developers and managers consider automating tests prior to producing the software to be tested

---

Recommendations

- **Prepare:**
  - ◆ Incorporate TDD into the test planning documentation and testing program.
- **Enable:**
  - ◆ Provide software developers and testers with training in TDD.
- **Perform:**
  - ◆ Give software developers responsibility for testing the units that they develop (either personally or as part of a pair-programming team).
  - ◆ Ensure that the software developers identify and develop unit test cases:
    - Either before or as the associated unit is designed and implemented
    - Before refactoring existing software that does not already have unit tests
    - Before debugging (that is, develop tests that would have found the bug)
  - ◆ Require software developers to iterate the unit test cases either before or at the same time as they iterate the associated unit.
- **Verify:**
  - ◆ Determine whether TDD has been incorporated into the test planning documentation and test program.
  - ◆ Determine whether the software developers are responsible for testing their own units.
  - ◆ Determine whether the software developers are identifying and developing unit-level test cases either before or at the same time as they design and implement the associated units.
  - ◆ Determine whether the software developers iterate their unit-level test cases either before or at the same time as they iterate the associated unit designs and implementations.

Related Pitfalls   Incomplete Test Planning (GEN-TPS-2), Testing at the End (GEN-TPS-6), Unclear Testing Responsibilities (GEN-STF-2), Inadequate Testing Expertise (GEN-STF-3), Testing and Engineering Processes Not Integrated (GEN-PRO-1), Conflict of Interest (TTS-UNT-2)

CONFLICT OF INTEREST (TTS-UNT-2)

Description   Nothing is done to address the following conflict of interest that exists when software developers test their own work products: They are being asked to demonstrate that their own software is defective.

Potential Applicability   This pitfall is potentially applicable anytime that a developer tests his or her own software, which is a very common industry practice. This pitfall is primarily applicable to software unit testing, but it also applies when:

- Requirements engineers test their own executable requirements models.
- Architects test their own executable architectural models.
- Designers test their own executable design models.

Characteristic Symptoms

- Software developers unit test the same units that they personally developed.
- Software developers and managers think that unit testing is not sufficiently important to require that professional testers perform it.
- Software developers spend far less time testing their software than developing it.
- There are few software unit-level test cases.
- The test cases concentrate heavily on demonstrating "sunny-day" paths and largely ignore verifying that "rainy-day" exceptional paths work properly.

Potential Negative Consequences

- Unit testing is poorly and incompletely performed.[86]
- Unit test cases are poorly maintained, in spite of their value for regression testing.
- An unacceptably large number of defects that should have been found during unit testing pass through to integration and system testing, which are thereby slowed down and made less efficient.

Potential Causes

- Developers tested the units that they personally developed.
- Developers expected their software to work correctly (an incorrect mindset), so:

- ◆ They tried to demonstrate that it works rather than show that it doesn't work.
- ◆ They developed as few test cases as practical.
- ▪ Developers felt that the testers would catch any defects they missed.[87]
- ▪ Developers thought that it was far more fun to write software than to test software.
- ▪ Managers or developers thought that unit testing is relatively unimportant, especially in relation to actually developing the software.

Recommendations

- ▪ **Prepare:**
  - ◆ Establish clear software unit testing success criteria that must be passed before the unit can be delivered for integration and integration testing.
- ▪ **Enable:**
  - ◆ Provide software developers with training in how to:
    - • Perform unit testing
    - • Be aware of and counteract their conflict of interest
  - ◆ Provide developers with tools to help with automated unit testing.
  - ◆ Ensure that the developers understand the importance of finding highly localized defects during unit testing, when they are much easier to localize, analyze, and fix.
- ▪ **Perform:**
  - ◆ Have units tested by peers of the software developers who produced them.
  - ◆ Institute pair programming.
  - ◆ Require that the software developers institute unit-level Test Driven Development (TDD).
  - ◆ Incentivize software developers to do a better job of testing their own software.
- ▪ **Verify:**
  - ◆ Determine whether the software developers are clear about their testing responsibilities.
  - ◆ Determine whether sufficient unit testing is taking place.
  - ◆ Determine (for example, via observation and conversation) whether the software developers are truly trying to identify defects (that is, break their own software).

Related Pitfalls   Wrong Testing Mindset (GEN-SIC-1), Unclear Testing Responsibilities (GEN-STF-2), Testing Does *Not* Drive Design and Implementation (TTS-UNT-1)

3.4.2 Integration Testing Pitfalls

Integration testing pitfalls can occur at different levels of integration: during the testing of a set of software or hardware units integrated into a component, a set of components integrated into a subsystem, a set of subsystems integrated into a system, or a set of systems integrated into a system of systems. While integration testing concentrates on verifying the interactions between the parts of the whole, it can also find defects that should have been found during unit testing or lower-level integration testing.

The following testing pitfalls are related to integration testing:

- Integration Decreases Testability Ignored (TTS-INT-1)
- Inadequate Self-Monitoring (TTS-INT-2)
- Unavailable Components (TTS-INT-3)
- System Testing as Integration Testing (TTS-INT-4)

INTEGRATION DECREASES TESTABILITY IGNORED (TTS-INT-1)

Description Nothing is done to address the fact that integration encapsulates the individual parts of the whole and the interactions between them, thereby making the internal parts of the integrated whole less observable and less controllable and, therefore, less testable.[88]

Potential Applicability This pitfall is potentially applicable anytime that the system is constructed by integrating smaller components.

Characteristic Symptoms

- It is difficult to establish test-case preconditions involving the internal parts of the integrated whole.
- It is difficult to observe the pretest and posttest states of the integrated whole.
- It is difficult to observe interactions within the integrated whole.
- It is difficult to stimulate the internals of the integrated whole with test inputs, especially exceptions or error codes.

Potential Negative Consequences

- The system or software fails to meet its testability requirements.[89]

- It takes an excessive amount of time and effort to set up and execute the integration test cases.
- It is difficult to determine the location of the defect that causes a test to fail:
  - The new or updated operational software under test
  - The new or updated operational hardware under test
  - The COTS operating system or middleware
  - The software test environments (for example, in software simulations of hardware)
  - The combined hardware and software test environments (for example, in hardware emulators or pre-production versions of the hardware)
  - The test cases (for example, in the test inputs, preconditions, expected outputs, or expected postconditions)
  - A configuration or version mismatch among test cases
- It takes an excessive amount of time and effort to localize defects.
- Errors in defect localization cause the wrong fix (for example, the wrong changes or changes to the wrong components) to be made.
- It takes an excessive amount of time and effort to show adequate test-case coverage of interactions between integrated parts.

Potential Causes
- Integration naturally decreased *controllability* as increasingly larger parts were integrated, because integration makes it increasingly difficult to control the internals of the integrated whole:
  - Establish test-case preconditions (for example, system state or mode and database values)
  - Stimulate the integrated whole with test inputs (for example, messages, data flows, exceptions, and error codes)
- Integration naturally decreased *observability* as increasingly larger parts were integrated, because integration makes it increasingly difficult to observe the internals of the integrated whole:
  - Verify that test preconditions were established by observing the pretest state of the integrated whole
  - Verify that internal interactions (involving messages, data flows, exceptions, and error codes) occurred as expected
  - Verify that test postconditions were achieved by observing the posttest state of the integrated whole
- The integrated whole did not incorporate:
  - Sufficient test hooks and interfaces[90]

- ◆ Built-in test (BIT), including PowerUp BIT (PupBIT), Interrupt-driven BIT (IBIT), Periodic BIT (PBIT), User-initiated BIT (UBIT), and Shutdown BIT (SBIT), whereby BIT is often also referred to as Built-In Self Test (BIST)
  - ◆ System prognostics and health management (PHM) function or subsystem
  - ◆ Logging support to provide adequate observability
  - ◆ Support for test mode(s)
- The testers did not have access to testing tools that increase controllability and observability.

Recommendations

- **Prepare:**
  - ◆ Train testers in how to overcome the decreased controllability and observability caused by integration.
- **Enable:**
  - ◆ Testers should review the requirements for appropriate testability including both controllability and observability.
  - ◆ Testers should review the architecture and design for appropriate support for controllability and observability.
  - ◆ Testers should review interface design documents to ensure that the system-internal interfaces are well defined, and that they include both syntax and semantics.
  - ◆ Testers should review the architecture and design to determine whether the system or software under test (SUT) incorporates test hooks and interfaces, BIT, PHM, Error logging and reporting capabilities, and support for test modes.
  - ◆ Testers should have sufficient test tools to enable adequate controllability and observability.
- **Perform:**
  - ◆ Perform sufficient unit testing and lower-level integration testing so that higher-level testing can concentrate on the interactions of the integrated parts of the whole.
  - ◆ Where appropriate, incorporate a test mode that logs information about errors, faults, and failures to support defect identification and localization.
  - ◆ Because a single type of defect often occurs in multiple locations, check similar locations for the same type of defect once a defect has been localized.
- **Verify:**
  - ◆ Determine whether sufficient unit testing and lower-level integration testing are taking place.

TTS-INT-1   Integration Decreases Testability Ignored

- Determine whether integration testing concentrates on testing the interactions between the parts of the integrated whole.
- Determine whether the system or software under test includes test hooks and interfaces, BIT, PHM, adequate logging, and support for test modes.
- Determine whether the testers have adequate tool support for integration testing.

Related Pitfalls   Wrong Testing Mindset (GEN-SIC-1)

INADEQUATE SELF-MONITORING (TTS-INT-2)

Description   Testers are unprepared for addressing the difficulty of testing encapsulated components due to a lack of system- or software-internal self-tests.

Potential Applicability   This pitfall is always potentially applicable.

Characteristic Symptoms
- There are no requirements for:
  - Sufficient test hooks and interfaces
  - Built-in test (BIT) including PowerUp BIT (PupBIT), Interrupt-driven BIT (IBIT), Periodic BIT (PBIT), User-initiated BIT (UBIT), and Shutdown BIT (SBIT)
  - System prognostics and health management (PHM) function or subsystem
  - Error logging and reporting capabilities
  - Support for test mode(s)
- The architecture does not include sufficient start-up health checks, BIT, status logging, PHM, or error-reporting capabilities.
- The design and code do not include significant error reporting via exception handling.

Potential Negative Consequences

- Faults that occur during testing are difficult to observe, localize, and reproduce.
- Fault tolerance hides underlying defects, thereby preventing them from being discovered, localized, diagnosed, and fixed.

- The defects associated with failures that occur during testing are difficult to observe, localize, and reproduce.
- It takes an excessive amount of time, effort, and funding to perform integration testing, potentially exceeding the test schedule.

Potential Causes

- Few, if any, self-monitoring capabilities were incorporated into the system.
- Associated reliability, robustness, safety, or security requirements did not exist.

Recommendations

- **Prepare:**
  - Testers should ensure that appropriate reliability, robustness, safety, and security requirements are specified (for example, as members of the requirements team or as reviewers of the requirements).
- **Enable:**
  - Testers should review the architecture and design to determine whether the system or software under test (SUT) incorporates test hooks and interfaces, BIT, PHM, Error logging and reporting capabilities, and support for test modes.
  - Ensure that testers have adequate test tools to provide adequate observability.
- **Perform:**
  - Where appropriate, incorporate a test mode that logs information about errors, faults, and failures to support defect identification and localization.
- **Verify:**
  - Determine whether any start-up health checks, BIT, status logging, PHM function or subsystem, or error-reporting capabilities are functioning correctly.

Related Pitfalls Integration Decreases Testability Ignored (TTS-INT-1)

UNAVAILABLE COMPONENTS (TTS-INT-3)

Description Integration testing must be postponed due to the unavailability of (1) system hardware or software components or (2) test environment components.

Potential Applicability This pitfall is potentially applicable anytime that the system is constructed by integrating smaller components.

Characteristic Symptoms

- Integration testing is postponed because the lack of one or more of the following necessary components makes it impossible to integrate the system, subsystem, or software to be tested:
  - The correct versions of the prototype software, simulation software, or actual operational software
  - The correct versions of the prototype hardware, emulation hardware, or actual operational hardware (for example, sensors, actuators, and network devices)
  - The correct versions of components for the test environments
- Integration testing is postponed because a lack of one or more of the following necessary components makes it impossible to create the integration test environment:
  - Computers (clients and servers) and networks
  - Test tools
  - The correct version of some test software (for example, to simulate hardware)
  - The correct version of some test hardware (for example, prototype hardware)
  - Test facilities

Potential Negative Consequences

- Integration testing cannot begin until the missing components:
  - Become available
  - Have been integrated into the subsystem under test or a test environment
- To remain on schedule, testing uses components that have lower fidelity until the intended components are available for integration.
- Integration testing is neither completed nor on schedule.

Potential Causes

- There was insufficient funding to purchase the needed components of the test environments or test beds.
- There were insufficient facilities in which to build the test environments or test beds.
- Software developers were behind schedule.
- Hardware developers were behind schedule.

- Hardware components that were originally intended for the test environment needed to be used to build prototype systems, such as during a Low Rate of Initial Production (LRIP) phase.

Recommendations

- **Prepare:**
  - ◆ Include the effort and time required to develop and install the simulation software and test hardware in the project budget and schedule.
  - ◆ Plan for sufficient prototype hardware to be produced to ensure an adequate supply for producing the test environments.
- **Enable:**
  - ◆ Provide sufficient resources (for example, staffing, budget, and schedule) to obtain or produce the components to be integrated into the system or software under test and the test environment(s) in time for integration testing to be performed.
- **Perform:**
  - ◆ Ensure that the operational software, simulation software, test hardware, and actual hardware components are available for integration into the test environments prior to scheduled integration testing.
  - ◆ If necessary, obtain components with lower fidelity (for example, prototype or simulation software or prototype or emulation hardware) for initial testing.
- **Verify:**
  - ◆ Determine whether there are sufficient resources to produce the components to be integrated in time for integration testing to be performed.
  - ◆ Determine whether there are no significant schedule delays with regard to developing the components to be integrated.
  - ◆ Determine whether sufficient components are available to integrate so that integration testing can begin.
  - ◆ Determine whether the quality of any simulation (software) or emulation (hardware) components is sufficiently high to be useful.

Related Pitfalls   Poor Fidelity of Test Environments (GEN-TTE-6)

System Testing as Integration Testing (TTS-INT-4)

Description   Testers are actually performing system-level tests of system functionality when they are supposed to be performing integration testing of component interfaces and interactions.

Potential Applicability   This pitfall is potentially applicable anytime the system is constructed by integrating smaller components.

Characteristic Symptoms

- Insufficient test cases exist to verify the interactions between integrated components.
- System tests fail due to defects that should have been identified as a result of integration testing.

Potential Negative Consequences

- Important aspects of the interactions between system components are either not tested or not sufficiently tested. Specifically, there are inadequate test cases that determine whether a component in the integrated system or software responds correctly:
  - To messages when the:
    - Messages use an incorrect protocol and therefore have the incorrect structure
    - Message parameters have both valid data types and ranges and invalid data types and ranges[91]
    - Messages contain error codes
    - Messages arrive at the wrong time (for example, too frequently, too early, out of order, too late, or never)
    - Messages are repeated (possibly as part of a man-in-the-middle or denial-of-service attack)
    - Messages arrive when the component is in the wrong state
    - Messages are encrypted, contain digital signatures, or hash codes (for example, to verify that the component provides adequate confidentiality, integrity, and non-repudiation)
  - When exceptions are raised (thrown) to it
- Component interaction defects are not found during integration testing.
- Test failures due to component interaction defects take an excessive amount of time to diagnose, fix, and retest.

Potential Causes

- Integration testing was adequately addressed in any of the test planning documentation.
- The testers were not adequately trained in integration testing.[92]

- The testers mistakenly assumed that system-level tests would naturally exercise a sufficient amount of the interactions between integrated components.
- Testers mistakenly assumed that if a component passed component testing, it would also continue to work properly when integrated with other components.
- The testers did not have time to perform adequate integration testing and therefore needed to start system testing before integration testing was complete.
- The testers were trying too hard to generate integration test cases that could be reused as system test cases and therefore ended up emphasizing system test cases over integration test cases.
- The testers did not have test tools to enable them to adequately test a component's response to exceptions being returned to it.

Recommendations

- **Prepare:**
    - Adequately address integration testing in the test planning documentation or in the testing sections of the SEMP or SDP.
- **Enable:**
    - Train the testers in integration testing techniques.
    - Provide test tools that specifically support integration testing (for example, by enabling exceptions as test inputs).
    - Provide sufficient time to properly perform integration testing.
- **Perform:**
    - Test component-to-component interactions under both normal and abnormal circumstances
- **Verify:**
    - Determine whether integration testing is adequately addressed in the test planning documentation or in the testing sections of the SEMP or SDP.
    - Determine whether the testers have adequate training and expertise in integration testing techniques.
    - Determine whether both normal and exceptional component interactions have been verified.

Related Pitfalls   Incomplete Test Planning (GEN-TPS-2), Inadequate Test Schedule (GEN-TPS-5), Inadequate Test Resources (GEN-MGMT-1), Inadequate Testing Expertise (GEN-STF-3), Developers Responsible for All Testing (GEN-STF-4)

3.4.3   Specialty Engineering Testing Pitfalls

The following testing pitfalls are related to the specialty engineering testing of quality-specific characteristics and their attributes. These pitfalls are highly

TTS-INT-4 System Testing as Integration Testing

similar in nature although they vary significantly in detail. This section could be much larger, because there are many different quality characteristics and associated attributes that each has its own associated potential symptoms, consequences, and causes. The following pitfalls were chosen, though, as they are typically some of the most important and commonly occurring ones:

- Inadequate Capacity Testing (TTS-SPC-1)
- Inadequate Concurrency Testing (TTS-SPC-2)
- Inadequate Internationalization Testing (TTS-SPC-3)
- Inadequate Interoperability Testing (TTS-SPC-4)
- Inadequate Performance Testing (TTS-SPC-5)
- Inadequate Reliability Testing (TTS-SPC-6)
- Inadequate Robustness Testing (TTS-SPC-7)
- Inadequate Safety Testing (TTS-SPC-8)
- Inadequate Security Testing (TTS-SPC-9)
- Inadequate Usability Testing (TTS-SPC-10)

Note that specialty engineering tests tend to find the kinds of defects that are both difficult and costly to fix (for example, because often they involve making architectural changes). Even though these are system-level quality characteristics, waiting until system testing is generally a bad idea. These types of testing (or other verification approaches) should begin relatively early during development.

INADEQUATE CAPACITY TESTING (TTS-SPC-1)

Description   Testers perform little or no capacity testing to determine the degree to which the system or software degrades gracefully as capacity limits are approached, reached, and exceeded.

Potential Applicability   This pitfall is applicable when there are specified or unspecified capacity requirements.

Characteristic Symptoms
- There is little or no testing to determine if performance degrades gracefully as capacity limits are approached, reached, and exceeded.
- There is little or no verification of adequate capacity-related computational resources (for example, processor, memory, or bus utilization).
- There are few, if any, tests traced back to capacity requirements.

Potential Negative Consequences

- Capacity testing is incomplete.
- Testing fails to uncover some capacity defects.
- Trustworthy test data to enable the estimation of system or software capacity are not collected.
- The system or software does not meet all of its capacity requirements.
- The system or software has inadequate capacity.
- Management, developers, and other stakeholders have false confidence that the system or software has sufficient capacity.
- Capacity failures occur, sometimes catastrophically, especially when initial usage far exceeds estimated initial usage.
- Capacity defects are uncovered during acceptance testing, operational testing, and once the system or software has been placed into operation.

Potential Causes

- Capacity testing was not addressed in any of the test planning documentation.
- Too many capacity requirements were not specified or were poorly specified, without any verifiable thresholds.
- Testers did not have sufficient training and expertise in:
  - Capacity and its quality attributes
  - Common capacity defects, faults, and failures
  - Commonly used architectural patterns to achieve adequate capacity
  - Capacity testing
- Testing capacity requirements was more difficult than testing functional requirements.
- Testers had inadequate tool support for performing capacity tests (for example, for creating large data sets or for achieving high input rates).
- There was confusion about who was responsible for testing capacity requirements: the development integrated product teams (IPTs), the independent test team(s), or the specialty engineering capacity engineer(s).
- Testing quality requirements (including capacity requirements):
  - Was considered less important than testing functional requirements
  - Had to wait until testing functional requirements was complete

- Capacity testing was never allocated sufficient resources because there were insufficient resources to do normal integration and system testing of the functional requirements.

Recommendations

- **Prepare:**
  - Address capacity testing in the test planning documentation or in the testing sections of the SEMP or SDP.
  - Read the capacity requirements.
  - Determine how the system architecture supports meeting the capacity requirements.
- **Enable:**
  - If needed, provide testers with training in capacity requirements and capacity testing.
  - Ensure that all necessary capacity requirements are properly specified.
  - Ensure that an adequate test environment for capacity testing is available.
- **Perform:**
  - Perform sufficient capacity testing to verify compliance with the capacity requirements.
  - Use capacity-specific testing approaches:
    - Use large data sets
    - Use large numbers of client computers to drive large numbers of transactions to simulate large numbers of users
- **Verify:**
  - Determine whether capacity testing is adequately addressed in the test planning documentation.
  - Determine whether the testers have adequate expertise in and experience with capacity requirements, commonly used architectural decisions to meet capacity requirements, types of capacity-related defects and failures, and how to perform capacity testing.
  - Determine whether the capacity requirements have been sufficiently specified to drive capacity testing.
  - Determine whether the architecture has been sufficiently documented to drive capacity testing.
  - Determine whether testing techniques appropriate for capacity testing are being correctly used.
  - Determine whether adequate test environment(s) and test tools exist for performing capacity testing.
  - Determine whether the capacity requirements have been sufficiently tested.

Related Pitfalls Incomplete Test Planning (GEN-TPS-2)

INADEQUATE CONCURRENCY TESTING (TTS-SPC-2)

Description   Testers perform little or no concurrency testing to determine the degree to which the system or software achieves a sufficient level of freedom from concurrency faults and failures.

Potential Applicability   This pitfall is potentially applicable anytime the system includes logically or physically concurrent components (for example, components with multiple executing processes or threads or software components running on multiple computers, computers with multiple processors, and multi-core computers).

Characteristic Symptoms

- There is little or no testing performed explicitly to uncover the defects that cause the common types of concurrency faults and failures: deadlock, livelock, starvation, priority inversion, race conditions, inconsistent views of shared memory, and unintentional infinite loops.
- Any concurrency testing that is performed is based on a random rather than a systematic approach to test-case identification (for example, based on interleaving threads).
- Any concurrency testing is performed manually.
- Concurrency faults and failures are identified only when they happen to occur while unrelated testing is being performed.
- Concurrency faults and failures occur infrequently, intermittently, and are difficult to reproduce.
- Concurrency testing is performed using a low-fidelity environment with regard to concurrency:
  - Threads rather than processes
  - Single computers rather than multiple computers
  - Computers with single rather than multiple processors
  - Computers with multicore processors
  - Deterministic rather than probabilistic drivers and stubs
  - Software simulation or hardware emulation rather than actual hardware

Potential Negative Consequences

- Any concurrency testing is both ineffectual and labor intensive.

- Many defects that can cause concurrency faults and failures are not found and fixed until final system testing, operational testing, or system operation, when they are much more difficult to reproduce, localize, and understand.

Potential Causes

- Concurrency testing was not addressed in any of the test planning documentation.
- Too many concurrency-related architectural constraints were not specified or were poorly specified, without any verifiable thresholds.
- Testers did not have sufficient training and expertise in:
  - Concurrency
  - Common concurrency defects, faults, and failures
  - Commonly used architectural patterns to support concurrency
  - Concurrency testing
- Testing concurrent behavior was more difficult than testing sequential implementations of functional requirements.

Recommendations

- **Prepare:**
  - Address concurrency testing in the test planning documentation.
  - Determine how the system architecture addresses concurrency.
- **Enable:**
  - If needed, provide testers with training in concurrency defects, faults, and failures.
  - Ensure that an adequate test environment for concurrency testing is available.
- **Perform:**
  - Use concurrency testing techniques that enable systematically selecting a reasonable number of test cases (for example, ways of interleaving the threads) from the impractically large number of potential test cases.
  - For testing threads sharing a single processor, use a concurrency testing tool that provides control over thread creation and scheduling.
  - When such tools are unavailable or inadequate, develop scripts that:
    - Automate testing deadlock and race conditions
    - Enable the reproducibility of test inputs
    - Record test results for analysis
  - To the extent possible, do not rely on merely throwing large numbers of random simultaneous inputs or requests[93] at the system when performing concurrency testing.

- Verify:
  - ◆ Determine whether concurrency testing is adequately addressed in the test planning documentation.
  - ◆ Determine whether the testers have adequate expertise in and experience with commonly used architectural decisions to address concurrency, types of concurrency defects and failures, and how to perform concurrency testing.
  - ◆ Determine whether the architecture is sufficiently documented to drive concurrency testing.
  - ◆ Determine whether adequate test environment(s), including test tools, exist for concurrency testing.
  - ◆ Determine whether testing techniques appropriate for concurrency testing are being correctly used.
  - ◆ Determine whether concurrent behavior is sufficiently tested.

Related Pitfalls   Incomplete Test Planning (GEN-TPS-2), Inadequate Performance Testing (TTS-SPC-4)

INADEQUATE INTERNATIONALIZATION TESTING (TTS-SPC-3)

Description   Testers perform little or no internationalization testing to determine the degree to which the system or software is configurable to function appropriately in multiple countries.

Potential Applicability   This pitfall is potentially applicable if the system or software under test (SUT) needs to support multiple languages, the laws and regulations of multiple countries, international symbols, and if it needs to address multicultural sensitivities (for example, words and colors that have radically different implications in different countries).

Characteristic Symptoms

- The system must handle input, output, stored, and configuration data in multiple languages.
- The system must conform to the laws and regulations (for example, tax rates) of multiple countries.
- The system must properly handle international symbols (for example, monetary symbols such as $, £, €, and ¥).
- The user interface does not correctly display foreign characters and text.
- Printed reports do not correctly display foreign characters and text.
- There are few, if any, tests traced back to internationalization requirements.

Potential Negative Consequences

- Internationalization testing is incomplete.
- Testing fails to uncover some internationalization defects.
- Trustworthy test data to enable the verification of system or software internationalization are not created.
- The system or software does not meet all of its internationalization requirements.
- The system or software has inadequate support for internationalization.
- Management, developers, and other stakeholders have false confidence that the system or software sufficiently supports internationalization based on it having passed tests that are written in the developers' native language (for example, English).
- Internationalization failures occur and the associated defects are uncovered during acceptance testing, operational testing, and once the system or software has been placed into operation.

Potential Causes

- Internationalization testing was not addressed in any of the test planning documentation.
- Too many internationalization requirements were not specified or were poorly specified, without any verifiable thresholds.
- Testers did not have sufficient training and expertise in:
  - Internationalization and its quality attributes
  - Common internationalization defects, faults, and failures
  - Commonly used architectural patterns to achieve adequate internationalization
  - Internationalization testing
- No native foreign-language speakers were part of or available to support the test team.
- Testing internationalization requirements required subject-matter experts in the relevant foreign languages, customs, and laws.
- There was confusion about who is responsible for testing internationalization requirements: the development integrated product teams (IPTs), the independent test team(s), or the specialty engineering subject-matter experts (SMEs).
- Testing quality requirements (including internationalization requirements):
  - Was considered less important than testing functional requirements

- ♦ Had to wait until the testing of functional requirements was complete
- Internationalization testing was never allocated sufficient resources because there were insufficient resources to do normal integration and system testing of the functional requirements.

Recommendations
- Prepare:
  - ♦ Address internationalization testing in the test planning documentation.
  - ♦ Search the requirements database for internationalization requirements.
- Enable:
  - ♦ If practical, add a native speaker of each of the required languages to the test team. Otherwise, obtain ready access to such native speakers for the duration of testing.
- Perform:
  - ♦ Develop foreign-language and symbol test data.
  - ♦ Execute tests covering the internationalization requirements using this internationalization test data.
- Verify:
  - ♦ Determine whether the test planning documentation adequately addresses internationalization testing.
  - ♦ Determine whether the test teams have identified all internationalization requirements.
  - ♦ Determine whether the test teams either have one or more foreign SMEs as members of their team or have access to such SMEs.
  - ♦ Determine whether the test teams are developing test cases using foreign data as inputs.
  - ♦ Determine whether testing techniques appropriate for internationalization testing are being correctly used.
  - ♦ Determine whether the internationalization tests are being executed.

Related Pitfalls   Incomplete Test Planning (GEN-TPS-2)

INADEQUATE INTEROPERABILITY TESTING (TTS-SPC-4)

Description   Testers perform little or no interoperability testing to determine the degree to which the system or software successfully interfaces and collaborates with other systems.

Potential Applicability   This pitfall is potentially applicable whenever the system or software under test (SUT) must interoperate with other systems.

Characteristic Symptoms

- Interoperability requirements are missing, ambiguous, or superficial.
- Interface requirements are missing, incomplete, or ambiguous.
- Testing of data/control interfaces is incomplete.
    - Data/control interfaces are not verified at the semantic level, only at the syntax or protocol level.
    - Data types of input and output data are not verified.
    - The content and format of input and output data or files are not verified.
    - Fault and failure tolerance at the system boundary is not verified (for example, compatibility of error codes and exceptions).
    - Testing of data/control interfaces is stopped after verifying that a handshake was established without checking associated data's content and format.
- Data/control interface protocols are not verified at all seven layers of the Open Systems Interconnection (OSI) model.
- Testing of electrical interfaces is incomplete:
    - Electrical interfaces may not be verified in terms of voltage, amperage ranges, AC versus DC, frequency, conditioning (for example, lack of surges, spikes, and slumps), and so on.
    - Developers or testers may believe that if the plugs match (that is, if you can physically connect the wires), then the electrical characteristics are compatible.
- Hydraulic interfaces may not be checked in terms of pressure compatibility.
- There are few, if any, tests traced back to interoperability requirements.

Potential Negative Consequences

- Interoperability and interface testing is incomplete.
- Testing fails to uncover some interoperability and interface defects.
- Trustworthy test data to verify system or software interoperability are not created.
- The system or software does not meet all of its interoperability requirements.
- The system or software has inadequate interoperability.
- Management, developers, and other stakeholders have false confidence that the system or software is sufficiently interoperable.

- Interoperability and interface failures occur and the associated defects are uncovered during acceptance testing, operational testing, and once the system or software has been placed into operation.

Potential Causes

- Interoperability and interface testing were not addressed in any of the test planning documentation.
- Too many interoperability and interface requirements were not specified or were poorly specified.
- Testers did not have sufficient training and expertise in:
  - Interoperability and its quality attributes
  - Common interoperability defects, faults, and failures
  - Commonly used architectural patterns to achieve adequate interoperability
  - Interoperability and interface testing
- Testing was rushed due to schedule pressures; so external interfaces were only minimally tested.

Recommendations

- **Prepare:**
  - Address interface and interoperability testing in the system or software test plans.
- **Enable:**
  - Ensure that all interoperability and interface requirements are properly identified and specified.
  - Ensure that the relevant test environments either connect to the external systems or properly simulate or emulate the external systems.
- **Perform:**
  - Test the protocols, syntax, and semantics of system-external interfaces.
  - Test whether the inputs from external systems enable the SUT to meet its requirements.
  - Test whether the outputs of the SUT enable external systems to meet their requirements.
- **Verify:**
  - Determine whether the test planning documentation adequately addresses testing of interoperability and interface requirements.
  - Determine whether adequate interoperability and interface requirements are specified to enable testing them.
  - Determine whether testing techniques appropriate for interoperability testing are being correctly used.

TTS-SPC-4   Inadequate Interoperability Testing

- Determine whether adequate interoperability and interface testing is being performed.

Related Pitfalls Incomplete Test Planning (GEN-TPS-2)

INADEQUATE PERFORMANCE TESTING (TTS-SPC-5)

Description Testers perform little or no performance testing to determine the degree to which the system or software has adequate levels of the performance quality attributes: event schedulability, jitter, latency, response time, and throughput.

Potential Applicability This pitfall is always potentially applicable, especially when there are performance requirements or when testing a hard- or soft-real-time system.

Characteristic Symptoms

- Performance requirements are not specified for all performance quality attributes, and little or no testing of these attributes is performed: event schedulability, jitter, latency, response time, and throughput.
- There is little or no performance testing or testing to determine if performance degrades gracefully.
- There is little or no verification of adequate performance-related computational resources.[94]
- Performance testing is performed using a low-fidelity environment.
- There are few, if any, tests traced back to performance requirements.

Potential Negative Consequences

- Performance testing is incomplete.
- Testing fails to uncover some performance defects.
- Trustworthy test data to enable estimating system or software performance are not collected.
- The system or software does not meet all of its performance requirements.
- The system or software has inadequate performance.
- Management, developers, and other stakeholders have false confidence that the system or software has sufficient performance based on adequate performance under normal testing involving nominal loads and only a subset of operational profiles.

- Performance failures occur and the associated defects are uncovered during acceptance testing, operational testing, and once the system or software has been placed into operation.

Potential Causes

- Performance testing was not addressed in any of the test planning documentation.
- Too many performance requirements were not specified or were poorly specified without any verifiable thresholds.
- Testers did not have sufficient training and expertise in:
  - Performance and its quality attributes, including jitter, latency, response time, schedulability, and throughput
  - Common performance defects, faults, and failures
  - Commonly used architectural patterns to achieve adequate performance
  - Performance testing
- Testing performance requirements was more difficult than testing functional requirements.
- Testers had inadequate tool support for executing performance tests.
- There was confusion about who was responsible for testing performance requirements: the development independent product teams (IPTs), the independent test team(s), or the specialty engineering performance engineer(s).
- Testing quality requirements (including performance requirements):
  - Was considered less important than testing functional requirements
  - Had to wait until testing functional requirements was complete
- Performance testing was never allocated sufficient resources because there were insufficient resources to do normal integration and system testing of functional requirements.

Recommendations

- Prepare:
  - Address performance testing in the test planning documentation.
  - Read the performance requirements.
  - Determine how the system architecture supports meeting the performance requirements.
- Enable:
  - Create realistic workload models under all relevant operational profiles.
  - Ensure that all performance requirements are properly identified and specified.
  - Evaluate performance testing tools for adequacy when testing performance requirements.

- **Perform:**
  - Create or use existing (for example, COTS or open source) performance tools, such as a <u>System Level Exerciser</u> (SLE), to manage, schedule, perform, monitor, and report the results of performance tests.
  - As appropriate, run single thread, multi-thread, and multi-processor (or core) tests.
  - Measure performance under both nominal conditions and exceptional (that is, fault- and failure-tolerance) conditions, as well as under conditions of peak loading and graceful degradation.
- **Verify:**
  - Determine whether performance testing has been adequately addressed in the test planning documentation.
  - Determine whether the testers have adequate expertise in and experience with performance requirements, commonly used performance architectural decisions, types of performance defects and failures, and how to do performance testing.
  - Determine whether the performance requirements have been sufficiently specified to drive performance testing.
  - Determine whether the architecture has been sufficiently documented to drive performance testing.
  - Determine whether sufficient test environment(s), including associated test tools, exist for executing performance tests.
  - Determine whether performance testing (for example, test-case selection and test-case completion criteria) is based on a proper performance analysis.
  - Determine whether testing techniques appropriate for performance testing are being correctly used.
  - Determine whether all performance requirements have been adequately tested, including all relevant performance attributes, operational profiles, and credible workloads.

Related Pitfalls   Incomplete Test Planning (GEN-TPS-2), Inadequate Concurrency Testing (TTS-SPC-2)

INADEQUATE RELIABILITY TESTING (TTS-SPC-6)

Description   Testers perform little or no long-duration reliability testing under operational profiles and based on the results of any reliability models to determine the degree to which the system or software continues to function over time without failure.[95]

Potential Applicability   This pitfall is always potentially applicable, especially when there are reliability requirements.

Characteristic Symptoms

- There is little or no long-duration reliability testing.
- Any reliability testing is not performed under operational profiles and is not based on the results of any reliability models.
- There are few, if any, tests traced back to reliability requirements.

Potential Negative Consequences

- Reliability testing is incomplete.
- Testing fails to uncover some reliability defects.
- Trustworthy test data to enable estimating system or software reliability are not collected.
- The system or software does not meet all of its reliability requirements.
- The system or software is insufficiently reliable.
- Management, developers, and other stakeholders have false confidence that the system or software is sufficiently reliable.
- Reliability failures occur and the associated defects are uncovered during acceptance testing, operational testing, and once the system or software has been placed into operation.

Potential Causes

- Reliability testing was not addressed in any of the test planning documentation.
- Too many reliability requirements were not specified or were poorly specified; that is, without any verifiable thresholds.
- Testers did not have sufficient training and expertise in:
  - Reliability and its quality attributes
  - Common reliability defects, faults, and failures
  - Commonly used architectural patterns to achieve adequate reliability
  - Reliability testing
- Testing reliability requirements is more difficult than testing functional requirements.
- Testers had inadequate tool support for performing reliability tests (that is, for performing long-term endurance testing).

- There was confusion about who was responsible for testing reliability requirements: the development IPTs, the independent test team(s), or the specialty engineering reliability engineer(s).
- Testing quality requirements (including reliability requirements):
  - Was considered less important than testing functional requirements
  - Had to wait until the functional requirements testing was complete
- There were insufficient resources to do normal integration and system testing of functional requirements, and reliability testing was thus never allocated sufficient resources.

Recommendations

- **Prepare:**
  - Address reliability testing in the test planning documentation.
  - Read the reliability requirements.
  - Determine how the system architecture supports meeting the reliability requirements.
- **Enable:**
  - Ensure that all reliability requirements are properly identified and specified.
  - Evaluate reliability testing tools for adequacy when testing reliability requirements.
- **Perform:**
  - Perform sufficient reliability testing to verify the reliability requirements.
  - To the degree that testing, as opposed to analysis, is practical as a verification method, perform reliability testing using credible operational profiles and credible workloads.
  - Perform reliability testing for a sufficiently long duration (also known as soak tests).
- **Verify:**
  - Determine whether reliability testing has been adequately addressed in the test planning documentation.
  - Determine whether the testers have adequate expertise in and experience with reliability requirements, commonly used architectural decisions to achieve adequate reliability, types of reliability defects and failures, and how to perform reliability testing.
  - Determine whether the reliability requirements have been sufficiently specified to drive reliability testing.
  - Determine whether the architecture has been sufficiently documented to drive reliability testing.

TTS-SPC-6   Inadequate Reliability Testing

- Determine whether sufficient test environment(s), including associated test tools, exist for performing reliability testing.
- Determine whether reliability testing (for example, test-case-selection and test-case-completion criteria) is based on proper reliability analysis, such as abnormal (that is, fault, degraded mode, and failure) use case paths, Event Tree Analysis (ETA), Fault Tree Analysis (FTA), or Failure Modes Effects and Criticality Analysis (FMECA).
- Determine whether all reliability requirements have been adequately tested using credible operational profiles and credible workloads.

Related Pitfalls   Incomplete Test Planning (GEN-TPS-2), Inadequate Robustness Testing (TTS-SPC-7)

INADEQUATE ROBUSTNESS TESTING (TTS-SPC-7)

Description   Testers perform little or no robustness testing based on the results of robustness models to determine the degree to which the system or software exhibits adequate error, fault, failure, and environmental tolerance.

Potential Applicability   This pitfall is always potentially applicable, especially when there are robustness requirements.

Characteristic Symptoms
- There is little or no *robustness* testing, such as:
  - **Error-tolerance testing** to determine whether the system properly detects and reacts to input errors (for example, input data of the wrong type or outside of the correct ranges, inputs received while the system is in an inappropriate state or mode)
  - **Fault-tolerance testing** to determine whether the system properly detects and reacts to system faults (for example, incorrect internal states or incorrect internal data)
  - **Failure-tolerance testing** to determine whether the system properly detects and reacts to system failures (that is, the system does not meet its requirements)
  - **Environmental-tolerance testing** to determine whether the system properly detects and reacts to dangerous environmental conditions (such as ambient temperatures, pressures, radiation levels, vibration, acceleration, and the presence of corrosive salt water).
- The robustness test cases are postponed until all of the normal (sunny-day) paths through the system's mission threads and use cases are implemented and tested, which does not provide sufficient time to do adequate robustness testing.[96]

- There are few, if any, tests traced back to robustness requirements.
- Robustness testing is not based on robustness analysis such as abnormal (that is, fault, degraded mode, and failure) use case paths, Event Tree Analysis (ETA), Fault Tree Analysis (FTA), or Failure Modes Effects Criticality Analysis (FMECA).

Potential Negative Consequences

- Robustness testing is incomplete.
- Testing fails to uncover some robustness (that is, error-, fault-, failure-, and environmental-tolerance) defects.
- Trustworthy test data to enable estimating system or software robustness are not collected.
- The system or software does not meet all of its robustness requirements.
- The system or software has inadequate robustness and does not properly:
  - Detect all errors, faults, or failures
  - Handle all errors, faults, or failures (for example, exceptions are not raised or error messages are either not communicated at all or are cryptic)
- Management, developers, and other stakeholders have false confidence that the system or software is sufficiently robust.
- Robustness failures occur and the associated defects are uncovered during acceptance testing, operational testing, and once the system or software has been placed into operation.

Potential Causes

- Robustness testing was not addressed in any of the test planning documentation.
- Too many robustness requirements were not specified or were poorly specified, without any verifiable thresholds.
- Testers did not have sufficient training and expertise in:
  - Robustness and its quality attributes, such as fault and failure tolerance
  - Common robustness defects, faults, and failures
  - Commonly used architectural patterns to achieve adequate robustness
  - Robustness testing
- Testing robustness requirements (rainy-day situations) is more difficult than testing sunny-day functional requirements.

- There was insufficient time to perform boundary-value testing that checks (among other things) how the system handles inputs at and just outside of the boundaries of equivalence classes of test input data.

- Once the system is integrated, its internals are encapsulated, which decreases testability by making it more difficult to:
  - Cause internal faults (that is, less controllability)
  - Observe the handling of internal faults (that is, less observability)

- Testers had inadequate tool support for performing robustness tests (that is, for inputting exceptions or for observing exception handling).

- Testers had inadequate test environments and facilities to test environmental tolerance (for example, ionizing and nonionizing radiation, temperature, vacuum, and vibration).

- There was confusion about who is responsible for testing robustness requirements: the development integrated product teams (IPTs), the independent test team(s), or the specialty engineering robustness engineer(s).

- Testing quality requirements (including robustness requirements):
  - Was considered less important than testing functional requirements
  - Had to wait until the functional requirements testing was complete

- Robustness testing was not allocated sufficient resources because there were insufficient resources to do normal integration and system testing of the functional requirements.

Recommendations

- **Prepare:**
  - Address robustness testing in the test planning documentation.
  - Read the robustness (that is, error-, fault-, failure-, and environmental-tolerance) requirements.
  - Determine how the system architecture supports meeting the robustness requirements.

- **Enable:**
  - Ensure that all robustness requirements are properly identified and specified.
  - Ensure that testers are aware of programming approaches to handling invalid data (for example, input data validation and exception handling) and testing techniques for performing associated testing (for example, boundary-value testing).
  - Evaluate robustness testing tools (for example, tools to raise exceptions or cause assertions to be violated) for adequacy when testing robustness requirements.

- **Perform:**
  - Base the test cases on an analysis of credible off-nominal situations.

- Perform sufficient robustness testing to verify
  - Robustness requirements
  - That the system exhibits sufficient error, fault, failure, and environmental tolerance
  - Behavior at and just outside of the boundaries of valid input data
- Where appropriate, incorporate test hooks, built-in test (BIT), fault logging (possibly triggered by exception handling, prognostics and health management (PHM) function or subsystem, or some other way to overcome information hiding in order to verify test-case preconditions and postconditions.
- To the extent practical, test the system's support for robustness during unit and integration testing when it is easier to provide off-nominal test inputs (for example, raise exceptions) and observe the system's responses.
- Use a test or logging system mode (if one exists).

- **Verify:**
  - Determine whether robustness testing is adequately addressed in the test planning documentation.
  - Determine whether the testers have adequate expertise in and experience with robustness requirements, including commonly used architectural decisions to achieve adequate robustness, types of robustness defects and failures, and how to perform robustness testing.
  - Determine whether the robustness requirements have been sufficiently specified and whether associated architecture and design decisions have been sufficiently documented to drive and support robustness testing.
  - Determine whether sufficient test environment(s), including associated test tools, exist for performing robustness testing.
  - Determine whether adequate test-tool support exists or whether sufficient robustness (including error-, fault-, and failure-logging) is incorporated into the system to enable adequate testing for tolerance (for example, by causing encapsulated errors and faults and observing the resulting robustness).
  - Determine whether robustness testing (for example, test-case-selection and test-case-completion criteria) is based on proper robustness analysis, including such methods or techniques as abnormal (that is, fault, degraded-mode, and failure) use case paths, Event Tree Analysis (ETA), Fault Tree Analysis (FTA), or Failure Modes Effects Criticality Analysis (FMECA).
  - Determine whether all robustness requirements have been adequately tested using credible off-nominal conditions and events.

Related Pitfalls   Incomplete Test Planning (GEN-TPS-2)

INADEQUATE SAFETY TESTING (TTS-SPC-8)

Description   Testers perform little or no safety testing based on the results of a safety or hazard analysis to determine the degree to which the system or software is safe from causing or suffering accidental harm.

Potential Applicability   This pitfall is always potentially applicable, especially when there are safety requirements.

Characteristic Symptoms

- There is little or no:
  - ◆ Testing based on safety analysis (for example, abuse or mishap cases, event tree analysis [ETA], or fault tree analysis [FTA])
  - ◆ Testing of safeguards (for example, interlocks)
  - ◆ Testing of fail-safe behavior
  - ◆ Safety-specific testing, such as:
    - **Vulnerability Testing** to expose system vulnerabilities (that is, defects or weaknesses that can lead to accidents)[97]
    - **Hazard Testing** to determine if the system creates any hazards
    - **Mishap Testing** to determine if the system can trigger accidents or near misses

Potential Negative Consequences

- Safety testing is incomplete.
- Testing fails to uncover some safety defects (vulnerabilities).
- Trustworthy test data to enable estimating the system or software's degree of safety are not collected.
- The system or software does not meet all of its safety requirements.
- The system or software is not sufficiently safe.
- Management, developers, and other stakeholders have false confidence that the system or software is sufficiently safe.
- Safety failures (that is accidents and near misses) occur and the associated defects are uncovered during acceptance testing, operational testing, and once the system or software has been placed into operation.

Potential Causes

- Safety testing was not addressed in any of the test planning documentation.
- Too many safety requirements were not specified or were poorly specified, without any verifiable thresholds (for example, how safe the SUT needed to be or an acceptable hazard frequency).
- Testers did not have sufficient training and expertise in:
  - Safety and its quality attributes
  - Common safety defects, faults, and failures
  - Commonly used architectural patterns to achieve adequate safety
  - Safety testing
- Testing safety requirements was more difficult than testing typical functional requirements.
- Testers had inadequate tool support for performing safety tests (for example, modeling specific hazards or mishaps).
- There was confusion about who is responsible for testing safety requirements: the development integrated product teams (IPTs), the independent test team(s), or the specialty engineering safety engineer(s).
- Testing quality requirements (including safety requirements):
  - Was considered less important than testing functional requirements
  - Had to wait until the functional requirements testing was complete
- Sufficient resources were not allocated to safety testing because there were insufficient resources to do normal integration and system testing of functional requirements.

Recommendations

- Prepare:
  - Address safety testing in the test planning documentation.
  - Read the safety-related requirements (for example, requirements that imply potential vulnerabilities or hazards, safety subsystem- or function requirements, and safety constraints).
  - Determine how the system architecture supports meeting these safety-related requirements.
- Enable:
  - If it hasn't already been done, the requirements team should properly identify and specify all safety-related requirements.
  - If it hasn't already been done, the architecture team should properly incorporate safety and safeguards into the architecture.
  - Identify and profile all safety-related system actors not already identified and profiled by the requirements and architecture teams

- **Perform:**
  - Base the test cases on a proper safety analysis, including:
    - Methods such as asset analysis, mishap analysis, vulnerability analysis, misuser analysis, hazard analysis, safeguard analysis, and safety risk analysis
    - Techniques such as misuse cases, Event Tree Analysis (ETA), Fault Tree Analysis (FTA), Failure Modes Effects Criticality Analysis (FMECA), and Systems-Theoretic Accident Model and Processes (STAMP)
  - Perform sufficient black-box testing of all safety requirements and sufficient white-box testing of safeguards (for example, interlocks) and fail-safe behavior.
  - Perform sufficient safety testing to verify
    - The safety requirements
    - That the system conforms to the safety aspects of its architecture (for example, safeguard selection)
- **Verify:**
  - Determine whether safety testing has been adequately addressed in the test planning documentation.
  - Determine whether the testers have adequate expertise in and experience with safety requirements, commonly used architectural decisions to achieve adequate safety, types of safety vulnerabilities and failures, and how to perform safety testing.
  - Determine whether the safety requirements have been sufficiently specified to drive safety testing.
  - Determine whether the architecture has been sufficiently documented to support safety testing.
  - Determine whether appropriate test environment(s) exist for performing safety testing.
  - Determine whether safety testing (for example, test-case-selection and test-case-completion criteria) is based on the results of a safety analysis.
  - Determine whether testing techniques appropriate for safety testing are being correctly used.
  - Determine whether all safety requirements and architectural safeguards have been adequately tested using credible vulnerabilities and hazards.

Related Pitfalls Incomplete Test Planning (GEN-TPS-2), Inadequate Security Testing (TTS-SPC-9)

TTS-SPC-8   Inadequate Safety Testing

INADEQUATE SECURITY TESTING (TTS-SPC-9)

Description   Testers perform little or no security testing based on the results of a security or threat analysis to determine the degree to which the system or software is secure from causing or suffering malicious harm.

Potential Applicability   This pitfall is always potentially applicable, especially when there are security requirements.

Characteristic Symptoms

- There is little or no:
  - ◆ Testing based on security analysis (for example, attack trees, or abuse or misuse cases)
  - ◆ Testing of security controls (for example, access control, encryption or decryption, or intrusion detection)
  - ◆ Fail-secure behavior testing
  - ◆ Security-specific testing, such as:
    - • **Penetration Testing** to determine the degree to which an attacker can penetrate the system's defenses
    - • **Red Teaming,** in which a separate group plays the role of attackers and performs *authorized* attacks on the SUT to identify its vulnerabilities so that they can be removed or mitigated
    - • **Anti-Tamper Testing** to determine the degree to which the system is tamper-resistant[98] and tamper-evident and thereby whether the system meets its anti-tamper requirements
    - • **Vulnerability Testing** to identify system vulnerabilities (that is, defects or weaknesses)

Potential Negative Consequences

- Security testing is incomplete.
- Testing fails to uncover some security defects (vulnerabilities).[99]
- Trustworthy test data to enable estimating the system or software's degree of security are not collected.
- The system or software does not meet all of its security requirements.
- The system or software is not sufficiently secure.

- Management, developers, and other stakeholders have false confidence that the system or software is sufficiently secure.
- Security failures occur and the associated defects are uncovered during acceptance testing, operational testing, and once the system or software has been placed into operation.

Potential Causes

- Security testing was not addressed in any of the test planning documentation.
- Too many security requirements were not specified or were poorly specified, without any verifiable thresholds (for example, how secure the SUT needed to be or a maximum acceptable vulnerability frequency).
- Testers did not have sufficient training and expertise in:
  - Security and its quality attributes
  - Common security defects, faults, and failures
  - Commonly used architectural patterns to achieve adequate security
  - Security testing (for example, penetration tests)
- Testing security requirements is more difficult than testing typical functional requirements.
- Testers had inadequate tool support for performing security tests (for example, tools for information gathering, network scanning, port scanning, password cracking, vulnerability scanning, privilege escalation, and reverse engineering).
- Testers were not granted written authority and a directive to "attack" a test version of the system.
- There was confusion about who was responsible for testing security requirements: the development integrated product teams (IPTs), the independent test team(s), or the specialty engineering security engineer(s).
- Testing quality requirements (including security requirements):
  - Was considered less important than testing functional requirements
  - Had to wait until functional requirements testing was complete
- Security testing was not allocated sufficient resources because there were insufficient resources to do normal integration and system testing of the functional requirements.

Recommendations

- Prepare:
  - Address security testing in the test planning documentation.
  - Read the security-related requirements (for example, requirements that imply potential vulnerabilities or threats, security subsystem or function requirements, and security constraints).

- Determine how the system architecture supports meeting these security-related requirements.
- **Enable:**
  - If it hasn't already been done, the requirements team should properly identify and specify all security-related requirements.
  - If it hasn't already been done, the architecture team should properly incorporate security and countermeasures into the architecture.
  - Identify and profile all security-related system actors (for example, attackers) not already identified and profiled by the requirements and architecture teams.
- **Perform:**
  - Base the test cases on a proper security analysis, including:
    - Methods such as asset analysis, misuse analysis, vulnerability analysis, misuser analysis, threat analysis, countermeasure analysis, and security risk analysis
    - Techniques such as abuse cases, attack surface identification, attack trees, and Systems-Theoretic Accident Model and Processes (STAMP)
  - Use static-vulnerability analysis tools to identify commonly occurring security vulnerabilities.
  - Perform sufficient:
    - Black-box testing of all security requirements
    - White-box testing of security features or subsystems, countermeasures (for example, access control, encryption) and fail-secure behavior
  - Perform sufficient security testing to verify:
    - The security requirements
    - That the system conforms to the security aspects of its architecture (for example, countermeasure selection and placement)
- **Verify:**
  - Determine whether security testing has been adequately addressed in the test planning documentation.
  - Determine whether the testers have adequate expertise in and experience with security requirements, commonly used architectural decisions to achieve adequate security, types of security vulnerabilities and failures, and how to perform security testing.
  - Determine whether the security requirements have been sufficiently specified to drive security testing.
  - Determine whether the architecture has been sufficiently documented to support security testing.
  - Determine whether appropriate test environment(s) exist for performing security testing.

- Determine whether security testing (for example, test-case-selection and test-case-completion criteria) is based on the results of a proper security analysis.
- Determine whether testing techniques appropriate for security testing are being correctly used.
- Determine whether all security requirements and architectural countermeasures have been adequately tested using credible vulnerabilities and threats.

Related Pitfalls   Incomplete Test Planning (GEN-TPS-2), Inadequate Safety Testing (TTS-SPC-8)

INADEQUATE USABILITY TESTING (TTS-SPC-10)

Description   Testers or usability engineers perform little or no usability testing to determine the degree to which the system's human-machine interfaces meet the system's requirements for usability, manpower, personnel, training, human factors engineering (HFE), and habitability.

Potential Applicability   This pitfall is always potentially applicable, especially when there are usability requirements (for example, whenever humans interact with the system).

Characteristic Symptoms
- Instead of actual usability testing, the user interface is prototyped, shown to potential users, and iterated until it is deemed acceptable.
- There is little or no explicit usability testing of the system's or software's human-machine interfaces, including testing the:
  - **Usability requirements and architecture**, or the quality attributes of usability, such as: accessibility, attractiveness (or engageability, preference, and stickiness[100]), credibility (trustworthiness), differentiation, ease of entry, ease of location, ease of remembering, effectiveness, effort minimization, error minimization, predictability, learnability, navigability, retrievability, suitability (appropriateness), understandability, and user satisfaction.
  - **Manpower requirements**, or the number and types of personnel (roles played) needed to properly train, operate, and maintain or sustain the system
  - **Personnel requirements**, such as the expertise (knowledge and skills), experience, and physical abilities needed to properly train, operate, and maintain or sustain the system
  - **Training requirements**, including the required knowledge and skills that different personnel need to properly train, operate, and maintain or sustain the system

- **Human factors engineering (HFE) requirements and architecture,** which address human capabilities and limitations (for example, cognitive, physical, sensory, and social) and their effect on people's ability to properly train, operate, and maintain or sustain the system
    - **Habitability requirements and architecture,** or the system-internal living and working conditions needed for human health, comfort, and morale. [101]
- There are no usability requirements on which to base usability testing.
    - Usability defects are based on user complaints during operational testing and operation rather than on violations of usability requirements.
    - The testers are writing new usability requirements based on user complaints.

Potential Negative Consequences

- Usability testing is incomplete.
- Testing fails to uncover some usability defects.
- Trustworthy test data to enable estimating the system or software's usability are not collected.
- The system or software does not meet all of its usability requirements.

    - The system or software is not sufficiently usable.
- Management, developers, and other stakeholders have false confidence that the system or software is sufficiently usable.
- Usability failures occur and the associated defects are uncovered during acceptance testing, operational testing, and once the system or software has been placed into operation.

Potential Causes

- Usability testing was not addressed in any of the test planning documentation.
- Too many usability requirements were not specified or were poorly specified, without any verifiable thresholds (for example, how usable the SUT needed to be, and usable in what ways).
- Testers did not have sufficient training and expertise in:
    - Usability and its quality attributes
    - Common usability defects, faults, and failures

TTS-SPC-10   Inadequate Usability Testing

- ◆ Commonly used architectural patterns to achieve adequate usability
  - ◆ Usability testing (for example, A/B testing and hallway intercept testing)
- Testing usability requirements was more difficult than testing typical functional requirements.
- Testers had inadequate stakeholder support for performing usability tests (for example, access to representative users).
- There was confusion about who was responsible for testing usability requirements: the development integrated product teams (IPTs), the independent test team(s), or the specialty engineering usability or human factors engineer(s).
- Testing quality requirements (including usability requirements):
  - ◆ Was considered less important than testing functional requirements
  - ◆ Had to wait until functional requirements testing was complete
- Usability testing was not allocated sufficient resources because there were insufficient resources to do normal integration and system testing of the functional requirements.
- Usability defects slipped past developmental testing to operational testing because development testers did not have experience using similar or earlier versions of the SUT and therefore had difficulty spotting usability defects.

Recommendations

- **Prepare:**
  - ◆ Address usability testing in the test planning documentation.
  - ◆ Read the usability requirements.
  - ◆ Determine how the system architecture and user-interface design support meets the usability requirements.
- **Enable:**
  - ◆ Ensure that all usability requirements are properly identified and specified with thresholds (that is, acceptance criteria).
- **Perform:**
  - ◆ Perform sufficient usability testing of the human interfaces, including testing for all relevant usability attributes such as accessibility, attractiveness (engageability, preference, and stickiness), credibility (trustworthiness), differentiation, ease of entry, ease of location, ease of remembering, effectiveness, effort minimization, error minimization, learnability, navigability, retrievability, suitability (appropriateness), understandability, and user satisfaction.
  - ◆ Temporarily use operator training as a workaround for usability defects that slip through usability testing.

TTS-SPC-10 Inadequate Usability Testing

- Verify:
    - Determine whether usability testing is adequately addressed in the test planning documentation.
    - Determine whether the testers have adequate expertise in and experience with usability requirements, commonly used architectural and design patterns to achieve adequate usability, types of usability defects and failures, and how to perform usability testing.
    - Determine whether the usability requirements have been sufficiently specified to drive usability testing.
    - Determine whether the architecture and design is sufficiently documented to support usability testing.
    - Determine whether appropriate test environment(s) exist for performing usability testing.
    - Determine whether testing techniques appropriate for usability testing are being correctly used.
    - Determine whether all usability requirements and usability-related architectural and design decisions have been adequately tested using typical and atypical operational profiles.

Related Pitfalls   Incomplete Test Planning (GEN-TPS-2), Inappropriate External Pressures (GEN-MGMT-2), Inconvenient Test Results Ignored (GEN-MGMT-5)

3.4.4   System Testing Pitfalls

The very nature of system testing often ensures that at least one of these pitfalls cannot be eliminated. At best, the recommended solutions can only mitigate their negative consequences.

The following testing pitfalls are specifically related to system testing:

- Test Hooks Remain (TTS-SYS-1)
- Lack of Test Hooks (TTS-SYS-2)
- Inadequate End-to-End Testing (TTS-SYS-3)

TEST HOOKS REMAIN (TTS-SYS-1)

Description   Testers fail to remove temporary test hooks after completing testing, so they remain in the delivered or fielded system.

Potential Applicability   This pitfall is potentially applicable whenever temporary test hooks are incorporated to support testing.

Characteristic Symptoms

- An attack that exploits an overlooked test interface is detected.
- The system fails as a result of maintenance during which the test interface is removed, which thereby breaks later-added software that unfortunately depended on the test interface.
- The remaining test interface is discovered during a code review (for example, during an impact analysis made prior to changing baselined software).

Potential Negative Consequences

- The test hooks become security vulnerabilities (for example, trapdoors) that provide attackers with a way to access the system that bypasses existing countermeasures. Such vulnerabilities are design or implementation defects.
- Developers may come to rely on these "temporary" test interfaces so that their software breaks when the test interface is removed.

Potential Causes

- The testers were careless when removing temporary test interfaces.
- The testers were rushed due to inadequate time for testing prior to delivery.
- A tester maliciously incorporated a trapdoor that he or she could misuse later (for example, to perform sabotage if fired).
- For various reasons, the system could not be certified as safe or secure because the delivered system would be different from the system tested once the test hooks were removed after testing was complete.

Recommendations

- **Prepare:**
  - Decide how to avoid this pitfall during test planning.
- **Enable:**
  - Keep an up-to-date record of all test interfaces so that none fall through the cracks when it is time to remove them.
- **Perform:**
  - Remove all temporary test interfaces prior to user acceptance testing, operational testing, and delivery.

- ◆ Where practical, use test tools that automatically insert and remove test interfaces rather than relying on manual insertion and removal, which is susceptible to human error.
- ▪ Verify:
  - ◆ Determine whether all temporary test interfaces have been removed prior to user acceptance testing, operational testing, and delivery.

Related Pitfalls   Lack of Test Hooks (TTS-SYS-2)

LACK OF TEST HOOKS (TTS-SYS-2)

Description   Testers fail to take into account how a lack of test hooks makes it more difficult to test parts of the system that are hidden via information hiding. [102]

Potential Applicability   This pitfall is potentially always applicable.

Characteristic Symptoms

- ▪ Incorporating test hooks such as test interfaces and test modes is prohibited by architecture and design guidelines (for example, for safety and security reasons).
- ▪ Test hooks have been removed prior to system testing (for example, for performance, safety, or security reasons).

Potential Negative Consequences

- ▪ The lack of test hooks makes it difficult to test requirements, architecture, and design decisions that are encapsulated and hidden behind the system's external interfaces.
- ▪ Such locally implemented requirements, architecture, and design decisions are not verified at the system level because of decreased testability due to the resulting low controllability and observability.

Potential Causes

- ▪ The lack of test hooks made it difficult to test encapsulated software and locally implemented requirements.

Recommendations

- **Prepare:**
  - ◆ Address how to overcome the limitations of encapsulation during system testing in the system-level functional testing part of the system test planning documentation.
- **Enable:**
  - ◆ Obtain test tools that provide test access to encapsulated software.
  - ◆ Add a testing mode to the system.
  - ◆ Update the system architecture to add:
    - Built-in test (BIT) capabilities
    - Prognostics and Health Management (PHM) functions or subsystem(s)
    - Error logging and reporting capabilities
- **Perform:**
  - ◆ Use one of the previously mentioned approaches to compensate for the encapsulation resulting from system integration.
  - ◆ Use unit and integration testing to adequately test locally implemented and encapsulated requirements that are difficult to verify during system testing.
- **Verify:**
  - ◆ Determine whether unit and integration testing have been used to adequately test locally implemented and encapsulated requirements, architecture, and design decisions.

Related Pitfalls   Test Hooks Remain (TTS-SYS-1)

INADEQUATE END-TO-END TESTING (TTS-SYS-3)

Description   Testers perform inadequate system-level functional testing of a system's end-to-end support for its missions.

Potential Applicability   This pitfall is always potentially applicable, especially when the system must interact with multiple external actors (that is, roles played by people and other systems) to achieve its missions (that is, when mission threads weaving multiple use cases are needed to model overall system behavior).[103]

Characteristic Symptoms

- There is little or no testing of end-to-end mission threads.
- Testing system functionality is based on individual use case paths.

Potential Negative Consequences

- Testing does not elicit system failures due to the improper interaction of multiple functions and external actors needed to support an overall system mission.
- Such subtle defects are not identified until after the system is placed into operation.

Potential Causes

- Functional testing was based on individual, specifically detailed functional requirements, whereby multiple functional requirements must be properly implemented to support an overall system mission.
- Tests of system functionality were based on use case modeling rather than mission-thread modeling.
- Schedule slippage caused end-to-end mission-thread system testing to be greatly limited, eliminated completely, or postponed until acceptance testing or operational testing.

Recommendations

- Prepare:
  - Incorporate mission-thread-based testing in the test planning documentation.
- Enable:
  - Train the system test team in mission-thread modeling.
  - Ensure that the requirements team collaborates with the testing team to perform sufficient mission-thread modeling during requirements analysis.
- Perform:
  - Perform mission-thread modeling as a part of test analysis if it is not performed during requirements analysis.
  - Develop test cases that exercise both nominal and off-nominal mission threads in order to verify the system's end-to-end support for its missions.
  - Perform the associated mission-thread testing.
- Verify:
  - Determine whether mission-thread testing is addressed in the test planning documentation.

- Determine whether the test team has sufficient training and expertise in mission-thread-based modeling and testing.
- Determine whether sufficient mission-thread modeling is being performed.
- Determine whether sufficient mission-thread testing is taking place.
  - Determine whether sufficient off-nominal mission threads have been adequately tested.

Related Pitfalls   Inadequate SoS Test Planning (TTS-SoS-1), Unclear SoS Testing Responsibilities (TTS-SoS-2), Inadequate Resources for SoS Testing (TTS-SoS-3)

3.4.5   System of Systems (SoS) Testing Pitfalls

The term *system of systems* (SoS) usually means more than merely what the words imply (that is, any collection of interacting systems). Usually the term is restricted to mean only systems composed of independently governed (that is, separately developed, funded, and scheduled) systems. Therefore, the term usually does not apply to a system that is either developed by a single prime contractor or integrated by a single system integrator using subsystems developed by subcontractors or vendors.

The following SoS-level pitfalls have very similar and analogous system-level pitfalls. For example, Inadequate SoS Test Planning (TTS-SoS-1) is highly related to No Separate Test Planning Documentation (GEN-TPS-1) and GEN-TPS-2 Incomplete Test Planning. However, the situation with a system of systems is sufficiently different from that of individual systems as to deserve its own pitfalls. For example, whereas a system-development project is highly likely to perform system-level testing, this is often not the case with SoS-level testing.

The following testing pitfalls are related to SoS testing and are not applicable unless one is concerned with testing an SoS:

- Inadequate SoS Test Planning (TTS-SoS-1)
- Unclear SoS Testing Responsibilities (TTS-SoS-2)
- Inadequate Resources for SoS Testing (TTS-SoS-3)
- SoS Testing Not Properly Scheduled (TTS-SoS-4)
- Inadequate SoS Requirements (TTS-SoS-5)
- Inadequate Support from Individual System Projects (TTS-SoS-6)
- Inadequate Defect Tracking Across Projects (TTS-SoS-7)
- Finger-Pointing (TTS-SoS-8)

TTS-SYS-3   Inadequate End-To-End Testing

INADEQUATE SoS TEST PLANNING (TTS-SoS-1)

Description Testers and SoS architects perform an inadequate amount of SoS test planning and fail to appropriately document their plans in SoS-level test planning documentation.

Potential Applicability This pitfall is potentially applicable anytime that an SoS is being tested.

Characteristic Symptoms

- There is *no* separate SoS-level test planning documentation.
- There is no SoS System Engineering Management Plan (SEMP) or SoS Development Plan (SoSDP) that addresses plans for SoS-level testing.
- There are only incomplete high-level overviews of SoS testing in the SoS SEMP or SoSDP.

Potential Negative Consequences

- There are no clear test responsibilities, objectives, methods, techniques, and completion or acceptance criteria at the SoS level.
- It is unclear which project, organization, team, or individual is responsible for performing the different SoS testing tasks.
- Adequate resources (funding, staffing, and schedule) are not made available for SoS testing.
- SoS testing is inadequate.
- There are numerous system-to-system interface defects causing end-to-end mission threads to fail.

Potential Causes

- There was little, if any, governance at the SoS level.
- Little or no test planning occurred above the individual system level.
- The SoS testing tasks were not determined, planned for, or documented.

Recommendations

- Prepare:
  - ◆ Determine the level of testing that is taking place at the system level.
  - ◆ Reuse or create a standard template and content or format standard for the SoS test planning documentation.
  - ◆ Include the SoS test planning documentation as a deliverable work product in the SoS integration project's contract.
  - ◆ Include the delivery of the SoS test planning documentation in the SoS project's master schedule (for example, as part of major milestones).
- Enable:
  - ◆ To the extent practical, ensure close and regular communication (for example, via status or working meetings and participation in major reviews) between the various system-level test organizations or teams.
- Perform:
  - ◆ Perform sufficient test planning at the SoS level.
  - ◆ Create SoS test planning documentation to ensure that sufficient test planning has occurred at the SoS level.
- Verify:
  - ◆ Determine whether SoS test planning documentation exists and is complete.

Related Pitfalls   No Separate Test Planning Documentation (GEN-TPS-1), Incomplete Test Planning (GEN-TPS-2)

UNCLEAR SoS TESTING RESPONSIBILITIES (TTS-SoS-2)

Description   Managers or testers fail to clearly define and document the responsibilities for performing end-to-end system of systems (SoS) testing.

Potential Applicability   This pitfall is potentially applicable anytime that an SoS is being tested.

Characteristic Symptoms

- No system of systems test planning documentation exists.
- No project or test team is explicitly tasked with testing end-to-end SoS behavior.
- There is disagreement among different project teams regarding who is responsible for performing system of systems testing.

Potential Negative Consequences

- No project has planned to provide the needed resources (for example, staffing, budget, and time in the schedule) for SoS testing.
- Adequate SoS testing is unlikely to be performed.
- The operational SoS includes SoS-integration-level defects.
- The SoS is unlikely to meet its schedule for deployment of new or updated capabilities.

Potential Causes

- There was no overall SoS-level test planning documentation.
- The overall SoS had neither centralized nor coordinated governance.

Recommendations

- **Prepare:**
  - Develop SoS test planning documentation that explicitly documents which organization(s) and team(s) are responsible for what parts of SoS-level testing.
- **Enable:**
  - To the extent practical, ensure close and regular communication (for example, via status or working meetings and participation in major reviews) between the various system-level test organizations or teams.
- **Perform:**
  - Create an SoS-level test organization or team that is specifically responsible for performing end-to-end SoS-level testing.
  - Provide the SoS-level test organization with the resources needed to perform SoS-level testing, including adequate:
    - Staffing
    - Budget
    - Schedule
    - Test tools, environments or test beds, and labs or facilities
  - Explicitly assign the individual system development or system update projects the responsibility for coordinating and collaborating with the SoS test organization or team.
  - Clearly communicate the responsibilities of the SoS test organization or team and the individual projects to all stakeholders.

- Verify:
    - Determine whether SoS-level test planning documentation exists.
    - Determine whether SoS-level test planning documentation adequately addresses the responsibilities of the projects, organizations, and teams responsible for SoS testing.
    - Determine whether regular communication concerning SoS-level testing is occurring.
    - Determine whether this communication is adequate to coordinate the testing efforts of the relevant projects, organizations, and teams.
    - Determine whether SoS-level test organization(s) and team(s) exist.
    - Determine whether these organization(s) and team(s) have adequate resources to properly perform SoS-level testing.
    - Determine whether responsibilities for performing and supporting SoS-level testing has been explicitly assigned, documented, and communicated.

Related Pitfalls   Unclear Testing Responsibilities (GEN-TOP-2)

INADEQUATE RESOURCES FOR SOS TESTING (TTS-SOS-3)

Description   Management fails to provide adequate resources for system of systems (SoS) testing.

Potential Applicability   This pitfall is potentially applicable anytime that an SoS is being tested.

Characteristic Symptoms

- If one or more SoS test organizations or team(s) exist:
    - There is inadequate staffing assigned to the SoS test organization or team(s).
    - The staffing assigned to the SoS test organization or team(s) has inadequate training, expertise, and experience to properly perform SoS-level testing.
    - Inadequate funding has been provided to SoS test organization or team(s).
    - Inadequate schedule has been allocated to SoS test organization or team(s).
    - Inadequate test environments and tools have been provided to SoS test organization or team(s).
- If the test teams of the individual projects have been assigned the responsibility of either performing or supporting SoS-level testing, then:
    - There is inadequate staffing assigned to these projects for this purpose.
    - The project staffing responsible for SoS-level testing has inadequate training, expertise, and experience to properly perform SoS-level testing.

- Inadequate funding has been provided to these projects for this purpose.
- Inadequate schedule has been allocated to these projects for this purpose.
- Inadequate test environments and tools have been provided to these projects for this purpose.

Potential Negative Consequences

- Little or no end-to-end SoS testing is performed.
- It is likely that residual system-to-system interface defects will cause failure end-to-end mission threads to fail.

Potential Causes

- No funding sources existed at the SoS-level.
- There was no policy or set of memoranda of understanding (MOUs) that required the separate system's projects to contribute funding to the SoS-level testing.
- No acquisition or development organization was responsible for the overall SoS and, therefore, testing the SoS.
- SoS-level testing was overlooked by the system-level projects.
- Stakeholders mistakenly assumed that the SoS would be adequately tested if its component systems passed system-level testing.

Recommendations

- Prepare:
  - Explicitly assign the responsibilities for performing and supporting SoS-level testing.
- Enable:
  - Communicate the importance of SoS-level testing to those who will potentially provide the resources for SoS-level testing.
- Perform:
  - Provide sufficient staffing to the organization(s) or team(s) responsible for SoS-testing.
  - Ensure that these people have adequate training, expertise, and experience to properly perform SoS-level testing.
  - Provide sufficient funding to the organization(s) or team(s) responsible for SoS-level testing.

- ◆ Provide sufficient time in the schedule for the organization(s) or team(s) responsible for SoS-level testing.
  - • Coordinate the SoS-level test schedule with the schedules of the individual system-level schedules.
- ◆ Provide sufficient test environments and tools to the organization(s) or team(s) responsible for SoS-level testing.

- ▪ **Verify:**
  - ◆ Determine whether the responsibilities for performing and supporting SoS-level testing has been officially determined, documented, and verbally communicated to all relevant stakeholders.
  - ◆ Determine whether those who will potentially provide the resources for SoS-level testing understand the importance of SoS-level testing and of providing sufficient resources for performing and supporting SoS-level testing.
  - ◆ Determine whether the organization(s) or team(s) responsible for SoS-testing have sufficient:
    - • Staffing
    - • Funding
    - • Time in the schedule
    - • Test environments and tools

Related Pitfalls   Lack of Stakeholder Commitment to Testing (GEN-SIC-3), SoS Testing Not Properly Scheduled (TTS-SoS-4)

SoS Testing Not Properly Scheduled (TTS-SoS-4)

Description   System of system testing is not properly scheduled and coordinated with the individual systems' testing and delivery schedules.

Potential Applicability   This pitfall is potentially applicable anytime that an SoS is being tested.

Characteristic Symptoms
- ▪ SoS testing is not in the individual systems' integrated master schedules.
- ▪ There is no SoS-level master schedule.
- ▪ SoS testing is being forced to fit into the uncoordinated schedules of the projects developing or updating the individual systems comprising the SoS.
- ▪ System-level integration and system testing is not coordinated among the system-level projects.

Potential Negative Consequences

- SoS testing that is not scheduled is unlikely to be performed.
- It is very difficult to obtain the correct versions of the different systems that comprise the SoS, which are needed in order to construct the test environments and execute the SoS-level tests.
- The configuration control of the SoS tests is unnecessarily complex in terms of the proper configurations of the component systems making up the overall SoS.
- If performed at all, it is likely that testing will be rushed, incomplete, and inadequate, with more mistakes than are typical.
- The operational SoS is likely to contain more SoS-integration defects and end-to-end mission-thread defects than is appropriate.

Potential Causes

- There was no overall acquisition or development organization responsible for the overall SoS.
- The individual system-level projects refused to give up independent control of their own project-level schedules, making it difficult to produce an overall test schedule that was consistent with the test and delivery schedules of the individual systems.
- There was a lack of schedule coordination:
  - Among the testing efforts of the individual system development projects
  - Between the testing efforts of the SoS project and the system projects

Recommendations

- Prepare:
  - Clearly communicate to the individual system development or system maintenance organizations their responsibilities regarding performing or supporting SoS-level testing.
- Enable:
  - To the extent practical, ensure close and regular communication (for example, via status or working meetings and participation in major reviews) between the various system-level test organizations or teams.
- Perform:
  - Include SoS testing on the SoS master schedule.
  - Coordinate SoS testing with the schedules of the individual systems.

- Include SoS testing on the individual systems' integrated master schedules so that support for SoS testing can be planned.
- **Verify:**
  - Determine whether the responsibilities for performing and supporting SoS testing have been explicitly assigned and clearly communicated.
  - Determine whether close and regular communication is taking place between the various system-level test organizations or teams.
  - Determine whether SoS testing is included on the SoS master schedule.
  - Determine whether SoS testing is on the individual systems' integrated master schedules.
  - Determine whether the schedule for SoS testing is being coordinated with the schedules of the individual systems.

Related Pitfalls   Inadequate Test Schedule (GEN-TPS-5)

INADEQUATE SOS REQUIREMENTS (TTS-SOS-5)

Description   Many SoS-level requirements are missing, are of poor quality, or are never officially approved or funded.

Potential Applicability   This pitfall is potentially applicable anytime that an SoS is being tested.

Characteristic Symptoms

- Little or no requirements exist above the system level.
- Many of the SoS-level requirements that do exist do not exhibit all of the characteristics of good requirements.
- The SoS-level requirements are not officially approved.
- The SoS-level requirements are ignored by the system-level projects.

Potential Negative Consequences

- Requirements-based SoS testing is difficult to perform because there is no officially approved set of SoS requirements to verify.
- System-level projects do not see the SoS requirements as relevant requirements and therefore feel that they can safely ignore them or indefinitely

postpone them to future increments. It is hard to develop test cases and to determine the corresponding expected test outputs.

- It is likely that system-to-system interface defects will cause end-to-end mission threads to fail.

Potential Causes

- There was inadequate funding and staff to engineer the SoS requirements.
- There was no SoS-level funding to pay the system-level projects to implement the SoS "requirements" (for example, because all funding exists at the system level).
- The SoS was "governed" by an organization that does not have the authority to mandate requirements on the individual component systems.
- The "requirements" for the SoS were whatever the individual systems do, as well as any emergent behavior.

Recommendations

- **Prepare:**
  - Provide the team(s) responsible for performing end-to-end SoS testing with access to any SoS requirements.
- **Enable:**
  - Establish a SoS requirements team.
  - Establish a working group to coordinate these requirements with the requirements of the individual systems.
  - The team(s) responsible for performing end-to-end SoS testing determine whether sufficient SoS requirements exist to drive testing.
- **Perform:**
  - Engineer any missing SoS requirements necessary to drive end-to-end SoS testing.
- **Verify:**
  - Determine whether sufficient SoS requirements exist to drive end-to-end SoS testing.

Related Pitfalls Ambiguous Requirements (GEN-REQ-1), Missing Requirements (GEN-REQ-3), Incorrect Requirements (GEN-REQ-5)

INADEQUATE SUPPORT FROM INDIVIDUAL SYSTEM PROJECTS (TTS-SoS-6)

Description   Test support from individual system development or system maintenance projects is inadequate to perform system of systems testing.

Potential Applicability   This pitfall is potentially applicable anytime that an SoS is being tested.

Characteristic Symptoms

- All available system-level test resources (for example, staffing, funding, and test environments) are already committed to system testing.
- System-level project managers and testers notify the SoS project manager(s) and testers that they cannot provide (timely) support to the SoS testers.

Potential Negative Consequences

- It is difficult or impossible to obtain the necessary test resources from individual projects to support SoS testing.
- SoS testing is less effective and efficient, thereby leading to SoS budget and schedule overruns.

Potential Causes

- Supporting SoS testing was not addressed in the individual systems':
  - ◆ Contracts or statements of work (SOWs)
  - ◆ Test planning documentation
  - ◆ Testing processes
- The individual system projects could not adequately support SoS testing because they did not have adequate allocated resources (such as funding, schedule, staffing, and test environments or facilities) to do so.
- Management and testers of the individual system development or maintenance projects were neither evaluated nor rewarded based on their support for SoS testing.

Recommendations

- **Prepare:**
  - ◆ Address performing and supporting SoS testing in contracts, plans, and testing processes of the individual systems.
- **Enable:**
  - ◆ Provide the individual system development or system update projects with sufficient support for SoS testing.
  - ◆ Ensure that these resources are not committed elsewhere, especially when the individual projects themselves run low on resources.
- **Perform:**
  - ◆ Ensure that the individual projects provide sufficient test resources to support SoS testing.

- ◆ Include support for SoS testing in the performance evaluations of relevant individuals in the individual system development or system update projects.
- ◆ When appropriate, provide incentives (for example, contract-award fees) based on support for SoS testing.

- ■ Verify:
  - ◆ Determine whether SoS testing is addressed in the contracts, plans, and testing processes of the individual systems.
  - ◆ Determine whether the individual system development or system update projects have sufficient resources to properly support SoS testing.
  - ◆ Determine whether these resources are being used for other purposes.
  - ◆ Determine whether the individual projects are providing sufficient test resources to support SoS testing.
  - ◆ If inadequate support is provided:
    - • Determine whether support for SoS testing is included in the performance evaluations of relevant individuals in the individual system development or system update projects.
    - • Determine whether incentives (for example, contract-award fees) are used to ensure adequate support for SoS testing.

Related Pitfalls   Lack of Stakeholder Commitment to Testing (GEN-SIC-3)

INADEQUATE DEFECT TRACKING ACROSS PROJECTS (TTS-SoS-7)

Description   Defect tracking across individual system development or maintenance projects is inadequate to support system of systems (SoS) testing.

Potential Applicability   This pitfall is potentially applicable anytime that an SoS is being tested.

Characteristic Symptoms

- ■ There is little or no coordination of defect tracking, defect fixing, and associated regression testing across the multiple projects making up the system of systems.
- ■ Different projects collect different types and amounts of information concerning defects identified during testing.

Potential Negative Consequences

- The same defect occurs in multiple systems.
- The same defect is fixed in only one or some of the systems in which it occurs.
- It is unnecessarily difficult to synchronize system- and SoS-level defect tracking.
- Defect localization and allocation of defects to individual or sets of systems are difficult to perform.

Potential Causes

- There was no budget or schedule set aside for SoS defect tracking.
- There was no SoS defect tracking.
- There was no coordination among the multiple system-level defect-tracking efforts.
- The different systems were using different defect-tracking processes and tools.
- The different systems were storing different information about defects in different formats in different tools or repositories.
- There was no overall SoS change control board (CCB) that kept track of the associated change requests or ensured SoS-wide impact analysis.

Recommendations

- Prepare:
  - Address the coordination of system- and SoS-level defect tracking in the:
    - Individual system development projects' planning documentation
    - Overall SoS planning documents
- Enable:
  - Mandate that the different system development projects:
    - Record the same information about defects in the same format
    - Use the same defect-tracking process and tool(s)
  - Set up an SoS testing coordination group and a change control board (CCB).
  - Develop a consensus concerning how to address defect reporting and tracking across the systems making up the SoS.

TTS-SoS-7 Inadequate Defect Tracking Across Projects

- **Perform:**
  - ◆ Coordinate defect tracking across system boundaries.
  - ◆ Document this consensus in all relevant test planning documentation for both SoS and individual systems.
- **Verify:**
  - ◆ Determine whether defect tracking and associated regression testing across the individual projects of the systems making up the SoS are adequately coordinated and reported.

Related Pitfalls   None

FINGER-POINTING (TTS-SoS-8)

Description   Different system development or maintenance projects assign the responsibility for finding and fixing defects to other projects.

Potential Applicability   This pitfall is potentially applicable anytime that an SoS is being tested.

Characteristic Symptoms

- There is a significant amount of finger-pointing across project boundaries regarding whether something is a defect (or feature), or where defects lie (that is, in which systems or in which project's testing work products).

Potential Negative Consequences

- Time and effort are wasted in allocating defects to individual or sets of systems.
- Defects take longer than appropriate to be fixed and verified.

Potential Causes

- Test planning documentation for the individual system development projects did not address who is responsible for fixing SoS-level defects.
- Individual system development projects typically do not allocate sufficient (or any) schedule and budget to fixing SoS-level defects.
- SoS-level requirements are often poor or missing, so it becomes easy for individual project teams to say that their system does not violate any SoS-level requirements and that therefore any defects must be some other project's responsibility.

- There is no SoS change control board (CCB) to officially mandate which system(s) need to be fixed.

Recommendations
- **Prepare:**
  - Address fixing SoS-level defects in the individual system development projects' planning documents.
- **Enable:**
  - Set up an SoS CCB if one does not already exist.
  - Grant the SoS CCB the authority to allocate defects to system-level projects for fixing.
  - Work to develop an SoS mindset among the members of the individual system development projects.
- **Perform:**
  - Assign representatives of the individual system projects to the SoS CCB and involve them in SoS defect allocation.
- **Verify:**
  - Determine whether an SoS CCB exists and has adequate authority to allocate defects to individual systems.

Related Pitfalls   Inadequate Support from Individual System Projects (TTS-SoS-6)

3.4.6   Regression Testing Pitfalls

The following pitfalls are specific to performing regression testing, including testing during maintenance:

- Inadequate Regression Test Automation (TTS-REG-1)
- Regression Testing Not Performed (TTS-REG-2)
- Inadequate Scope of Regression Testing (TTS-REG-3)
- Only Low-Level Regression Tests (TTS-REG-4)
- Test Resources Not Delivered for Maintenance (TTS-REG-5)
- Only Functional Regression Testing (TTS-REG-6)

INADEQUATE REGRESSION TEST AUTOMATION (TTS-REG-1)

Description   Testers and developers have automated an insufficient number of tests to enable adequate regression testing.[104]

Potential Applicability   This pitfall is potentially applicable anytime regression testing is needed (that is, almost always).

Characteristic Symptoms

- Many or even most of the tests are being performed manually.

Potential Negative Consequences

- Manual regression testing takes so much time and effort that it is not done.
- If performed, regression testing is rushed, incomplete, and inadequate to uncover a sufficient number of defects.
- Testers make an excessive number of mistakes while manually performing the tests.
- Defects introduced while making changes in previously tested subsystems or software remain in the operational system.
- The lack of adequate test automation prevents the use of an agile evolutionary (iterative and incremental) development cycle.

Potential Causes

- Testing stakeholders (for example, managers and the developers of unit tests):
  - Mistakenly believed that regression testing is neither necessary nor cost effective because:
    - Most changes are minor in scope.
    - System testing will catch any inadvertently introduced integration defects.
    - They are overconfident that their changes have not introduced any new defects.
  - Were not aware of the:
    - Importance of regression testing
    - Value of automating regression testing
    - Dependence of agile evolutionary development processes on test automation
- Automated regression testing was not an explicit part of the testing process.
- Automated regression testing was not incorporated into the test planning documentation.
- The schedule contained little or no time for developing and maintaining automated tests.
- Tool support for automated regression testing was lacking (for example, due to insufficient test budget) or impractical to use.

- The initially developed automated tests were not maintained.
- The initially developed automated tests were not delivered with the system.
- The system was locked down (for example, Apple iPad and iPhone), thereby making it difficult to perform automated installation and testing.

Recommendations

- **Prepare:**
  - Explicitly address automated regression testing in the project's:
    - Test planning documentation
    - Test process documentation (for example, procedures and guidelines)
    - Master schedule
    - Work Breakdown Structure (WBS)
- **Enable:**
  - Provide training or mentoring to the testing stakeholders in the importance and value of automated regression testing.
  - Provide sufficient time in the schedule for automating and maintaining the tests.
  - Provide sufficient funding to pay for tools that support test automation.
  - Ensure that adequate resources (staffing, budget, and schedule) are planned and available for automating and maintaining the tests.
- **Perform:**
  - Have testers and developers collaborate on automating regression testing whereby each plays the role for which they have adequate expertise and experience:[105]
    - Testers determine types of regression testing; test-case-selection criteria; test cases, including test preconditions, inputs, postconditions, and outputs; test-completion criteria, and so on.
    - Developers create automated regression tests, including configuring the test automation tools, programming in the test cases, writing test scripts, and whatever else is necessary.
  - Automate as many of the regression tests as is practical.
  - Make running the regression tests as easy as is practical so that they can be run frequently (for example, every night).
  - Where appropriate, use commercially available test tools to automate testing.
  - Ensure that both automated and manual test results are integrated into the same overall test results database so that test reporting and monitoring are seamless.
  - Maintain the automated tests as the system changes.
  - Deliver the automated tests with the tested system.

- Verify:
  - ◆ Determine whether the test planning documentation, test process documentation, and WBS adequately address automated regression testing.
  - ◆ Determine whether the schedule provides sufficient time to automate and maintain the tests.
  - ◆ Determine whether a sufficient number of the tests have been automated.
  - ◆ Determine whether the automated tests function properly.
  - ◆ Determine whether the automated tests are properly maintained.
  - ◆ Determine whether the automated tests are delivered with the system.

Related Pitfalls No Separate Test Planning Documentation (GEN-TPS-1), Incomplete Test Planning (GEN-TPS-2), Inadequate Test Schedule (GEN-TPS-5), Unrealistic Testing Expectations (GEN-SIC-2), Inadequate Test Resources (GEN-MGMT-1), Inadequate Maintenance of Test Assets (GEN-PRO-9), Over-Reliance on Manual Testing (GEN-TTE-1), Test Assets Not Delivered (GEN-TTE-8), Inadequate Test Configuration Management (GEN-TTE-9)

REGRESSION TESTING NOT PERFORMED (TTS-REG-2)

Description Testers and maintainers perform insufficient regression testing to determine if new defects have been accidentally introduced when changes are made to the system.[106]

Potential Applicability This pitfall is potentially applicable anytime regression testing is needed (that is, almost always).

Characteristic Symptoms
- No regression testing is being performed.
- Parts of the system are not retested after they are changed (for example, additions, modifications, and deletions due to refactoring and defect fixes).
- Appropriate parts of the system are not retested after interfacing parts are changed.
- Previously tested software is being reused without modification.
- Defects trace to previously tested changed components and components interfacing with changed components.

Potential Negative Consequences

- Defects are introduced into previously tested subsystems or software while making changes.
- The reused software fails, potentially catastrophically, when integrated with the system's new software and hardware or placed into operation in a new environment.
- These new defects:
    - Are not found due to a lack of regression testing
    - Remain in the operational system

Potential Causes

- Testing stakeholders (for example, managers and the developers of unit tests):
    - Mistakenly believed that performing regression testing was neither necessary nor cost effective because:
        - Most changes are minor in scope.
        - A change would have only local effects and thus could not affect the rest of the system.
        - The reused software did not need to be retested because it wasn't changed.
        - System testing would catch any inadvertently introduced integration defects.
        - They were overconfident that their changes had not introduced any new defects.
    - Were not aware of the:
        - Importance of regression testing
        - Value of automating regression testing
- Regression testing was not an explicit part of the testing process.
- Regression testing was not incorporated into the test planning documentation.
- The schedule contained little or no time for performing and maintaining automated tests.

TTS-REG-2 Regression Testing Not Performed

- Regression tests were not automated.
- The initially developed automated tests were not maintained.
- The initially developed automated tests were not delivered with the system.
- There was insufficient time and staffing to perform regression testing, especially if it had to be performed manually.
- Change-impact analysis:
  - Was not performed (for example, because of inadequate configuration management)
  - Did not address the impact on regression testing
- The architecture and design of the system was overly complex, with excessive coupling and insufficient encapsulation between components, thereby hiding interactions that might be broken by changes.

Recommendations

- **Prepare:**
  - Explicitly address regression testing in the project's:
    - Test planning documentation
    - Test process documentation (for example, procedures and guidelines)
    - Master schedule
    - Work Breakdown Structure (WBS)
  - Provide sufficient time in the schedule for performing and maintaining the regression tests.
- **Enable:**
  - Provide training or mentoring to the testing stakeholders in the importance and value of automated regression testing.
  - Automate as many of the regression tests as is practical.
  - Maintain the regression tests.
  - Deliver the regression tests with the system.
  - Provide sufficient time in the schedule to perform the regression testing.
  - Collect, analyze, and distribute the results of metrics concerning regression testing.
- **Perform:**
  - Perform change-impact analysis to determine what part of the system needs to be regression tested.
  - Perform regression testing on the potentially impacted parts of the system.
  - Resist efforts to skip regression testing unless a change-impact analysis has determined that retesting is really not necessary.
- **Verify:**
  - Determine whether the test planning documentation, test process documentation, and WBS adequately address automated regression testing.

- Determine whether the schedule provides sufficient time to automate and maintain the tests.
- Determine whether a sufficient number of the tests have been automated.
- Determine whether the automated tests function properly.
- Determine whether the automated tests are properly maintained.
- Determine whether the automated tests are delivered with the system.
- Determine whether change-impact analysis is being performed and whether it addresses the impact of the change on regression testing.
- Determine whether sufficient regression testing is being performed:
  - Repeat the testing of every component that is changed.
  - Repeat integration testing involving the component that is changed and every component that interacts with that component (covering all inputs and outputs, including exception handling of the component that changed).
  - Repeat system testing of every test involving the component that changed, including verification of both functional requirements and relevant nonfunctional requirements).

Related Pitfalls   No Separate Test Planning Documentation (GEN-TPS-1), Incomplete Test Planning (GEN-TPS-2), Inadequate Test Schedule (GEN-TPS-5), Unrealistic Testing Expectations (GEN-SIC-2), Inadequate Test Resources (GEN-MGMT-1), Inadequate Maintenance of Test Assets (GEN-PRO-9), Over-Reliance on Manual Testing (GEN-TTE-1), Test Assets Not Delivered (GEN-TTE-8), Inadequate Test Configuration Management (GEN-TTE-9)

INADEQUATE SCOPE OF REGRESSION TESTING (TTS-REG-3)

Description   The scope of regression testing is insufficiently broad.

Potential Applicability   This pitfall is potentially applicable anytime regression testing is needed (that is, almost always).

Characteristic Symptoms

- Regression testing is restricted to only the subsystems or software that has changed.[107]
- Potentially relevant parts of the system are not retested after parts that they interface with are changed (for example, additions, modifications, and deletions).
- Defects are unexpectedly discovered in components that had previously passed testing but were *not* retested because managers, developers, or testers did not think that changes made in interfacing components would affect them.

TTS-REG-3   Inadequate Scope of Regression Testing

Potential Negative Consequences

- Defects introduced into previously tested components while making changes:
  - Are not found during regression testing
  - Remain in the operational system

Potential Causes

- Testing stakeholders (for example, managers and the developers of unit tests):
  - Mistakenly believed that regression testing is neither necessary nor cost effective because:
    - Most changes are minor in scope.
    - A change would have only local effects and thus couldn't affect the rest of the system.
    - System testing would catch any inadvertently introduced integration defects.
    - They were overconfident that their changes did not introduce any new defects.
  - Were under significant budget and schedule pressure to minimize regression testing
- Determining the proper scope of regression testing was not an explicit part of the testing process.
- Change-impact analysis:
  - Was not performed (for example, because of inadequate configuration management)
  - Did not address the impact on regression testing
- The schedule contained little or no time for the performing and maintaining regression tests.
- Regression tests were not automated.
- The initially developed automated tests were not maintained.
- The initially developed automated tests were not delivered with the system.
- There was insufficient time and staffing to perform regression testing, especially when it had to be performed manually.
- The architecture and design of the system was overly complex with excessive coupling and insufficient encapsulation between components, thereby hiding interactions that might be broken by changes.

Recommendations

- **Prepare:**
  - Explicitly address the proper scope of regression testing in the project's test process documentation (for example, procedures and guidelines).
  - Provide sufficient time in the schedule for performing and maintaining the regression tests.
- **Enable:**
  - Provide training or mentoring to the testers in the proper scope of regression testing.
  - Automate as many of the regression tests as is practical.
  - Maintain the regression tests.
  - Deliver the regression tests with the system.
  - Provide sufficient time in the schedule to perform regression testing.
  - Collect, analyze, and distribute the results of metrics concerning regression testing.
- **Perform:**
  - Perform change-impact analysis to determine what part of the system needs to be regression tested.
  - Perform regression testing on the potentially impacted parts of the system.
  - Resist efforts to skip regression testing unless a change-impact analysis has determined that retesting is actually unnecessary.
- **Verify:**
  - Determine whether the test process documentation addresses the proper scope of regression testing.
  - Determine whether the schedule provides sufficient time to automate and maintain the tests.
  - Determine whether a sufficient number of the tests have been automated.
  - Determine whether the automated tests function properly.
  - Determine whether the automated tests are properly maintained.
  - Determine whether the automated tests are delivered with the system.
  - Determine whether change-impact analysis is being performed and whether it addresses the impact of the change on regression testing.
  - Determine whether sufficient regression testing is being performed:
    - Repeat the testing of every component that is changed.
    - Repeat integration testing involving the component that is changed and every component that interacts with that component (covering all inputs and outputs, including exception handling of the component that changed).

- Repeat system testing of every test involving the component that changed, including verification of both functional requirements as well as relevant nonfunctional requirements).

Related Pitfalls   No Separate Test Planning Documentation (GEN-TPS-1), Incomplete Test Planning (GEN-TPS-2), Inadequate Test Schedule (GEN-TPS-5), Unrealistic Testing Expectations (GEN-SIC-2), Inadequate Test Resources (GEN-MGMT-1), Inadequate Maintenance of Test Assets (GEN-PRO-9), Over-Reliance on Manual Testing (GEN-TTE-1), Test Assets Not Delivered (GEN-TTE-8), Inadequate Test Configuration Management (GEN-TTE-9), Regression Testing Not Performed (TTS-REG-2), Only Low-Level Regression Tests (TTS-REG-4)

ONLY LOW-LEVEL REGRESSION TESTS (TTS-REG-4)

Description   Only low-level (for example, unit-level and possibly integration) regression tests are rerun so there is no system, acceptance, and operational regression testing and no SoS regression testing.

Potential Applicability   This pitfall is potentially applicable anytime regression testing is needed (that is, almost always).

Characteristic Symptoms

- Regression testing is restricted to unit testing (and possibly some integration testing).
- Regression testing does not include system testing, acceptance testing, operational testing, and system of systems (SoS) testing.

Potential Negative Consequences

- Integration defects introduced while changing existing, previously tested subsystems or software remain in the operational system because they are not found during regression testing.

Potential Causes

- High-level regression tests were not adequately automated.
- High-level regression tests were not addressed in the test planning documentation.

- The developers believed that high-level regression testing was not necessary given that:
  - The system passed the low-level regression tests.
  - The developers felt that no integration defects were introduced.
- There was management pressure to minimize regression testing as much as possible due to its cost and schedule impacts.

Recommendations

- **Prepare:**
  - Address high-level regression testing in the test planning documentation.
- **Enable:**
  - Include all levels of regression testing in the metrics plan and process.
  - Allocate sufficient time in the schedule and budget to enable high-level regression testing to take place.
  - Use software engineering techniques (for example, abstraction and information hiding, modular architectures, open key interfaces, exception handling, and design by contract) to decouple subsystems so that defects in one subsystem will not propagate to other subsystems.
- **Perform:**
  - Automate as many of these high-level regression tests as is practical so that it will be practical to rerun them.
  - Ensure that all relevant and appropriate levels of regression testing (for example, unit, integration, system, specialty, and SoS) are rerun when changes are made.
- **Verify:**
  - Determine whether sufficient high-level regression testing is being performed:
    - Repeat the testing of every component that is changed.
    - Repeat integration testing involving the component that is changed and every component that interacts with that component (covering all inputs and outputs, including exception handling of the component that changed).
    - Repeat system testing of every test involving the component that changed, including verification of both functional requirements and relevant nonfunctional requirements).

Related Pitfalls   Inadequate Scope of Regression Testing (TTS-REG-3)

Test Resources Not Delivered for Maintenance (TTS-REG-5)

Description   The test resources produced by the development organization are not made available to the maintenance organization to support testing new capabilities and regression testing changes.

Potential Applicability   This pitfall is potentially applicable when the software is being released by a development organization to a maintenance organization.

Characteristic Symptoms

- The development organization did not deliver the test environments, test software, test data, and test procedures along with the developed system.
- The maintenance organization does not have access to the development organization's test resources (for example, test work products, including test tools, test environments, test software, test data, and test procedures).
- The development organization delivers test documents and test data in a form that is either not easily reusable (for example, documents as PDF files rather than as MS Word files and test data in documents rather than in data files or databases).

Potential Negative Consequences

- Insufficient resources are made available to adequately support maintenance testing.
- Maintenance testing is unnecessarily labor intensive and expensive.
- Test documents and data must be translated into a usable format prior to reuse and maintenance.
- Testing is delayed while either the existing testing resources are obtained from the development organization or new resources are obtained or produced.

Potential Causes

- Delivery of testing work products to the maintenance organization was not required by the maintenance organization's contract, statement of work (SOW), or memorandum of understanding (MOU).
- The development organization was not required (for example, by the contract, SOW, or MOA) to deliver the testing work products along with the

delivered system to the acquisition organization. And even if these testing work products were delivered to the acquisition organization, they were not passed on to the maintenance organization.

- The maintenance organization was not provided with sufficient funding to recreate these testing work products.

Recommendations

- Prepare:
  - ◆ Remember maintenance testing when considering development testing.
- Enable:
  - ◆ Include delivery of the testing work products to the acquisition organization in the development contract, SOW, or MOU.
- Perform:
  - ◆ The development organization properly delivers the testing work products to the acquisition organization.[108]
  - ◆ The acquisition organization properly furnishes these testing resources to the maintenance organization so that they can be used for testing the operational system as it is maintained.
- Verify:
  - ◆ Determine whether the development contract, SOW, or MOU specifies delivery of the testing work products to the acquisition organization.
  - ◆ Determine whether the development organization's test planning documentation addresses the delivery of the test resources along with the system.
  - ◆ Determine whether the development organization properly delivers the testing work products to the acquisition organization.
  - ◆ Determine whether the acquisition organization properly furnishes these testing resources to the maintenance organization.

Related Pitfalls   Incomplete Test Planning (GEN-TPS-2), Test Assets Not Delivered (GEN-TTE-8)

ONLY FUNCTIONAL REGRESSION TESTING (TTS-REG-6)

Description   Testers and maintainers only perform regression testing to determine if changes introduce functionality-related defects.

Potential Applicability   This pitfall is potentially applicable anytime regression testing is needed (that is, almost always).

Characteristic Symptoms

- New regression tests test only the functionality of the system or software (and possibly the system's external interfaces).
- Regression tests do not include any specialty engineering tests or tests of the system's quality requirements (that is, support for sufficient levels of the various quality characteristics and attributes).
- There are no new regression tests of architecture, design, and implementation constraints.

Potential Negative Consequences

- Any changes that cause the system to fail to meet its quality requirements are not found by the regression tests.
- The development or maintenance organization is unaware that its support for important quality characteristics and their quality attributes is becoming degraded.

Potential Causes

- Functional tests are easier to design and run than tests for quality requirements, quality characteristics, and their quality attributes, so the quality tests were not addressed.
- There was not sufficient time in the schedule to develop all of the regression tests and to automate the appropriate ones.

Recommendations

- Prepare:
  - Ensure that the development organization's test planning documentation addresses the inclusion of specialty engineering or quality testing in regression testing.
- Enable:
  - Provide adequate tools for specialty engineering or quality testing.
- Perform:
  - Incorporate sufficient specialty engineering or quality test cases in the regression suite of test cases.

- Verify:
  - Determine whether the planning documents include specialty engineering or quality testing in regression testing.
  - Determine whether the regression suite of test cases incorporates sufficient specialty engineering or quality test cases.

Related Pitfalls   Inadequate Capacity Testing (TTS-SPC-1), Inadequate Concurrency Testing (TTS-SPC-2), Inadequate Internationalization Testing (TTS-SPC-3), Inadequate Performance Testing (TTS-SPC-4), Inadequate Reliability Testing (TTS-SPC-5), Inadequate Robustness Testing (TTS-SPC-6), Inadequate Safety Testing (TTS-SPC-7), Inadequate Security Testing (TTS-SPC-8), Inadequate Usability Testing (TTS-SPC-9)

TTS-REG-6 Only Functional Regression Testing

CHAPTER 4

CONCLUSION

Testing is a critically important verification method that takes up a very large portion of a project's resources, including schedule, budget, staffing, and facilities. Unlike the many constructive activities of systems engineering, testing is relatively unique because it is inherently destructive. Its primary purpose is to force the system or its components to fail so that the defects that caused the failure can be uncovered and then fixed. In addition to defect detection, testing is also performed to provide sufficient objective evidence to justify confidence in the system's quality, fitness for purpose, and readiness for being accepted and placed into operation.

Unfortunately, people have come up with many ways in which to unintentionally make testing less effective, less efficient, and more frustrating to perform. These inappropriate decisions, mindsets, actions, and failures to act comprise the 92 commonly occurring testing pitfalls that are the subject of this book. Look at any project's testing program and you are almost guaranteed to observe that the project has fallen into several of these pitfalls.

The primary goal of this book is to provide you with the information you need to:

- Avoid falling into any of these commonly occurring testing pitfalls.
- Recognize when you have already fallen into one or more of these testing pitfalls.
- Escape from these pitfalls while minimizing the resulting negative consequences.

4.1   Future Work

The contents of this book are not the result of a formal, academic study. Rather, they were derived from the experience of real testers working on real projects as well as the experience of testing subject-matter experts who have performed technical assessments of actual testing programs.

As such, the current qualitative document leaves several important quantitative questions unanswered:

- **Frequency** Which of these testing pitfalls occurs most often? More specifically, what is the probability distribution of the frequencies with which these pitfalls occur?
- **Impact** Which testing pitfalls cause the most harm? What are the probability distributions of the negative consequences caused by each of these pitfalls?
- **Risk** Based on the frequency and severity of these testing pitfalls, which ones represent the greatest risks? Given these risks, how should an organization prioritize the limited project resources to minimize a project's test-related risks?
- **Distribution** Finally, what factors influence the frequency, severity, and risks associated with the different pitfalls? How do the frequencies, severities, and risks of the testing pitfalls differ in different application domains such as commercial versus governmental, civilian versus military, web versus IT versus embedded systems, and so on?

I hope that more formal studies and industry surveys based on these testing pitfalls will be performed to answer these questions.

4.2 Maintaining the Lists of Pitfalls

With 92 common testing pitfalls organized into 14 categories, this taxonomy of testing pitfalls should be relatively complete. However in spite of its size, it is also quite likely that additional pitfalls and even missing categories of pitfalls will be identified over time as testers read this book and compare it to their personal experiences. As an enhancement to the print edition, we have provided the following location on the web where readers can find major additions and modifications to this taxonomy of pitfalls: http://donald.firesmith.net/home/common-testing-pitfalls

Please send any recommended changes and additions to dgf (at) sei (dot) cmu (dot) edu, and I will consider them for publication both on the website and in future editions of this book.

APPENDIX A

GLOSSARY

The following glossary is provided as an easy reference to testing terms used within this book.

A/B testing Using two versions (A and B) of the user interface to accomplish identical tasks so that the resulting usability metrics can be compared to determine which version of the user interface is more usable[109]

analysis (verification) The verification method in which established technical or mathematical models or simulations, algorithms, or other scientific principles and procedures are used to provide evidence that a work product (for example, a document, a software application, or a system) meets its specified requirements

beta testing Any form of operational testing in which one or more beta (that is, near-final) versions of the system are released to a relatively limited number of representative users (also known as beta testers) for actual trial usage in an operational environment in order to identify residual defects that have slipped through the testing that was performed by the development organization(s)

black-box testing (also known as interface testing) Any testing, either functional or nonfunctional, without reference to the internal structure of the component or system; this testing is restricted to the externally visible behavior and characteristics of the thing being tested.

boundary-value testing The testing technique in which test cases are selected just inside, on, and just outside each boundary of an equivalence class of potential test cases[110]

branch coverage Code coverage defined in terms of the percentage of branches that have been exercised by a test suite, whereby a branch is a basic block that can be selected for execution based on a program construct in which one of two or more alternative program paths is available, for example case, jump, go-to, if-then-else

built-in test (BIT) Test software that is embedded in the operational software, including:

- PowerUp built-in test (PupBIT), which runs during system startup
- Periodic built-in test (PBIT), which regularly runs as a background task
- Interrupt-driven built-in test (IBIT), which runs when predefined events (for example, the detection of a fault) occur
- User-initiated built-in test (UBIT), which runs when requested by a user or operator
- Shutdown built-in test (SBIT), which runs during system shutdown

cloud testing Testing in which the cloud (that is, computing resources on the Web provided as a service) is used as part of the test environment; for example, the cloud can be used to provide testing as a service (TaaS) by providing test inputs for performing stress testing, capacity testing, load testing, performance testing, compatibility or interoperability testing, and so on.

code coverage Any analysis method that determines which parts of the software have been executed (covered) by the test suite and which parts have not been executed; for example, statement coverage, decision coverage, and condition coverage

concurrent development cycle Any development cycle in which multiple activities or tasks occur concurrently rather than sequentially (for example, requirements engineering and testing, test-case development and test execution)

condition coverage (also known as predicate coverage) Code coverage defined in terms of the percentage of condition outcomes that have been exercised by a test suite[111]

crowdsource testing The type of informal operational testing that is outsourced to a large number of independent organization-external testers who are paid only on a per-defect-found basis

decision coverage Code coverage defined in terms of the percentage of decision outcomes that have been exercised by a test suite, where a decision is a program point at which the control flow has two or more alternative routes

defect Any flaw in a component or system that can cause the component or system to fail to perform its required function, for example, an incorrect statement or data definition; any flaw resulting from an error made during development that will cause the system to perform in an unintended or unwanted manner if executed (possibly only under certain circumstances); any flaw in a model or document[112]

demonstration The verification method in which a system or subsystem is observed during operation under specific scenarios to provide visual evidence of whether it behaves properly

derived requirement Any requirement that is implied or inferred from other requirements or from applicable standards, laws, policies, common practices, management and business decisions, or constraints

developmental testing Any formal or informal testing conducted during the development of the system

emulator Any system or component that replaces another system or component by duplicating the externally visible behavior of the other system or component; an emulator produces the same relevant outputs given the same relevant inputs. Emulators tend to be combinations of hardware and software and used as part of the test environment during integration testing to replace system components that are unavailable for testing (for example, components that are still being developed or are used to create deliverable systems)

entry/exit coverage Code coverage defined in terms of the percentage of possible function calls and returns exercised by a test suite

error Any human mistake (for example, an incorrect, missing, extra, or improperly timed action) that can cause erroneous input or a defect[113]

erroneous input Any incorrect input (for example, values that do not match the actual or required values, incorrect commands, commands entered in an incorrect order, or commands entered at the wrong time, such as when the system is in an inappropriate state)

error tolerance The degree to which the system detects erroneous input (for example, from a human or a failed sensor) and responds properly to avoid faults and failures

failure Any event or situation in which the system ceases to meet one or more of its requirements (that is, it fails to exhibit a mandatory behavior or characteristic)[114]

failure tolerance The degree to which the system detects the existence of failures and reacts appropriately to avoid harm (for example, by going into a degraded mode or failing into a safe and secure state)

false-negative test result This test result implies that no underlying defect exists, although a defect actually exists (that is, the test fails to expose the defect).[115]

false-positive test result This test result implies the existence of an underlying defect, although no such defect actually exists.[116]

fault Any abnormal system-internal condition (for example, incorrect stored data value, incorrect subsystem state, or execution of the wrong block of code) that may cause the system to fail[117]

fault tolerance The degree to which the system detects the existence of faults and reacts appropriately to avoid failures

function coverage Code coverage defined in terms of the percentage of function (also known as procedure, method, or subroutine) calls executed by a test suite

functional requirement Any requirement that specifies a mandatory behavior of a system or subsystem

functionality testing Any testing intended to verify functionality by causing the implementation of a system function to fail in order to identify associated defects

fuzz testing The testing technique in which random inputs are used to cause the system to fail

gray-box testing Any testing via the interfaces of a system or software under test (SUT) (as in black-box testing) whereby the selection and design of the test cases are informed by knowledge of the internals of the SUT (as in white-box testing)

hallway intercept testing The testing technique in which random samples of users (as in: People in a hallway are intercepted while walking past the testing room.) are brought in to use the user interface in an effort to discover usability problems or to compare different versions of the user interface

incremental development cycle Any development cycle in which the development process (including testing) is repeated to add additional capabilities

inspection The verification method in which a static work product is observed using one or more of the five senses, simple physical manipulation, and mechanical and electrical gauging and measurement to determine if it contains defects

integration testing The incremental testing of larger and larger subsystems as they are integrated to form the overall system

interoperability the degree to which the system operates (that is, interfaces *and* collaborates) effectively with specified (types of) external systems by successfully providing data, information, material, and services to those systems and using data, information, material, and services provided by those systems

iterative development cycle Any development cycle in which all or part of the development process (including testing) is repeated to modify an existing subsystem or software component, typically to correct defects or make improvements (for example, refactoring the architecture or design or replacing existing components)

load testing Testing a system to determine (1) if the system meets its requirements (especially capacity and performance) under normal load and (2) if the system's performance degrades gracefully as its anticipated peak load is approached;[118] contrast with stress testing.

loop coverage Code coverage defined in terms of test cases executing every loop zero times, once, and more than once in the software under test

metadata Any data describing other data; for example, who created it, when, where, and any other relevant information

operationally relevant testing Testing the final operational system (including the actual deliverable software, hardware, and data) in the actual physical environment(s) where the system is intended to operate[119]

operational testing Testing the "completed" system in the actual physical environment under actual conditions and in accordance with operational profiles in order to:

- Identify residual defects that have slipped through the testing performed by the development organization(s)
- Determine operational suitability and effectiveness
- Determine readiness to transition from low rate of initial production (LRIP) to full-rate production (FRP)
- Determine readiness for deployment and operation
- Operational testing is also known as in-the-wild testing. Examples of operational testing include beta testing, crowdsource testing, flight testing, and the sea trials of new and modified ships.

path coverage Code coverage in terms of the percentage of possible routes through the software under test that are executed by a test suite[120]

penetration testing The testing technique in which a tester plays the role of an attacker and tries to penetrate the system's defenses

postcondition Any assertion that must hold following the successful execution of the associated function (for example, use case path)

precondition Any assertion that must hold prior to the successful execution of the associated function (for example, use case path)

quality attribute Any major measureable component of a quality characteristic (for example, the quality attributes of performance include jitter, latency, response time, schedulability, and throughput)

quality characteristic Any high-level characteristic or property of a system or architectural component that characterizes an aspect of its quality (for example, availability, maintainability, performance, portability, reliability, robustness, safety, security, and usability)

quality requirement Any requirement that specifies a mandatory quality characteristic in terms of a minimum acceptable level of some associated quality attribute

regression testing The testing of a previously tested unit, component, or system following modification to determine if defects have been introduced or uncovered in changed areas as a result of the changes made

requirement A single capability (that is, behavior or characteristic) that a product or process must exhibit in order to meet a stakeholder need

requirements management tool Any tool used to (1) store requirements and requirements metadata and (2) control changes to the requirements

requirements metadata Any data about a given requirement, such as its unique identifier, its source, its verification method, or its type

requirements trace Any mapping between:
- Higher- and lower-level requirements
- Requirements and architectural components
- Requirements and design components
- Requirements and software or hardware units
- Requirements and tests

sensor drift The slow degradation of sensor properties over time, causing incorrect sensor output and necessitating sensor recalibration

simulator Any system or component that models another system or component by duplicating the externally visible behavior of the other system or component, whereby the simulator produces the same outputs given the same inputs; software simulators are often used to simulate the intended behavior of a missing system component or external system.

statement coverage Code coverage defined in terms of the percentage of statements in the software under test that are executed by the test suite

stress testing Testing a system to determine whether it meets its requirements (especially capacity and performance) under loads exceeding peak load; contrast with load testing.

structural testing Synonym for white-box testing

sunny-day testing Testing that only verifies nominal behavior (for example, nominal paths through use cases) and thus does not test error, fault, or failure tolerance behavior (such as raising, throwing, and handling exceptions); also known as golden-path testing and nominal-case testing

System Engineering Management Plan (SEMP) The technical plan of the project that documents the system engineering processes (such as those for requirements engineering, architecture engineering, design, implementation, integration, and testing) and the associated tools that will be used to produce the system; the SEMP identifies other, more detailed plans such as the risk management plan, configuration management plan, and test and evaluation master plan. It also documents the project's organization, including the responsibilities of teams.

system testing The black-box testing of an integrated system against its requirements

test Any execution of the system or software under test (SUT) that is triggered by inputs under controlled preconditions (for example, pretest stored data and pretest mode and states) where actual outputs and postconditions (for example, posttest stored data and posttest mode and states) are compared with expected or required outputs and postconditions

testability The degree of ease with which testing can be used to determine if a system meets its specified requirements; testability can be decomposed into controllability and observability.

test asset Any test work products such as:
- Test documentation, such as test planning documentation, test procedures, and test reports
- Test tools, test environments or test beds, and test facilities or test labs
- Test software such as test cases, test drivers or scripts, test stubs, and test tools

test bed Synonym for test environment

test case Any single atomic test consisting of test preconditions, test inputs, expected test outputs, and expected test postconditions

test-case-selection criteria Criteria that are used to determine the actual test cases to create and run

test-completion criteria Criteria that are used to determine when sufficient testing (of a specific type) has been performed

test driven development (TDD) The development approach in which the development of tests largely precedes the design and implementation of the system, subsystem, or software being tested[121]

test driver Any software or hardware unit that was developed for unit or integration testing, that sends input commands and associated data to the component under test (CUT), and that records any resulting outputs or exceptions raised by the CUT; test drivers typically execute test scripts.

test engineer (1) The role played by a person when performing testing-related tasks such as developing test assets, executing tests, and reporting test results; (2) the job title or profession of someone responsible for performing test-related tasks

test environment (also known as test bed) An integrated environment for testing consisting of both hardware (for example, computers, network devices, sensors, and actuators) and software (for example, operating systems, middleware, test tools, and test scripts)

test and evaluation master plan (TEMP) The system engineering plan that documents how the system and its components will be tested and evaluated (for example, via demonstration, inspection, or review); the TEMP includes both developmental and operational testing and evaluations. It also includes major testing milestones as well as required testing resources and organizational responsibilities for testing and evaluation.

tester Any person who performs testing tasks

test hook Any interface included to make a system, subsystem, or component more testable by enabling the tester to bypass encapsulation and thereby make local inputs and state/data changes (controllability) and to observe local outputs and state/data changes (observability)

testing The execution of a system, subsystem, or component under specific preconditions (for example, pretest mode, states, stored data, or external conditions) with specific inputs so that its actual behavior (outputs and postconditions) can be compared with its expected or required behavior[122]

testing effectiveness The percentage of defects found by testing, which is measured by the number of defects found divided by the estimated number of existing defects

testing method Any method describing the intended process for performing a specific type of testing

testing stakeholder Anyone with a legitimate interest in the completeness, effectiveness, or efficiency of testing

test input Any data, exceptions (for example, from stubs), or commands that are used as inputs during the execution of test cases

test oracle Any source of the information defining correct and expected system or software behavior and test postconditions

test output Any data, exceptions, or commands (for example, to stubs) that are produced by the system or component under test

test planning documentation Any documentation recording the results of the test planning process including the scope, approach(es), resources, and schedule of intended test activities (including major testing milestones, their entry and exit criteria, and their relationship to project's master schedule)

test script Any set of instructions that executes one or more test cases; a test script can be textual for manual execution or a software procedure for automatic execution.

test strategy Any high-level description of the test levels to be performed and the testing within those levels for an organization or program (one or more projects); the test strategy includes (among other things) the different types of testing (such as unit testing, integration testing, system testing, regression testing, and so on), how these types of testing will be performed (for example, test-case-selection criteria, and test-completion criteria), and the test resources (for example, test facilities, environments, and tools).

test strategy document Any document describing an organization's or program's test strategy

test stub Any software or hardware unit that simulates an actual software or hardware component on which the component under test depends

test tool (1) Any software tool that automates some of the testing tasks, typically including test execution, and recording of test results; (2) any hardware device used during testing to provide test inputs and display or record test outputs

trigger event Any initial input command or flow of data that marks the beginning of the validity of a corresponding requirement

unit testing The testing of individual units (for example, modules, procedures, and object-oriented classes)

use case Any named service that the system provides to one or more primary actors that enables them to achieve a single specific functional goal (and thereby provides them with something of measurable value); a use case models a functionally cohesive set of use case paths.

use case path Any named set of usage scenarios (that is, a series of interactions between the system and its actors) that all flow down the same course through the use case; a use case path can be considered an equivalence class of test cases.

validation Requirements validation is any activity used to determine if the requirements are correct (that is, they meet the stakeholders' needs). System validation is any activity used to determine if the correct system is being developed (that is, it meets its specified requirements). Validation can be performed using many techniques (for example, review and workshop).

verification Any activity used to determine if the system is being built or updated correctly (that is, the as-performed processes are in accordance with the as-planned methods); verification can be performed in many ways (for example, demonstration, inspection, review, and testing).

vulnerability Any system-*internal* weakness that can increase the likelihood or harm severity of one or more abuses (that is, mishaps or misuses)

vulnerability testing The testing technique the goal of which is to expose a system vulnerability (that is, defect or weakness) that can be exploited to cause a mishap or misuse

white-box testing (also known as structural and implementation testing) Testing based on an analysis of the internal structure of a component or system under test; testing the internal, typically encapsulated structures or workings of software as opposed to its externally visible behavior, often performed to meet some kind of code-coverage criteria[123]

Work Breakdown Structure An arrangement of work elements and their relationship to each other and to the end product; a WBS is typically used to show dependency relationships (for example, when one task has to be started or completed before another task can begin).

APPENDIX B

ACRONYMS

ALM	Application Lifecycle Management
BIST	Built-In Self Test (a common synonym for BIT)
BIT	Built-in Test
CCB	Change Control Board
CM	Configuration Management
COM	Communication
COQUALMO	Constructive QUALity Model
COTS	Commercial off-the-Shelf
CUT	Component under Test
ETA	Event Tree Analysis
FMECA	Failure Modes and Effects Criticality Analysis
FP	Function Point
FRP	Full Rate of Production
FTA	Fault Tree Analysis
GEN	General
GIG	Global Information Grid
GOTS	Government off-the-Shelf
HFE	Human Factors Engineering
IBIT	Interrupt-driven Built-in Test
INT	Integration test
IPT	Integrated Product Team
IRAD	Independent Research and Development
ISTQB	International Software Testing Qualification Board
LRIP	Low Rate of Initial Production
MGMT	Management
MOU	Memorandum of Understanding
NIPRNet	Non-classified Internet Protocol Router Network
OS	Operating System

OT	Operational Testing
PBIT	Periodic Built-in-Test
PDL	Program Design Language
PHM	Prognostics and Health Management
PMS	Project Master Plan
POST	Power-on Self-Test
PRO	Process
PupBIT	Power-up BIT
REG	Regression
REP	Requirements Engineering Plan
REQ	Requirements
SBIT	Shutdown BIT
SDC	System Development Cycle
SDP	Software Development Plan
SEMP	System Engineering Management Plan
SIC	Stakeholder Involvement and Commitment
SIPRNet	Secure Internet Protocol Router Network
SLE	System Level Exerciser
SME	Subject-matter Expert
SoS	System of Systems
SoSDP	SoS Development Plan
SOW	Statement of Work
SPC	Specialty engineering testing
STF	Staffing
STP	System Test Plan
SUT	System under Test
SYS	System testing
TaaS	Testing as a Service
TDD	Test Driven Development
TEMP	Test and Evaluation Master Plan
TPS	Test Planning and Scheduling
TSD	Test Strategy Document
TTE	Test Tools and Environments
TTS	Test-Type-Specific
UBIT	User-initiated Built-in Test
UNT	Unit Test
USB	Universal Serial Bus
WBS	Work Breakdown Structure

NOTES

1. Appendix E provides a checklist of pitfalls that can be used during the planning of a testing effort to assess the actual testing effort (that is, the as-planned and as-performed testing programs).

2. Not all testing pitfalls have the same probability or harm severity. These pitfall specifications are not intended to be used as part of a quantitative scoring scheme based on the number of pitfalls found. Instead, they are offered to support qualitative review and planning.

3. Note that the occurrence of a potential consequence may be a symptom by which the pitfall is recognized.

4. Causes are important to understand because recommendations should be based on the causes. Also, a recommendation to address root causes may be more important than proximate causes, because recommendations addressing proximate causes may not combat the root cause and therefore may not prevent the pitfall under all circumstances.

5. Some of the recommendations may no longer be practical after the pitfall rears its ugly head. It is usually much easier to avoid the pitfall—or nip it in the bud—rather than fixing it when the project is well along or near completion. For example, several possible ways exist to deal with inadequate time to complete testing, including (1) delay the test completion date and reschedule testing, (2) keep the test completion date and (a) reduce the scope of delivered capabilities, (b) reduce the amount of testing, (c) add testers, and (d) perform more parallel testing (for example, different types of testing simultaneously). Selection of the appropriate recommendations to follow, therefore, depends on the actual state of the project.

6. While avoiding certain pitfalls, most agile projects may suffer from other pitfalls, especially when used to develop large, complex, business- or mission-critical systems.

7. This does not mean that every test plan must include all of this information; test plans should include only the information that is relevant for the cur-

rent project. It is quite reasonable to reuse much or most of this information in multiple test plans; just because it is highly reusable does not mean that it is meaningless boilerplate that can be ignored. For example, the test plans can be used to estimate the amount of test resources (for example, time and tools) needed as well as the skills or expertise that the testers need.

8. This includes combinations such as testing system start-up when hardware or software components fail.

9. This includes testing error, fault, failure, and environmental tolerance.

10. Note that an evolutionary (for example, iterative, incremental, and concurrent) development or lifecycle greatly increases the amount of regression testing needed (although this increase in testing can be largely offset by highly automating regression tests). Although testing can never be exhaustive, more time is typically needed for adequate testing unless testing can be made more efficient. For example, fewer defects could be produced and these defects could be found and fixed earlier and thereby be prevented from reaching the current iteration.

11. When there is insufficient time to perform manual testing, it may be difficult to justify automating these tests. However, automating regression testing is not just a maintenance issue. Even during initial development, there should typically be a large amount of regression testing, especially if an iterative and incremental development cycle is used. Thus, ignoring the automation of regression testing because of the investment of staff and schedule is often a case of being pennywise and pound foolish.

12. An interesting example of this is the Hubble telescope. Testing the mirror's focusing capability was postponed until after launch, resulting in an incredibly expensive repair mission.

13. The primary goal of testing is not to prove that something works, but rather to demonstrate that it does not. A good tester assumes that there are always defects (an extremely safe assumption) and seeks to uncover them. Thus, a good test is one that causes the thing being tested to fail so that the underlying defect(s) can be found and fixed. Although tests that pass are often used as evidence that the system (or subsystem) under test meets its (derived and allocated) requirements, testing can never be exhaustive for even a simple system and therefore cannot "prove" that all requirements are met. However, system and operational testing can provide evidence that the system under test is "fit for purpose" and ready to be placed into operation. For example, certain types of testing may provide evidence required for safety and security accreditation and certification. Nevertheless, a tester must take a "show it fails" rather than a "show it works" mindset to be effective.

14. Note that testing cannot identify all defects because some defects (for example, failure to implement missing requirements) do not cause the system to fail in a manner detectable by testing.

15. Using testing to "prove" that their software works is most likely to become a pitfall when developers test their own software (for example, with unit testing and with small cross-functional or agile teams).

16. Developers typically do their own unit-level (that is, lowest-level) testing. With small, cross-functional (for example, agile) teams, it is becoming more common for developers to also do integration and subsystem testing.

17. Whereas tests that verify nominal behavior are essential, testers must keep in mind that there are typically many more ways for the system under test to fail than to work properly. Also, nominal tests must remain part of the regression test suite even after all known defects are fixed, because changes could introduce new defects that cause nominal behavior to fail.

18. Take care to avoid incentivizing developers to be careless or even insert defects into their own software so that they can then find them during testing. Also, be careful to not penalize testers who are assigned high-quality software that has few defects to find.

19. As documented in Table 1.2, testing is not as efficient as static analysis when it comes to detecting defects. As documented in Tables 1.3 and 1.4, the individual types of testing typically find less than half of all latent defects.

20. A single passed test case means little by itself. Even many passed test cases do not prove there are no residual defects. However, passing a large number of well-chosen and well-implemented test cases does increase one's confidence in the system's quality.

21. Note that this will help only if the test manager is not below the manager applying improper pressure.

22. The potential testing pitfalls analyzed in this book can be viewed as representing testing risks that, if relevant, probably should be officially entered into the project risk repository unless they already have been eliminated or sufficiently mitigated.

23. Note that the number of tests metric does not indicate the effort or complexity of identifying, analyzing, and fixing the associated defects.

24. COQUALMO (Constructive QUALity Model) is an estimation model that can be used for predicting the number of residual defects per thousands of source lines of code (KSLOC) or defects per Function Point (FP) in a software product.

25. There is typically a great deal of variability from one project to another in the number of initial defects per function point/KSLOC due to many factors beyond the control of the testers, such as the size and complexity of the sys-

tem, the type and rigor of the development process used, the quality of the requirements, and the expertise and experience of the requirements engineers, architects, designers, and programmers. This makes it difficult to use tester efficiency metrics such as the number of defects found per tester day to get more than a rough approximation of tester efficiency. Similarly, tester productivity metrics such as number of tests developed per tester day need to be taken with a grain of salt because individual tests can vary in terms of complexity, number of test cases, and the size and complexity of test inputs and outputs.

26. Clearly, rerunning the same tests should find fewer defects over time, as many more defects are identified and fixed than new ones inadvertently introduced during iteration.

27. For example, what are the percentages of defects that manage to slip by architecture reviews, design reviews, implementation inspections, unit testing, integration testing, and system testing without being detected?

28. Great care should be used when measuring test program productivity. First, it must take into account the number of latent defects. After all, even the best testing program finds fewer defects when there are fewer defects to be found. This is especially true if one intends to determine the productivity of individual testers because it is clearly unfair to penalize the testers who get high-quality code to test. This is why productivity should be measured in terms of the percentage of remaining defects found. This is further complicated by the fact that all defects are not equal. Finding one critical defect is often far more important than finding several insignificant defects.

29. You cannot and should not try to measure everything. Metrics can help you manage the test program but other issues (for example, schedule, budget, availability of test environments, and tester experience and expertise) are also important.

30. While it is clearly management's responsibility to weigh and make trade-offs between meeting schedule, coming in on budget, delivering capabilities, and ensuring high quality, it can be a major mistake to always make quality the lowest priority. While residual defects (including security vulnerabilities) may not be as obvious during development as meeting milestones, staying within budget, and delivering capabilities, it can become critical once the system is delivered and placed into operation. This is especially true if the system is business-, mission-, safety-, or security-critical.

31. This false sense of security is likely to be replaced by a sense of panic when the system begins to frequently fail operational testing or real-world usage after deployment.

32. Note that these recommendations apply regardless of whether the project uses separate testing teams or cross-functional teams that include testers.

33. While the actual testing of future capabilities must wait until those capabilities are delivered to the testers, one can begin to develop black-box test cases that are not currently needed because they are based on requirements allocated to future builds. On the other hand, some of these tests may never be needed if the associated requirements change or are deleted.

34. Just because testing functionality is overemphasized relative to other types of testing (for example, specialty engineering testing and testing interfaces and data requirements) does not mean that there will be adequate testing of functionality. There may be too little of all types of testing being performed.

35. Note that adequately testing quality requirements requires significantly more time to prepare for and perform than testing typical functional requirements.

36. Note that this can be largely true for some of the nonfunctional requirements (for example, interface requirements and performance requirements).

37. This is not to say that black-box testing is not more important than white-box testing. After all, it is more important that the system works the way it needs to (that is, black-box verification of requirements) than for the system to work the way that the developers think it should work (that is, white-box verification of architecture, design, and implementation). However, only a combination of black-box and white-box testing will uncover sufficient defects.

38. Individual major testing work products (for example, test planning documentation) should probably be evaluated. In other cases where there are numerous instances of a testing work product (for example, test cases, test results, and defect reports), it may make more sense to evaluate only a representative sample.

39. Although requirements traceability matrices can be used when the number of requirements and test cases are quite small, the use of a requirements management, test management, or configuration management tool is usually needed to document and maintain tracings between requirements and tests.

40. This will help combat the loss of project expertise due to the fact that many or most of the testers who are members of the development staff tend to move on after delivery. The same recommendation also applies to the following pitfalls: Inadequate Maintenance of Test Assets (GEN-PRO-9) and Lack of Requirements Trace (GEN-REQ-9).

41. Note that having a good tool can be necessary but may not be adequate, especially if there are a great number of requirements and the system itself is very large and complex. This is especially true of quality requirements that tend to be cross-cutting and are implemented by numerous components that are scattered across the architecture.

42. While this is useful with regard to any product that undergoes multiple internal or external releases, it is especially a good idea when an evolu-

tionary (iterative and incremental) development cycle produces numerous short-duration increments.

43. The pitfall is not so much that the testing is incomplete, but rather that it is inappropriately and unnecessarily incomplete. As was noted in Unrealistic Testing Expectations (GEN-SIC-2), testing can never be exhaustive. So the issue is really whether testing is sufficiently complete to minimize the risks associated with residual defects to an acceptably low level.

44. Code coverage is typically very important for software with safety or security ramifications. When software is categorized by safety or security significance, the mandatory rigor of testing (including the completeness of coverage) increases as the safety and security risk increases (for example, from function coverage through statement coverage, decision or branch coverage, and condition coverage to path coverage).

45. This can be especially prevalent on agile projects where developers perform testing and the amount and type of testing is determined for each build or increment or sprint on a case-by-case basis.

46. This may not be a pitfall if test automation is not practical for some reason (for example, the quick-and-dirty testing of a UI-heavy rapid prototype that will not be maintained).

47. While using testing tools can be very useful (especially to ensure code coverage, stress testing, and the automate regression tests), the tester needs to use the requirements, architecture, and design as the oracle rather than merely letting the tool identify test cases based on the software being tested.

48. A common example of this is a software application that is developed to run on all popular mobile devices (for example, laptops, tablets, and smart phones).

49. Note that it is okay and often mandatory to mask sensitive personal data or classified data during testing to ensure its confidentiality. Specifically, it is okay to replace confidential data with dummy test data so long as the format, range, and precision is the same. In fact, testers should verify that actual confidential data is masked before it is used as test data.

50. For example, a sensor in a test environment may produce out-of-range sensor data due to sensor drift. This could cause the system or software under test to perform the correct error handling and thereby provide appropriate output that nevertheless causes the test to appear to fail because it is not the behavior that the tester expected to occur.

51. Testing is often performed on clean test computers, whereas real programs often must compete with many other programs for limited resources, which results in resource contentions (for example, lack of memory, storage, bandwidth, and processing power) and indirect failure propagation (for example,

another application causes the operating system to crash, which causes the application under test to immediately "fail" or fail upon restart).

52. For example, the hardware could be from different vendors, be different models or versions, have a different number of processors, or have a different amount of memory. Again, consider applications that must run on numerous mobile devices. Also, testing may be performed using prototype hardware, software simulation of the operational hardware, or hardware emulation of the operational hardware. Testing also often unrealistically assumes unlimited resources.

53. The testing may be performed using new mobile devices whereas the operational devices might be old and have batteries that hold less of a charge, discharge faster, or produce lower voltages.

54. Examples of this are mobile devices inside buildings or located where signals are (partially) blocked by buildings, mountains, hills, or trees. Note that testing in a shielded room or using Wi-Fi often assumes ideal conditions that do not take into account bandwidth, latency, electromagnetic interference, and so on.

55. This is a common pitfall when testing an application intended to run on COTS mobile devices (for example, laptops, tablets, and smart phones) that are intended to simultaneously host and execute an arbitrary number of additional COTS, GOTS, Open Source, and developed applications, some of which may not even exist yet.

56. If a classified program has not yet passed testing, it may be prohibited from being connected to the classified network it must use once operational, thereby leading to a chicken-and-egg problem.

57. While it is naturally a major part of Operational Testing and Evaluation (OT&E), some operationally relevant testing can (and should probably) also occur at the end of Developmental Testing (DT).

58. This is primarily a pitfall with test environments and their components that are developed in-house.

59. Note that it may not be practical (for example, for performance reasons or code size) or permitted (for example, for safety or security reasons) to deliver the system with embedded test software. For example, embedded test software could provide an attacker with a back-door capability.

60. Note that a closely related pitfall would be that the subsystem under test (SUT) is not under configuration control. Incompatibilities will also occur if the SUT is informally updated with undocumented and uncontrolled "fixes" without the test team being aware.

61. Well-written code in a popular, readable, high-level language with adequate comments may be sufficiently self-documenting at the code level, but that

does not mean that it is sufficiently self-documented at the component and system level, where architecture documentation is critical.

62. This is especially a pitfall when the fault or failure is intermittent and inherently difficult to reproduce.

63. This is especially likely when a prime contractor or system integrator and subcontractors are involved in development.

64. It is critical to ensure that this review not become a bottleneck.

65. This includes the documents and models needed to determine test inputs, preconditions, steps, expected outputs, and expected postconditions.

66. Although this is primarily a pitfall with regression tests that are obsoleted by changes to the requirements, architecture, design, and software, it can also be a pitfall with developing new tests for new capabilities if these capabilities are not documented properly.

67. However, as stakeholders in these documents and models, the testers are responsible for expressing the importance of properly maintaining them and report any obsolete information they discover so that it can be updated.

68. As stated in Inadequate Test Configuration Management (GEN-TTE-10), these test documents also need to be placed under configuration control.

69. Good requirements are truly needed and not unnecessary architectural or design constraints.

70. There are actually quite a few characteristics that good requirements should exhibit. These are merely some of the more important ones with regard to testing.

71. At least, white-box testing will help to get the system to where it will run without crashing and thereby provide a stable system that can be modified when the customer finally determines what the true requirements are.

72. While the first five GEN-REQ pitfall types are violations of the characteristics of good requirements, there are many other such characteristics that are not listed in them. This inconsistency is because the first five tend to cause the most frequent and severe testing problems.

73. Because testers often begin outlining black-box test cases during requirements engineering based on initial requirements, they are in a good position to identify requirements ambiguity.

74. If the tester is familiar with the system under test or its application domain, the tester can make educated guesses about what the missing requirements are. The tester can then have the requirements team validate the new requirements created by the tester with the system's stakeholders to verify whether the tester's guesses were correct.

75. These requirements are often critical for achieving adequate reliability, robustness, and safety. While requirements often specify how the system should behave, they rarely specify how the system should behave in those cases in which it does not or cannot behave as it should. It is equally critical that testing verify that the system does not do what it should not do (that is, that the system meets its negative as well as positive requirements).

76. This is not to imply that testing normal paths is not necessary. However, it is often incorrectly assumed that it is sufficient. Software can misbehave in many more ways than it can work properly. Defects are also more likely to be triggered by boundary conditions or rainy-day paths than in sunny-day paths. Thus, there should typically be more boundary and invalid condition test cases than normal behavior test cases.

77. All of these components are not needed for each requirement. However, stakeholders and requirements engineers often assume them to be implicitly part of the requirements and thus unnecessary to state explicitly. However, tests that ignore these missing parts of incomplete requirements can easily yield incorrect results if they are not taken into account.

78. A requirement is incorrect when it specifies a system behavior or characteristic (for example, function, data, interface, or quality) that is neither needed nor wanted. An incorrect requirement may be unnecessary gold plating that is innocuous other than wasting development resources. It may also cause a harmful behavior or characteristic that makes it harder or impossible for the system to fulfill its mission in a safe and secure manner.

79. This testing pitfall is similar to but more general than the preceding pitfall, Incorrect Requirements, because fixing incorrect requirements is one potential reason that the requirements may be volatile. Other reasons may be that engineering missed requirements and that stakeholder needs changed.

80. There are times when the requirements are unclear, provisional, and should be subject to rapid iteration. Under these circumstances, testers must live with the volatile requirements. Other times, the requirements churn is unnecessary and needs to be stabilized.

81. Dealing with requirements changes due to project-external events (for example, new competing systems, rapidly changing threats, emergence of new technologies enabling new capabilities, and changing markets) is an inescapable problem that testers must deal with. The problem becomes a pitfall when these requirements changes are not properly managed, thereby adversely impacting testing (among other project activities).

82. Note that this may be impossible or impractical due to delivery schedules and the amount of testing required.

83. Note that this especially tends to be a pitfall with cross-cutting quality requirements as it is often difficult to allocate higher-level thresholds across multiple lower-level subsystems.

84. Note that each requirement may be individually allocated its own verification method(s). On the other hand, a group of requirements may all be allocated the same verification method(s).

85. There are multiple ways to specify verification methods, and the appropriate one(s) to use will depend on the requirements engineering process.

86. Another reason for not having people test their own software is because people are not as likely to discover their own mistakes as they are to discover the mistakes of others.

87. Note that because unit testing is typically the responsibility of the developers rather than professional testers, the general problem of inadequate testing expertise, experience, and training often applies.

88. To be testable, the tester needs to be able to control the system under test (for example, place it into the proper pretest state and stimulate it with test inputs). To be testable, the tester needs to be able to observe the internals of the system under test (for example, determine if the system is in the correct pretest state and if the test leaves the system in the correct posttest state). Thus controllability and observability are quality attributes of the quality characteristic testability. Integration increases encapsulation and information hiding and thus decreases controllability and observability. Decreased testability is thus a natural consequence of integration and will occur unless compensating steps are taken to eliminate or mitigate its effects.

89. Note that testability requirements may need to be traded off against other quality requirements, especially performance, safety, and security requirements.

90. Note that security and other concerns may prohibit the inclusion of support for increased controllability and observability.

91. Testers should consider boundary-value testing as a means of testing test-input verification.

92. Testers who are developers who are only used to performing unit tests on their code often do not have adequate expertise in higher-level testing such as integration testing (as well as system testing, acceptance testing, and operational testing).

93. Such tests may redundantly test the same interleaving of threads while leaving many interleavings untested. Unexpected determinism may even result in the exact same interleaving being performed over and over again.

94. Examples include network and disk I/O, bus or network bandwidth, processor utilization, memory (RAM and disk) utilization, and database performance.

95. Note that reliability (also known as load, stability, or endurance) testing are nominal tests in the sense that they are executed within the performance envelope of the System Under Test (SUT). Capacity (stress) testing, where you test for graceful degradation, is outside the scope of performance testing.

96. Postponing the development and testing of off-nominal (that is, rainy-day) behavior is especially a problem because there are many more ways that the system can fail than it can run properly. Thus, there should be more test cases verifying whether the system identifies and handles errors, faults, and failures than the test cases verifying whether the system handles normal functionality. Also, this can be problematic because the requirements specification is typically woefully inadequate when it comes to how the system should behave if it fails to behave as it should.

97. Note that the term vulnerability (meaning a weakness in the system) applies to both safety and security. Vulnerabilities can be exploited by an abuser (either unintentionally [safety] or intentionally [security]) and contribute to the occurrence of an abuse (either a mishap [safety] or misuse [security]).

98. Note that no system is truly "tamper-proof" if subject to an advanced, persistent threat (APT) in which the attack and attacker are sufficiently sophisticated and persistent.

99. Warning: Although a bad idea, security requirements are sometimes specified in a security document rather than in the requirements specification or repository. Similarly, security testing is sometimes documented in security rather than testing documents. This makes the security requirements and tests easier to overlook.

100. The term "stickiness" is typically used with reference to web pages and refers to how long users remain at (that is, remain stuck to) given web pages.

101. The other traditional parts of Human System Integration (HSI) include Environment, Safety, Health, and Survivability. Environment and Health are subsumed into Safety and Security. Survivability is at the same level as Safety and Security, all three of which are quality characteristics outside of and at the same level as usability.

102. The temporary hooks incorporated to promote testability typically have to be removed in order to achieve certain quality characteristics such as performance, safety, and security and to enable the associated types of testing.

103. For a system to support an overall mission, it often needs to properly support a sequence or network of use case paths (often involving multiple

actors and multiple use cases) and thereby implement numerous specific detailed functional requirements. For example, a mission planning system may need to support interactions with mission planners, flight planners, diplomatic clearance specialists, and other actors in order to create a complete mission plan and deliver it to the aircraft and flight crew. Unfortunately, it is possible for the system to interact properly with the individual actors (and thereby pass use case path-level testing) and still not be successful when all of these use case path interactions are integrated together to produce end-to-end mission threads.

104. Automating regression testing is especially important when an evolutionary (iterative, incremental, and parallel) development cycle is used. The resulting numerous, short-duration increments of the system must be retested because of changes due to iteration (for example, refactoring and defect correction) and the integration of additional components with existing components.

105. Many testers do not have sufficient expertise and experience to be highly productive at programming high-quality test scripts, and the like. Similarly, many developers do not have sufficient expertise and experience to generate an adequate set of high-quality test cases.

106. The proper amount of regression testing depends on many factors, including the criticality of the system, the potential risks associated with introducing new defects, the potential costs of fixing these defects, the potential costs of performing regression testing, and the resources available to perform regression testing. There is a natural tension between managers who want to minimize cost and schedule due to regression testing and testers who want to perform as much testing as practical within budget and schedule limitations.

107. Unfortunately, changes in one part of the system can sometimes impact other apparently unrelated parts of the system. Defects also often unexpectedly propagate faults and failures beyond their local scope.

108. This includes the complete set of testing work products (for example, test data, test scripts, configuration files, and test-related documentation). These work products need to be of usable quality with all necessary data rights.

109. Note that multivariate, or bucket, testing is analogous but involves simultaneously comparing more than two versions of the user interface.

110. All test inputs within the equivalence class are considered equivalent because they all follow the same path through the code with regard to branching, so the behavior should be basically the same based on the requirements or design.

111. Condition coverage does not necessarily imply decision coverage.

112. The defect could be in software (for example, incorrect statements or declarations), in hardware (for example, a flaw in material or workmanship or manufacturing defects), or in data (for example, incorrect hardcoded values

in configuration files). A software defect (also known as a bug) is the concrete manifestation within the software of one or more human errors. One error may cause several defects, and multiple errors may cause the same defect.

113. If an error occurs during development, it can create a defect. If the error occurs during operation, it can produce erroneous input.

114. Failure often refers to both the condition of not meeting requirements as well as the event that causes this condition to occur.

115. There are many reasons for false-negative test results. They are most often caused by selecting test inputs and preconditions that do not exercise the underlying defect.

116. A false-positive test result could be caused by bad test input data, incorrect test preconditions, incorrect test oracles (outputs and postconditions), defects in a test driver or test stub, improperly configured test environment, and so on.

117. A fault can be caused by erroneous input or execution of a defect. Unless properly handled, a fault can cause a failure.

118. Note that the load could refer to any type of capacity, such as the number of simultaneous users or the rate of input commands.

119. Operationally relevant testing during Developmental Testing (DT) may incorporate test data collection software that will not remain in the final delivered system; operationally relevant testing during Operational Testing and Evaluation (OT&E) tests the final system with nothing added. Alpha testing and flight testing (for aircraft) are typical DT examples, whereas beta testing and sea trials (for ship systems) are typical OT&E examples.

120. This level of code coverage is usually impractical or infeasible because of the combinatorial explosion of paths as branch points are added.

121. TDD is concerned with black-box testing because white-box testing relies on knowing the not-yet-determined internal structure of the thing being tested. TDD is similar to Design By Contract (DBC), which involves determining an operation's contract (that is, preconditions and postconditions) before designing and implementing that operation. This similarity is especially striking when one considers that preconditions (that is, pretest conditions) and postconditions (that is, required posttest conditions that make up part of the test oracle) are important components of a test case.

122. Testing is one of the standard verification approaches. There are numerous types of testing based on the scope of testing, the test-case-selection criteria, the test-completion criteria, the specific goals of the testing, and the time in the development cycle during which the testing takes place.

123. Typical code coverage criteria include branch, decision, path, and statement coverage.

APPENDIX D

REFERENCES

[Feiler et al. 2012]   Peter Feiler, John Goodenough, Arie Gurfinkel, Charles Weinstock, and Lutz Wrage, "Reliability Validation and Improvement Framework," Technical Report CMU/SEI-2012-SR-013, Software Engineering Institute, Carnegie Mellon University, 2012.

[ISTQB 2012]   Glossary Working Party, "Standard glossary of terms used in Software Testing," Version 2.2, International Software Testing Qualifications Board (ISTQB), 19 October 2012, p. 52.

[Jones 2013a]   Capers Jones, "Software Quality and Defect Removal Efficiency (DRE)" Report, personal email, 22 June 2013.

[Jones 2013b]   Capers Jones, "The Ranges and Limits of Software Quality," Namcook Analytics LLC, 23 June 2013.

[Jones 2013c]   Capers Jones, "Why "Cost Per Defect" Is Harmful for Software Quality," Namcook Analytics LLC, 23 June 2013.

[Mats 2001]   Lars Mats, "The Top Five Software-Testing Problems and How to Avoid Them," *EDN Systems Design*, EDN, 1 February 2001, pp. 107–110.

[McConnell 2004]   Steve McConnell, *Code Complete, A Practical Handbook of Software Construction, Second Edition* (Redmond, WA: Microsoft Press, 2004).

[NIST 2002]   National Institute of Standards and Technology (NIST), "The Economic Impacts of Inadequate Infrastructure for Software Testing, Final Report," May 2002, http://www.nist.gov/director/planning/upload/report02-3.pdf

PLANNING CHECKLIST

The following checklist can be used during initial planning (that is, as-planned) of a testing effort and during the assessment of the actual (that is, as-performed) testing effort.

Testing Pitfalls	Characteristic Symptom(s) Observed	Potential Consequence(s) Observed	Potential Cause(s) Identified	Recommendations Implemented
Test Planning and Scheduling Pitfalls				
No Separate Test Planning Documentation (GEN-TPS-1)				
Incomplete Test Planning (GEN-TPS-2)				
Test Plans Ignored (GEN-TPS-3)				
Test-Case Documents as Test Plans (GEN-TPS-4)				
Inadequate Test Schedule (GEN-TPS-5)				
Testing at the End (GEN-TPS-6)				
Stakeholder Involvement and Commitment Pitfalls				
Wrong Testing Mindset (GEN-SIC-1)				
Unrealistic Testing Expectations (GEN-SIC-2)				
Lack of Stakeholder Commitment to Testing (GEN-SIC-3)				

Testing Pitfalls	Characteristic Symptom(s) Observed	Potential Consequence(s) Observed	Potential Cause(s) Identified	Recommendations Implemented
Management-Related Testing Pitfalls				
Inadequate Test Resources (GEN-MGMT-1)				
Inappropriate External Pressures (GEN-MGMT-2)				
Inadequate Test-Related Risk Management (GEN-MGMT-3)				
Inadequate Test Metrics (GEN-MGMT-4)				
Inconvenient Test Results Ignored (GEN-MGMT-5)				
Test Lessons Learned Ignored (GEN-MGMT-6)				
Staffing Pitfalls				
Lack of Independence (GEN-STF-1)				
Unclear Testing Responsibilities (GEN-STF-2)				
Inadequate Testing Expertise (GEN-STF-3)				
Developers Responsible for All Testing (GEN-STF-4)				
Testers Responsible for All Testing (GEN-STF-5)				

Testing Pitfalls	Characteristic Symptom(s) Observed	Potential Consequence(s) Observed	Potential Cause(s) Identified	Recommendations Implemented
Test Process Pitfalls				
Testing and Engineering Processes Not Integrated (GEN-PRO-1)				
One-Size-Fits-All Testing (GEN-PRO-2)				
Inadequate Test Prioritization (GEN-PRO-3)				
Functionality Testing Over-emphasized (GEN-PRO-4)				
Black-Box System Testing Overemphasized (GEN-PRO-5)				
Black-Box System Testing Underemphasized (GEN-PRO-6)				
Too Immature for Testing (GEN-PRO-7)				
Inadequate Evaluations of Test Assets (GEN-PRO-8)				
Inadequate Maintenance of Test Assets (GEN-PRO-9)				
Testing as a Phase (GEN-PRO-10)				
Testers Not Involved Early (GEN-PRO-11)				
Incomplete Testing (GEN-PRO-12)				
No Operational Testing (GEN-PRO-13)				
Inadequate Test Data (GEN-PRO-14)				
Test-Type Confusion (GEN-PRO-15)				

Testing Pitfalls	Characteristic Symptom(s) Observed	Potential Consequence(s) Observed	Potential Cause(s) Identified	Recommendations Implemented
Test Tools and Environments Pitfalls				
Over-Reliance on Manual Testing (GEN-TTE-1)				
Over-Reliance on Testing Tools (GEN-TTE-2)				
Too Many Target Platforms (GEN-TTE-3)				
Target Platform Difficult to Access (GEN-TTE-4)				
Inadequate Test Environments (GEN-TTE-5)				
Poor Fidelity of Test Environments (GEN-TTE-6)				
Inadequate Test Environment Quality (GEN-TTE-7)				
Test Assets Not Delivered (GEN-TTE-8)				
Inadequate Test Configuration Management (GEN-TTE-9)				
Developers Ignore Testability (GEN-TTE-10)				
Test Communication Pitfalls				
Inadequate Architecture or Design Documentation (GEN-COM-1)				
Inadequate Defect Reports (GEN-COM-2)				
Inadequate Test Documentation (GEN-COM-3)				
Source Documents Not Maintained (GEN-COM-4)				
Inadequate Communication Concerning Testing (GEN-COM-5)				

Testing Pitfalls	Characteristic Symptom(s) Observed	Potential Consequence(s) Observed	Potential Cause(s) Identified	Recommendations Implemented
Requirements-Related Testing Pitfalls				
Ambiguous Requirements (GEN-REQ-1)				
Obsolete Requirements (GEN-REQ-2)				
Missing Requirements (GEN-REQ-3)				
Incomplete Requirements (GEN-REQ-4)				
Incorrect Requirements (GEN-REQ-5)				
Requirements Churn (GEN-REQ-6)				
Improperly Derived Requirements (GEN-REQ-7)				
Verification Methods Not Specified (GEN-REQ-8)				
Lack of Requirements Trace (GEN-REQ-9)				
Unit Testing Pitfalls				
Testing Does *Not* Drive Design and Implementation (TTS-UNT-1)				
Conflict of Interest (TTS-UNT-2)				
Integration Testing Pitfalls				
Integration Decreases Testability Ignored (TTS-INT-1)				
Inadequate Self-Monitoring (TTS-INT-2)				
Unavailable Components (TTS-INT-3)				
System Testing as Integration Testing (TTS-INT-4)				

Testing Pitfalls	Characteristic Symptom(s) Observed	Potential Consequence(s) Observed	Potential Cause(s) Identified	Recommendations Implemented
Specialty Engineering Testing Pitfalls				
Inadequate Capacity Testing (TTS-SPC-1)				
Inadequate Concurrency Testing (TTS-SPC-2)				
Inadequate Internationalization Testing (TTS-SPC-3)				
Inadequate Interoperability Testing (TTS-SPC-4)				
Inadequate Performance Testing (TTS-SPC-5)				
Inadequate Reliability Testing (TTS-SPC-6)				
Inadequate Robustness Testing (TTS-SPC-7)				
Inadequate Safety Testing (TTS-SPC-8)				
Inadequate Security Testing (TTS-SPC-9)				
Inadequate Usability Testing (TTS-SPC-10)				
System Testing Pitfalls				
Test Hooks Remain (TTS-SYS-1)				
Lack of Test Hooks (TTS-SYS-2)				
Inadequate End-to-End Testing (TTS-SYS-3)				

Testing Pitfalls	Characteristic Symptom(s) Observed	Potential Consequence(s) Observed	Potential Cause(s) Identified	Recommendations Implemented
System of Systems (SoS) Testing Pitfalls				
Inadequate SoS Test Planning (TTS-SoS-1)				
Unclear SoS Testing Responsibilities (TTS-SoS-2)				
Inadequate Resources for SoS Testing (TTS-SoS-3)				
SoS Testing Not Properly Scheduled (TTS-SoS-4)				
Inadequate SoS Requirements (TTS-SoS-5)				
Inadequate Support from Individual System Projects (TTS-SoS-6)				
Inadequate Defect Tracking Across Projects (TTS-SoS-7)				
Finger-Pointing (TTS-SoS-8)				
Regression Testing Pitfalls				
Inadequate Regression Test Automation (TTS-REG-1)				
Regression Testing Not Performed (TTS-REG-2)				
Inadequate Scope of Regression Testing (TTS-REG-3)				
Only Low-Level Regression Tests (TTS-REG-4)				
Test Resources Not Delivered for Maintenance (TTS-REG-5)				
Only Functional Regression Testing (TTS-REG-6)				

INDEX

A

AADL models. *See* Architecture Analysis and Design Language (AADL) models
abnormal behavior
residual defects, 45
testing, 41
abnormal use case paths, 193, 196
A/B testing, 243
abuse cases, 200, 202
acceptance testing, 31, 104
defects causing failures, 59–60
system testing as, 105
accidental regression testing, 104
accreditation testing, 115
acquirer representatives, 57
acquisition organizations, 141
acronym list, 33, 145–146
acronyms
listing, 253–254
undefined, 147
agile development, 4, 127–128
consulting, 95
cross-functional development teams, 71
denigrating documentation in favor of verbal communication, 133
developers' testing expertise, 72
integrated components, 87
project planning documentation, 96
schedules, 96
testing documentation, 136, 137
testing performed by non-testers, 73
test planning documentation, 38, 96
training, 95
working on different components and subsystems simultaneously, 4
ALM tool repositories. *See* Application Lifecycle Management (ALM) tool repositories
alpha testing, 100
alternative use case paths, 103, 151

Ambiguous Requirements (GEN-REQ-1), 19, 144–147, 220
characteristic symptoms, 144
description, 144
potential applicability, 144
potential causes, 145
potential negative consequences, 145
recommendations, 146–147
related pitfalls, 147
analysis, 243
Anti-Tamper Testing, 200
application domain, 70
Application Lifecycle Management (ALM) tool repositories
acquiring, 30
testing, xix
test planning information stored in, 29
apps, 120
architects, 141
insufficient architecture or design documentation, 131–133
testing executable architectural models, 167
architecturally significant requirements, 4
architecture
inadequate, 18
testing, 203
tests driving development, 165–166
undocumented changes to, 139
Architecture Analysis and Design Language (AADL) models, 3
architecture documents, 139–140
architecture engineering process, 160
architecture models, testing, 3
architecture teams, testers excluded from, 76
as-performed testing process
evaluating, xix
metrics-driven, 61
quality assurance evaluations, 92

Assessment and Control of Software Risks (Jones), xiv
asset analysis, 199, 202
attack surface identification, 202
attack trees, 200, 202
automated testing, 31, 70–71, 107–108, 166
difficulty developing, 18, 129–130
expertise required, 48
Proof of Concept study, 107
relying too heavily on, 108–110
return on investment (ROI), 107
test cases, 47
automating regression testing, 113, 226–227, 229–231

B

backward-looking testing metrics, 60
behaviors
exceptional, 104
failing to test, 17, 98–100
normal versus abnormal, 31, 104
testing documentation, 78
best practices, 70
beta testing, 100, 243
BIST. *See* Built-In Self Test
BIT. *See* built-in test
black-box system
little time for testing, 87
no metrics collected, 87
overemphasizing, 16, 85–86
testing, 31, 38, 86–88, 104
Black-Box System Testing Overemphasized (GEN-PRO-5)
characteristic symptoms, 85
description, 85
potential applicability, 85
potential causes, 85
potential negative consequences, 85
recommendations, 86
related pitfalls, 86

The SEI Series in Software Engineering

ISBN 0-321-46108-8

ISBN 0-321-22876-6

ISBN 0-321-11886-3

ISBN 0-201-73723-X

ISBN 0-321-50917-X

ISBN 0-321-15495-9

ISBN 0-321-17935-8

ISBN 0-321-27967-0

ISBN 0-201-70372-6

ISBN 0-201-70482-X

ISBN 0-201-70332-7

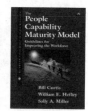

ISBN 0-201-60445-0

ISBN 0-201-60444-2

ISBN 0-321-42277-5

ISBN 0-201-52577-1

ISBN 0-201-25592-8

ISBN 0-321-47717-0

ISBN 0-201-54597-7

ISBN 0-201-54809-7

ISBN 0-321-30549-3

ISBN 0-201-18095-2

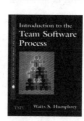

ISBN 0-201-54610-8

ISBN 0-201-47719-X

ISBN 0-321-34962-8

ISBN 0-201-77639-1

ISBN 0-201-73-1134

ISBN 0-201-61626-2

ISBN 0-201-70454-4

ISBN 0-201-73409-5

ISBN 0-201-85-4805

ISBN 0-321-11884-7

ISBN 0-321-33572-4

ISBN 0-321-51608-7

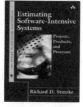

ISBN 0-201-70312-2

ISBN 0-201-70-0646

ISBN 0-201-17782-X

Please see our web site at informit.com/seiseries for more information on these titles.

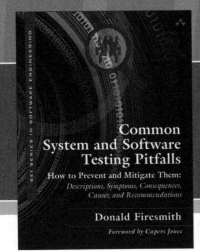

Safari
Books Online

FREE
Online Edition

Your purchase of **Common System and Software Testing Pitfalls** includes access to a free online edition for 45 days through the **Safari Books Online** subscription service. Nearly every Addison-Wesley Professional book is available online through **Safari Books Online**, along with thousands of books and videos from publishers such as Cisco Press, Exam Cram, IBM Press, O'Reilly Media, Prentice Hall, Que, Sams, and VMware Press.

Safari Books Online is a digital library providing searchable, on-demand access to thousands of technology, digital media, and professional development books and videos from leading publishers. With one monthly or yearly subscription price, you get unlimited access to learning tools and information on topics including mobile app and software development, tips and tricks on using your favorite gadgets, networking, project management, graphic design, and much more.

Activate your FREE Online Edition at
informit.com/safarifree

STEP 1: Enter the coupon code: YDKBOVH.

STEP 2: New Safari users, complete the brief registration form.
Safari subscribers, just log in.

If you have difficulty registering on Safari or accessing the online edition,
please e-mail customer-service@safaribooksonline.com